HACKING
CYBERSPACE

Polemics

Michael Calvin McGee and Barbara Biesecker,
University of Iowa

John M. Sloop, *Vanderbilt University*

HACKING
CYBERSPACE

<011000110101010101>

David J. Gunkel

Northern Illinois University

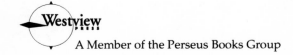

Westview
PRESS
A Member of the Perseus Books Group

Copyright © 2001 by Westview Press, A Member of the Perseus Books Group

Published in 2001 in the United States of America by Westview Press, 5500 Central Avenue, Boulder, Colorado 80301-2877, and in the United Kingdom by Westview Press, 12 Hid's Copse Road, Cumnor Hill, Oxford OX2 9JJ

Find us on the World Wide Web at www.westviewpress.com

Library of Congress Cataloging-in-Publication Data

Gunkel, David J.
  Hacking cyberspace/David J. Gunkel
    p. cm.—(Polemics)
  Includes bibliographical references and index.
  ISBN 0-8133-3669-4 (pbk.)
    1. Computer security. 2. Computer hackers. 3. System programming (Computer science).
I. Title. II. Polemics series.

QA76.9.A25 G86 2001
005.8—dc21

00-053180

The paper used in this publication meets the requirements of the American National Standard for Permanence of Paper for Printed Library Materials Z39.48-1984.

PERSEUS
POD
ON DEMAND   10   9   8   7   6   5   4   3   2

Contents

v

Acknowledgments

Hacking, like writing, is not a lonely or solitary occupation. Despite popular mythologies and persistent misconceptions, both are highly situated practices that rely on and are informed by networks of complex relationships. Acknowledging these associations and affiliations is a necessary but ultimately impossible task. The following, therefore, is only a partial list of the network of connections that contributes to and makes up *Hacking Cyberspace*.

This book began with a letter of invitation written by Cathy Murphy, then senior editor at Westview Press, on behalf of the series editors of Polemics. I thank the editors, Barbara Biesecker, Michael Calvin McGee, and John Sloop, for perceiving in a single article possibilities of which I was not even aware and for challenging me to transform that potential into a readable text. It was a thrill to respond to and work with scholars whose work had informed so much of my own research. I am also grateful for the patience and leadership exhibited by Cathy Murphy as she shepherded the project through the proposal, contract, manuscript, and initial review stages. The text has additionally benefited from the comments of an anonymous reader, who supplied much needed tweaking of my often tortured prose, and the editorial work of David McBride, David Pervin, and Jill Rothenberg, and the attentive copyediting provided by Geoffrey T. Garvey.

Nascent versions of the chapters that make up this text were presented at conferences and have appeared in various academic journals. A preliminary version of the introduction was presented at the Midwest Conference on Film, Language, and Literature held at Northern Illinois University in April 2000 and published in a special edition of the *Journal of Advanced Composition* (*JAC*;

November 2000). I am beholden to Michael Day, Martin E. Rosen-
berg, Eric Hoffman, and Matt Duncan for useful questions and
comments, Debbie Hawhee and John Muckelbauer for soliciting,
coordinating, and editing the special edition of *JAC,* and Barbara
Biesecker for her careful reading and remarkable insight.

Chapter 1 expands upon and develops theses initially presented
in a paper that I wrote in collaboration with Ann Hetzel Gunkel,
"Virtual Geographies: The New Worlds of Cyberspace." It was
presented at the Philosophy Interpretation Culture (PIC) conference held at SUNY Binghamton in November 1996 and subsequently published in a special edition of *Critical Studies in Mass
Communication (CSMC),* vol. 14, no. 2 (June 1997). I thank my coau-
thor for direction and insight, John Protevi, Jeff Nealon, and Rob
Wittig for comments and conversation at the PIC conference, and
Steve Jones and the reviewers at *CSMC* for assistance in developing the essay's arguments and conclusions.

Chapter 2 has benefited from comments received at a presentation delivered to the Broadcast Education Association's (BEA) annual convention in 2000. I graciously acknowledge Stan LaMuth,
who coordinated the session, Fritz Messere and Eun-mee Kim,
who provided thoughtful comments, and the anonymous readers
at the BEA who awarded the composition second place in the
open-paper competition.

Preliminary versions of Chapter 3 were presented at the Florida
State University Conference on Film and Literature (January 1997)
and the National Communication Association annual convention
in 1999. A draft of the current chapter was published in *Critical
Studies in Media Communication (CSMC),* vol. 17, no. 1 (March 2000)
under the title "Rethinking Virtual Reality: Simulation and the Deconstruction of the Image." I thank Rob Wittig, Ann Hetzel
Gunkel, Jeff Chown, Robert Self, Clark Germann, and Karen Lollar
for comments and questions at the conferences and James Chese-
bro and the reviewers at *CSMC* for their help in preparing the paper for publication.

A draft of Chapter 4 was presented at the DePaul University
conference From Microchip to Mass Media: Culture and the Tech-

nological Age (May 1996) and published in *Configurations,* vol. 7, no. 1 (1999). I am indebted to Randall Honold for organizing the conference, to Bill Martin for challenging questions and comments, and to James Bono and the reviewers at *Configurations* for crucial suggestions and direction.

A variant of Chapter 5 was presented at the second annual Ethics and Technology Conference held at Loyola University in Chicago, June 1997, and published under the title "Virtually Transcendent: Cyberculture and the Body" in the *Journal of Mass Media Ethics (JMME),* vol. 13, no. 2 (1998). I am appreciative of the questions and comments provided by the conference participants and the editorial advice supplied by Clifford G. Christians, Thomas W. Cooper, and the reviewers at JMME.

A form of Chapter 6 was presented at the annual convention of the National Communication Association held in Chicago, November 1997. I thank the other members of the panel, Julianne Lawson and Ed Rivas, for their participation and David Shulkin for his assistance in preparing the cyborg website for its public debut. A preliminary draft of this chapter was published under the title "We Are Borg: Cyborgs and the Subject of Communication" in *Communication Theory,* vol. 10, no. 3 (August 2000). I graciously acknowledge the insights and suggestions provided by the editor, Michael Cody, and several anonymous reviewers.

I owe a huge debt to my colleagues in the Department of Communication at Northern Illinois University for their unwavering support, encouragement, and time. My work has particularly benefited from the advice and experience of the department chair, Lois Self, and the expertise and guidance provided by the senior faculty: Ferald Bryan, Gary Burns, Jeffrey Chown, Martha Cooper, Richard Johannesen, Charles Larson, Mary Larson, Robert Miller, Orayb Najjar, Angela Powers, and Joseph Scudder. This book would not have been possible if it was not for the department's generous gift of a reduction in teaching load during the spring of 1997, 1998, 1999, and 2000. "The gift of time," as Jeff Nealon (1998) acknowledges, "should never be taken lightly or without acknowledgment" (*x*). Additional research funding was provided by two summer research grants issued by the College of Liberal Arts and Sciences and a travel grant provided by the Division of International Programs. I am also appreciative of the uncanny insights and critical observations of my undergraduate and graduate students in COMS 465, 496, 550, and 547. They not only indulged my particular mania but kept me on track by letting me know when I was full of it.

Most important, I thank my family and friends for their encouragement and patience throughout the research and writing process: Peter and Judith Gunkel, Marian and David Torkelson and their children Jared and Miranda, Juliet Gunkel and Stephen Bunge, Jennifer Gunkel, Florence Hetzel, Martha Dankowski and everyone at the cave, Al and Maria Hetzel and the Hetzel family, Murray Coffey, and Paul Sterczek. I am also thankful for the early-morning company of my dogs, Peaches, who slept while I wrote, and Pączek, who interrupted at the most inopportune times. Finally, I am forever thankful for the love and assistance of my wife, Ann Hetzel Gunkel, who inspires, sustains, and understands it all.

I dedicate this book to the memory of my grandparents, Adeline Krusick (1912–1994) and Sigmund Dolata (1910–1978) and Rose Kress (1902–1976) and Ernest Gunkel (1906–1974).

David J. Gunkel

INTRODUCTION: PROLEGOMENA— HACKING CYBERSPACE

> If there is a challenge here for cultural critics, then it might be presented as the obligation to make our knowledge about technoculture into something like a hacker's knowledge, capable of penetrating existing systems of rationality that might otherwise be seen as infallible.
>
> **Ross 1991b, 132**

Knowledge about cyberspace is shaped and delimited by the questions we ask and the kinds of inquiries in which we engage and are already engaged. Questioning, however, is never objective or neutral. As Martin Heidegger (1962) demonstrated, a question, no matter how carefully articulated, necessarily harbors preconceptions and preunderstandings that direct and regulate the inquiry (24). When we ask, for example, whether cyberspace portends a new world of opportunity that is uninhibited by the limitations of embodiment and physical existence, a techno-dystopia of alienation and surveillance where digital artifacts supersede lived reality, or something in between these two extremes, our query already affiliates with the terms and conditions of a well-established debate (cf. Critical Art Ensemble 1997; Mattelart 2000) and employs a complex set of assumptions concerning the essence, function, and significance of technology. This network of preconditions and assumptions usually does not appear as such within the space of a specific inquiry but constitutes the epistemological context in which any significant investigation is and must be situated. To continue to operate on the basis of these established systems is certainly understandable, completely rational, and potentially useful. Doing so, however, necessitates adherence to exigencies and prejudices that often remain unexamined, unquestioned, and essentially unknown.

If we are to know how we know cyberspace, we need to devise methods of investigation that target and question the network of preconditions and assumptions that already inform and delimit our modes of inquiry. What is required are procedures that do not simply conform to the conventional questions and debates but become capable of infiltrating the existing systems of rationality that structure these examinations and, as a result, are all too often taken for granted. What is necessary, as software manufacturers often describe it, is the ability to think outside the box. Such a procedure, following the suggestions of Andrew Ross (1991b), would transform existing knowledge about cyberspace into a hacker's knowledge. This knowledge would be "capable of penetrating existing systems of rationality that might otherwise be seen as infallible" and would be "capable of reskilling, and therefore of rewriting the cultural programs and reprogramming the social values that make room for new technologies" (132). Consequently, *hacking* suggests an alternative mode of examination that learns how to enter, explore, and rework the basic systems and programs that have informed and regulated investigations of cyberspace. It institutes, echoing Friedrich Nietzsche's (1966) characterization of *Beyond Good and Evil*, a fundamental revaluation of the values that have so far directed and regulated any and all evaluations of this subject matter (310).

Hacking Cyberspace proposes a method of investigation that infiltrates, reevaluates, and reprograms the systems that have shaped and delimited cyberspace. Despite this apparently simple description, these two words and their juxtaposition necessarily resonate with noisy complexities that complicate this preliminary formulation. First, neither *hacking* nor *cyberspace* designates activities, entities, or concepts that are univocal, easily defined, or immediately understood. In fact, both terms are riddled with apparently contradictory denotations that challenge, if not defy, conventional logic. *Hacking,* for example, designates an activity that is simultaneously applauded for its creativity and reviled for its criminal transgressions, while *cyberspace* constitutes a neologism that is pulled in every conceivable direction by every conceivable interest. Second, the juxtaposition of these two words complicates these initial difficulties, for hacking is an activity that is itself proper to and that operates within the contested zones of cyberspace. *Hacking Cyberspace,* however, suggests that hacking is to be expropriated from and turned against its proper and indigenous situation as some form of critical intervention. Whether this endeavor constitutes an operation that is creative, criminal, or both, one may not at this point be able to determine. What is certain, however, is that before detailing the parameters, procedures, and strategies of hacking cyberspace one should first consider both *hacking* and *cyberspace.* Such deliberation does not attempt to simplify the complexity with which these words are already associated but endeavors to learn how to take it into account.

Hacking

Hacker: Originally, a compulsive computer programmer. The word has evolved in meaning over the years. Among computer users, *hacker* carries a positive connotation, meaning anyone who creatively explores the operations of computer systems. Recently, it has taken on negative connotation, primarily through confusion with *cracker.*

Harper's Forum 1999, 128

Hacking does not have a single, discrete definition. According to Peter Ludlow (1996), the word is pulled in at least two seemingly opposite and irreducible directions. "Originally, a hacker was someone who liked to hack computer code (i.e., write programs) or, in some cases, hack electronic hardware (i.e., design and build hardware). Thanks to the news media, 'hacker' has also come to have a negative connotation, usually meaning those who illicitly hack their way into other people's computer systems. Some folks have tried to preserve the original (good) sense of 'hacker' by introducing the term *cracker* to cover cases of electronic trespassers, but like all attempts to fight lexical drift, their efforts have failed" (125). The word *hacking*, as currently understood, designates both creative innovation and a form of illicit behavior. It is an activity that occupies two extreme positions and is, for that reason, both celebrated for its insightful inventiveness and vilified for its monstrous deviations. Consequently, the hacker has played, and continues to play, the role of both hero and villain in the narratives of cyberspace.

This terminological equivocation is not, however, a form of polysemia caused by the word's (mis)use or what Bruce Sterling (1992) has called its "unfortunate history" (53). It is the result of an original and irreducible dissemination of meaning that has always and already affected the word. For the activities that compose what is called hacking are delimited not by strict methodological specification and rigorous conceptual formulation, but by particular practices and movements that only become manifest through specific performances. One becomes a hacker not by subscribing to certain tenets, methods, and doctrines, but by yielding to the "hands-on imperative" (Levy 1984, 27)—that is, engaging in and learning to perform "hacks." And one learns how to hack not by adhering to instructions provided in philes[1] or reading the text of a manifesto or two, but by engaging in the practice. In other words, as Emmanuel Goldstein explained it in *Harper's* Forum (1999), "there are no leaders and no agenda" (129). As a result, hacking only is what it does and what is done with it. The general accumulation and abstraction of these various and often highly particular practices comprises what has come to be called "the hacker ethic" (Levy 1984, 26). Here too, however, one is confronted with an insoluble multiplicity. "There is," as Acid Phreak pointed out in the *Harper's* (1999) discussion, "no one hacker ethic. Everyone has his own" (128). Hacking, therefore, comprises performances that not only resist univocal signification but are also highly situated and radically empirical.[2] It is this fundamental and irreducible differentiation that is constitutive of the practice of hacking and responsible for the term's seemingly unrestrained lexical drift and "unfortunate history."

Whether it denotes a form of creative debugging or a mode of unauthorized exploration and manipulation, hacking takes place as *parasitic activity*. It is an undertaking that always requires a host system in which and on which to operate. The logic of the parasite, however, is remarkably complex. It is not, as Jacques Derrida (1993) points out, "a logic of distinction or of opposition," for "a parasite is neither the same as nor different from that which it parasites" (96). The parasite, therefore, behaves according to another kind of logic, one that exceeds the simple dichotomies of inside/outside, legitimate/illegitimate, legal/illegal, cause/effect, etc. "The parasite," Derrida (1993) writes in a passage that responds to and remains parasitic on a text written by John Searle,

> is by definition never simply *external*, never simply something that can be excluded from or kept outside of the body "proper," shut out from the "familial" table or house. Parasitism takes place when the parasite (called thus by the owner, jealously defending his own, his *oikos*) comes to live *off the life* of the body in which it resides—and when, reciprocally, the host incorporates the parasite to an extent, willy nilly offering it hospitality: providing it with a place. The parasite then "takes place." And at bottom, whatever violently "takes place" or occupies a site is always *something* of a parasite. (90)

Parasitism constitutes an eccentric operation that exceeds the traditional logic of either/or or what is sometimes called the "law of noncontradiction." The parasite occupies a structurally unique position that is neither simply inside nor simply outside. It is the outside in the inside and the inside outside itself. Parasitism, therefore, takes place in a way that is never simply external nor externalizable. For this reason, it is difficult to describe the status or activities of a parasite without, as is already demonstrated here, using a kind of convoluted logic that operates at the very limits of language. This general characterization of parasitism contains several important consequences for understanding the activities of hacking.

First, as a parasite, hacking draws all its strength, strategies, and tools from the system on which and in which it operates. The hack does not, strictly speaking, introduce anything new into the system on which it works but derives everything from the host's own protocols and procedures. It does so not to neutralize or to confirm the system but to understand how it operates and to experiment with different manipulations that deploy it otherwise—that is, in excess of the restricted possibilities articulated by the system's initial programming. As Levy (1984) describes it, "hackers believe that essential lessons can be learned about the systems—about the world—from taking things apart, seeing how they work, and using this knowledge to create new and even more interesting things" (27). Consequently, hacking is a form of "exploring and manipulating" (Sterling 1992, 64) that not only learns how a specific system behaves but also discovers how to employ its tools and procedures against and in excess of the necessary limitations of its own programming. Donna Haraway (1991b) terms this curious form of exploration and manipulation *blasphemy*, which she immediately distinguishes from apostasy (149). Whereas apostasy designates a mere renunciation and abandonment by which one comes to occupy a position that literally stands apart or separated from something, blasphemy constitutes a calculated response that understands, acknowledges, and continually works within an established system. Like a parasite, the blasphemer is not an alien proceeding from and working on the outside. S/he is an insider, who not only understands the intricacies of the system but does so to such an extent that s/he becomes capable of fixating upon its necessary but problematic lacunae, exhibiting and employing them in such a way that disrupts the system to which s/he initially belongs and must continually belong. Although these operations can be reduced to and written off as mere adolescent pranks, they constitute more often than not a form of *serious play*.

Second, this parasitic and/or blasphemous operation is neither simply destructive nor simply corrective. On the one hand, hacking does not constitute a form of random violence or simple vandalism. Despite the word's dictionary definition, which reads "to cut with repeated irregular or unskillful blows," hacking constitutes a precise and calculated incision into a system, program, or network. If this incision appears to be "irregular" or "unskillful," it may be designated as such only from the perspective of the system that did not and could not see it coming. From the perspective of the hack, however, this occupation is always precisely calculated. Furthermore, in procuring access to a system, the hack does not aim at destroying the host on and in which it operates. To do so would mean nothing less than a form of suicide. This exigency, which is fundamental to all parasitic endeavors, has been codified in one of the (un)official hacker commandments: "thou shalt not destroy" (Slatalla and Quittner 1996, 40). Hacking, like any parasite, works within its host in a manner that simultaneously preserves and sustains that in which and on which it functions. Destruction of the host system is neither its purpose nor an acceptable alternative (Denning 1996, 146; Slatalla and Quittner 1996, 3). On the other hand, this apparently negative activity does not constitute a form of corrective criticism, which is how all negations of a system come to be reincorporated into and domesticated by that which they appear to negate. Although a number of hacks and hackers have been put to work for the enhancement of system security and administration, hacking in general resists this reemployment that has the effect of reappropriating so-called transgressions as a form of corrective criticism. Hacking deliberately exceeds recuperative gestures that would put its activities to work for the continued success and development of the host's system.

Hacking is content to be neither a friend nor an enemy. Either position only serves to reconfirm and justify the system in which and on which it operates. As Richard Stallman points out, hacking is often presented with two options, neither of which is adequate or appropriate: "One way is for hackers to become part of the security-maintenance establishment. The other, more subtle, way is for a hacker to become the security-breaking phreak the media portray. By shaping ourselves into the enemy of the establishment, we uphold the establishment" (*Harper's* Forum 1999, 128). Formulated as either a useful component of the established system or its dialectical opposite, hacking would serve and reconfirm the system in which and on which it works. Consequently, hacking endeavors to resist the gravitational pull of either option. It occupies a thoroughly eccentric position that is both in between these two extremes and neither one nor the other. Because hacking works against such recuperation that makes it serve the system as either negative counterpart or corrective critique, the "transgressions" of hacking, defined as such by the system that is hacked, must be described otherwise. "My crime," writes the Mentor (1986), "is that of outsmarting you, something you will never forgive me for" (3). Because hacking cannot be simply reduced to a destructive intervention or corrective criticism, its operations appear only as a kind of outsmarting and outmaneuvering of the system. "Outsmarting," however, is neither destructive nor critical. It is, in the usual sense of the words, neither good nor bad. Its logic and value remain otherwise. As a result, outsmarting cannot be forgiven, for it exceeds the very definition of wrongdoing that is the condition for any possibility of forgiveness.

Finally, hacking exceeds the traditional understanding of agency. Hackers cannot be praised or blamed in the usual manner for what it is they do or do not do. In other words, hackers do not, in any strict sense of the term, *cause* the disruptions or general system failures exhibited in and by the activities of hacking. Hacking only fixates on and manipulates an aporia, bug, and/or back door that is always and already present within and constitutive of the system itself. Emmanuel Goldstein, editor of *2600*,[3] has described this situation in the following way: "Hackers have become scapegoats: We discover the gaping holes in the system and then get blamed for the flaws" (*Harper's* Forum 1999, 130). According to this logic, any *hacker crackdown* is simply a form of "blaming the messenger." The hacker can be neither credited nor blamed for doing something (or not doing something) as an active and willful agent. Instead, the activities of hacking must be seen as highly attentive and even compulsive responses to specific systems that both call for and make the hack possible in and by their very systems design. If hacking admits of any form of agency, it can only be as a kind of *agent provocateur*. Hacking, therefore, is not some catastrophe that befalls an innocent and pure system as a kind of external threat and profound danger. It develops from a necessary and unavoidable deformity that always and already resides within and defines the proper formation of the system itself.[4] Hacking takes place as the teasing out of these deformations that, although constitutive of the system's original programming, often go undetected by the system in which and through which they first occur. Consequently, blaming or even crediting the hacker is as naïve and simplistic as trying to build impervious firewalls and security systems that keep the hacker outside. The situation is much more complex and necessarily exceeds the binary logic that typically distinguishes subject from object, active from passive, and inside from outside. Hacking, like a parasite, takes place in and by occupying and feeding off a host that always and already has made a place for it to take place. It is for this reason that, despite the valiant efforts of law enforcement, hacking cannot be stopped or even hindered by cracking down on and punishing individual hackers. As the Mentor (1986) warns in the conclusion to his manifesto, "I am a hacker, and this is my manifesto. You may stop this individual, but you can't stop us all" (3). Even if the authorities target and stop one hacker or even a formidable gang of hackers, hacking will persist. For it is not the result of individual agents with some kind of deviant and malicious intent but first and foremost arises out of the resources of the systems and programs to which individual hacks respond and with which they interact.

Cyberspace

Cyberspace must be one of the most contested words in contemporary culture. Wherever the term appears, it becomes the subject of speculation and controversy, as critics and proponents argue over its function and future. This tug of war over the terrain of cyberspace . . . has generated more confusion and revealed more paradoxes than it has clarified.

Kendrick 1996, 143

Technically speaking, "cyberspace" is not a technology or even an ensemble of technologies. Despite the fact that the word has been routinely employed to name recent advancements in computer technology, telecommunications networking, and immersion user-interface systems, cyberspace is neither the product of technological research and development nor a conglomeration of hardware and software. It is a fiction invented and prototyped in a work of science-fiction that was authored, so the story goes, by a self-proclaimed computer illiterate on a manual typewriter. Consequently, cyberspace is not the product of technological innovation developed in the dust-resistant white-rooms of government-sponsored research but comprises a constellation of ideas about technology and technoculture that was created and deployed in the low-tech, print and paper realm of William Gibson's imaginative *Neuromancer* (1984). In this work of fiction, Gibson introduced and first described cyberspace as a "consensual hallucination," that is, an artificially created perception or vision that is common to a specific community of users. Since its initial introduction in 1984, this curious neologism has come to be employed by a number of researchers, scholars, and practitioners to designate actual technologies and the possibilities for enhanced interaction and communication that have been and will be created by such systems. As Sterling describes it, "cyberspace is best considered as a generic term which refers to a cluster of different technologies, some familiar, some only recently available, some being developed and some still fictional, all of which have in common the ability to simulate environments within which humans can interact" (Featherstone and Burrows 1995, 5). Consequently, cyberspace in both its content and form comprises a *consensual hallucination*. The neologism is employed not only to name the techniques and technologies used for producing artificially created, interactive environments but to define a common vision of the current and future state of communication and information technology that has been proffered, developed, and shared by a community of researchers, theorists, and practitioners.

Although it names a kind of collective fantasy, cyberspace, as the word is currently employed and delimited, by no means admits of a single vision and/or univocal determination. It has been, from the moment of its fabrication, already open to and afflicted by a multiplicity of competing and complex designations. A small number of theorists and practitioners, such as Mike Featherstone and Roger Burrows (1995) and Frank Biocca and Mark Levy (1995b), understand the word to denote either a form of technology or a collection of technologies that have also been designated by other names like Internet, virtual reality, computer simulation, and computer-mediated communication; but for the vast majority, including Howard Rheingold (1993), William Mitchell (1995), Allucquere Rosanne Stone (1995), Mark Dery (1996), Steve Jones (1995), Rob Shields (1996), and Florian Rötzer (1998), it names not a technology or even an ensemble of technologies but the perceived, interactive environments that are and can be created by the hybrid of current and future communication and information systems. For some, like Nicholas Negroponte (1995), Mark Poster (1995), and Sherry Turkle (1995), these cyberspaces are unquestionably contemporary, futuristic, and even postmodern. For others, including Michael Heim (1993) and Michael Benedikt (1993b), they comprise ancient and familiar territory—an extension of Western metaphysics or a continuation of the age-old desire to live in an alternate, mythic realm. For many, including William Gibson (1984), Ziauddin Sardar and Jerome Ravetz (1996), and Zillah Eisenstein (1998), cyberspace comprises a dark and dystopic image of technological hegemony and colonization. For a number of optimists, such as Michael Benedikt (1993b), Howard Rheingold (1993), Esther Dyson et al. (1996), and John Perry Barlow (1997), it names new possibilities for democracy, virtual community, and global cooperation.

Cyberspace is not limited to extant, recently developed, or even fictitious technologies but comprises an entire system of ideas, practices, operations, and expectations that are not only derived from but circulate within a number of sources, not all of which are, technically speaking, a matter of technology. This has at least two consequences that are pertinent to any consideration of the topic. First, cyberspace is not simply a product of technological innovation but also a result of the various ways by which it is and has been addressed, investigated, and discussed. Because of this, what cyberspace is and what it can become is as much a function of new developments in the hardware and software of communi-

cation and information technology as it is of the various techniques used to examine, describe, and situate cyberspace in short
stories and novels, scholarly articles and technical specifications,
popular books and magazines, film narratives and television doc-
umentaries, comic books and art, and web-sites and online discussions. Consequently, the words, images, and various discursive techniques used to present and debate issues involving
cyberspace are not just representations of extant or developing
technology but constitute, as already demonstrated in Gibson's
Neuromancer, appropriate sites for the production of and struggle
over significance.

Second, cyberspace is not and cannot be limited to the sphere
of technology or applied science. Its various configurations and
manifold signification are always and already influenced by work
in a number of seemingly unrelated and not necessarily technological fields. This is immediately evident in the wide variety of
texts addressing the subject of cyberspace that have been published in the last two decades of what is called the second Christian millennium. These texts include works in philosophy (Heim
1993; Taylor and Saarinen 1994; Paul Virilio 1995; Dixon and Cassidy 1998; Hartmann 1999), geography and architecture (Benedikt
1993a; Mitchell 1995 and 1999; Boyer 1996; Spiller 1998; Hillis
1999), theology and religion (Zaleski 1997; Davis 1998; Wertheim
1999), anthropology and cultural studies (Dery 1996; Leeson 1996;
Sardar and Ravetz 1996; Shields 1996; Porter 1997), communication and media studies (Biocca and Levy 1995b; Jones 1995 and
1997b; Shields 1996; Morse 1998; Robins and Webster 1999; Mattelart 2000), sociology and psychology (Featherstone and Burrows
1995; Stone 1995; Turkle 1995; Schroeder 1996), political science
and women's studies (Haraway 1991b; Poster 1995; Balsamo 1996;
Eisenstein 1998; Hunter 1999), and art and fiction (Gibson 1984;
Sterling 1986; Stephenson 1993; Critical Art Ensemble 1994; Penny
1995; Druckrey and Ars Electronica 1999). This diversity means
that cyberspace is not only open to a wide variety of disciplines
and approaches but that no area can escape its reach. Or, as Benjamin Woolley (1992) has succinctly described the situation, "no

one can avoid becoming active citizens of cyberspace" (134). This fact not only complicates the examination of cyberspace by making it a thoroughly transdisciplinary object but disables in advance all attempts to avoid dealing with the topic by restricting it to a kind of technical quarantine in the disciplines of computer science, communication studies, or telecommunications practices.

Hacking Cyberspace

> This (therefore) will not have been a book. Still less, despite appearances, will it have been a collection of "essays."
>
> **Derrida 1981b, 3**

Hacking proposes a mode of investigation that both learns how to infiltrate systems that have usually gone unexamined and develops strategies for exploring their functions and reprogramming their operations. This undertaking, like other blasphemous and parasitic endeavors, does not aim at either confirming or refuting the systems in question, but works on and in them in order to learn how and why they function the way they do and to experiment with alternative deployments of their own programming. What is hacked in this case, however, are not individual computer components and programs but the various systems that structure, inform, and program cyberspace. Hacking cyberspace concerns an analysis that does not target technical equipment per se but works on and in the general infrastructure through which this technical equipment and the cultural context in which they appear have come to be determined, delimited, and debated. What is hacked, therefore, are the systems that connect and internetwork the various technologies, epistemologies, narrative techniques, research practices, texts, applications, and images that compose what is called cyberspace.

The hack is organized into six individual movements or chapters. These chapters, however, do not conform to what is usually expected of a book. They do not develop a single thought, pursue a univocal end, or practice what is usually understood and described as a formal method. Instead they constitute highly specific and individual incisions into the systems of cyberspace. Therefore, what they develop and how they do so will be specific to the programs and subroutines on which they work and from which they derive their energy and resources. Despite this diversity, they are all connected and internetworked through the general movement, occupation, and procedures of hacking. Accordingly, each chapter is designated with a *handle* that identifies the hack in a kind of code or discursive schematic. In the case of *Hacking Cyberspace*, these handles take the form of Latin phrases either expropriated from extant texts or synthesized by combining prefabricated linguistic components. The Latin phrases ensure that the handles not only communicate a certain content but also harbor a kind of linguistic excess that cannot be reduced and comprehended by the process of translation. That is, they contain a form of semantic noise that complicates and deforms every possible univocal specification. This is not the result of some obscure and cryptic pretense but is in both form and content directed and dictated by the exigencies of hacking.

The first chapter takes aim at and hacks a number of interrelated rhetorical techniques that had invaded and occupied cyberspace from the beginning. Immediately after its introduction in 1984, cyberspace was proclaimed the "electronic frontier" and a "new world." Terminology like this currently saturates the technical, theoretical, and popular understandings of cyberspace. From the "console cowboys" of Gibson's *Neuromancer* to the exciting "new worlds" announced by John Walker of Autodesk and from the pioneering work of Ivan Sutherland and Tom Furness to John Perry Barlow and Mitch Kapor's *Electronic Frontier Foundation*, the spirit of frontierism has infused the rhetoric and logic of cyberspace. Although certainly useful for explaining the implications and possibilities of new communication and information technology, these designations are not without significant limitations and consequences. In particular, they not only link the concept of cyberspace to the Columbian voyages of discovery and the wider network of European and American expansionism but communicate with the exercise of cultural power that is implied by these violent undertakings. Consequently, understanding and describing cyberspace through rhetorical devices that are explicitly connected to the age of exploration and the American West opens a discursive and ideological exchange between cyberspace and the hegemony of frontierism. The Latin handle designating this hack, *Terra Nova*, is of course adequately translated as "new world." However, in its Latin form, the handle harbors numerous vectors and lines of force that connect this seemingly innocent name to the European age of discovery, the Columbian invasion of the Americas, and the violent conquest and colonization of the American West. The first chapter not only traces the contours of these complex associations but suggests strategies by which to deploy counterhegemonic practices that contribute to a general decolonization of cyberspace.

The second chapter bears the handle *Ars Metaphorica*, which designates literally the "art or technique of metaphor." In its translated form, however, the title should be read as a double genitive. That is, it designates both the technique of metaphor and the metaphor of technique. What is at issue in the second hack is the conceptualization of cyberspace as a medium of communication. The computer and the computer network were not initially designed as a system of communication and information exchange. Indeed, as the name indicates, the computer was a machine that was to be employed for number crunching and calculation, and the computer network, which had its beginning with the mainframe computers of the late 1950s and early 1960s, was developed to permit time-shared access to computational devices. At some point, therefore, understanding of the computer and the network experienced a fundamental transformation. This point is demarcated by J. C. R. Licklider and Robert Taylor's influential article of 1968, "The Computer As a Communication Device." The most important word in the title of this article is deceptively small—the "as." For the "as" signifies a metaphorical operation wherein the computational apparatus became understood *in terms of* communication. This transference of meaning necessarily mobilized all kinds of preconceptions and ideas about what communication is or can be. As a result, Licklider and Taylor's article, in its very title, puts in play a network of ideas and expectations about the association of computers and communication. The second chapter hacks this system by taking aim at the metaphors of communication that have been imported into and that currently shape understandings of the computer and the network.

The third chapter examines the principles and technology of the virtual reality interface. The handle, *Veritatem Imitari*, which is a virtual contradiction, precisely indicates what is at stake. *Veritatem imitari* denotes "truthful image." It designates a kind of almost absolute realism through which a created image comes so close to approximating the truth of the matter that it can be and often is confused with the real thing. This is ostensibly what the VR (virtual reality) interface and researchers working in this new field seek to achieve; that is, imitations so realistic that they can fool the senses of the user, leading one to believe that s/he is confronting a real situation and scene. Technically speaking, however, *veritatem imitari* is a logical contradiction. For the image, since the time of Plato's *Republic*, has been not only distinguished from but absolutely unable to achieve proximity to the real. Juxtaposing *veritas* and *imitari* is, from the perspective of a certain tradition within Western thought, a violation of what is considered to be good logic. It is this gap between, on the one hand, the desire for perfect images and, on the other hand, the fundamental incongruity between images and reality that opens up all kinds of systemic and methodological problems in the art, science, and theories of virtual reality. This is precisely the object and task of the third hack. It inserts itself into the discipline and practice of VR, locates this complex aporia within its system, and releases this disturbing logic against that from which it is derived. As a result, the third hack not only deconstructs[5] the logical categories of real and imitation but elicits a new understanding of computer generated *simulation* that does not resolve into the one or the other.

Although its taxonomy is derived from a mathematical concept, the computer and the computer network do not comprise technologies that are simply limited to the task of computation. As early as the mid–1940s, computer scientists recognized that the essence of the information processor lay in its general ability to manipulate linguistic signs. The fourth chapter hacks this complex and often neglected relationship that is situated between the computer and language. This undertaking is entitled *Lingua ex Machina* and is directed by the mechanism of the Tower of Babel. If the collapse of the Tower of Babel marks the introduction of linguistic difference, the computer, it has been argued, promises to overcome linguistic variation through the mechanisms of machine translation and the various forms of what has been called "postsymbolic communication" (Lanier 1988, 1). The fourth chapter takes aim at the rhetoric and logic of this promise that not only accompanies but actually informs the very invention of the computer. The hack locates the point of entry into this system, which surprisingly is much older than one would think, understands how and why it functions in the manner that it does, and learns how to deploy its own protocols against itself by proposing an alternative interpretation of the Tower of Babel narrative. Once again, it is the preposition situated between the two nouns *lingua* and *machina* that does the work of signifying the complex issues that are at stake in this chapter. The Latin preposition *ex*, which is commonly translated as "from" or "out of," indicates a complex relationship between two or more terms that denotes either an order of precedence or a kind of general exclusion or expropriation. Understood in this way, *Lingua ex Machina* designates, on the one hand, language engendered by and proceeding from various techniques of mechanization and, on the other hand, languages that already ex-ceed and are ex-cluded from this form of technology.

The fifth chapter hacks the transcendentalism that belongs to and informs the subject matter of cyberspace. From its introduction in Gibson's *Neuromancer*, cyberspace has been considered to be a realm of pure thought that is disengaged from and uncontaminated by the "meat of the body" (Gibson 1984, 6), physical spaces, or even terrestrial limitations. This transcendentalism, however, is not anything technological but is informed and directed by concepts introduced and developed in Christianity and Western philosophy and science. It is for this reason that Nietzsche (1983a) grouped the various traditions that compose what is called Western thought under the general term "despisers of the body" (146). The fifth chapter hacks the *corpus amittere* (literally, losing the body) that has been and is continually uploaded into and employed by the systems of cyberspace. Because this transcendental ideology extends beyond the realm of cyberspace into theology and philosophy, the hack takes aim not only at the material of cyberspace but at the *doctrine of dualism* that is articulated in the history of Western thought. In pursuing this course, the hack comes to rely on an important body of work in the field of feminism that targets and analyzes the phallocentric aversion to the body and corporeality in general. The chapter is designated *Corpus Amittere* because cyberspace has not only been determined to be a place of virtual disembodiment and liberation from the constraints of corporeal existence but in doing so has always and has already been open to a loss and negligence that threatens to undermine its very material and subject matter.

The sixth and final chapter hacks the concept of humanism that has been rampant in the theories and practices of cyberspace. The hack takes aim at the *cyborg*, a monstrous hybrid of human and machine that, on the one hand, names the current state of what used to be called "human nature" as it becomes wired into new forms of communication and information technology and, on the other hand, indicates a potential threat that appears to undermine the very definition and dignity of the "human." In addressing this complex entity, the hack of humanism does not seek to resolve, to confront, or even to resist this apparently monstrous figure. Like the Borg of *Star Trek*, it knows that resistance is futile, that the cyborg is not a possible future but is already part and parcel of the humanist past, and that those entities who deceptively thought themselves human were always already and nothing more or less than cyborg. As a result, the final hack does not introduce the cyborg as some catastrophic crisis that could be resisted with any amount of strength or conservative energy. It simply locates and points out a fundamental monstrosity that is already constitutive of the system of humanism that it subsequently appears to threaten. This monstrous logic is immediately announced in the chapter's title, *Ecce Cyborg*, which translates into the apparently simple "behold the cyborg." This title, however, cites and makes reference to Nietzsche's *Ecce Homo* (1969), a work which in turn cites and makes reference to Pilate's indictment of Jesus Christ in the Gospel of John (19:5). Nietzsche's curious autobiographical text not only presents "a different image of humanity" (Kaufmann 1969, 204) that marks significant deviations from that of Western onto-theology but, what is more important, demonstrates, as Nietzsche's subtitle indicates, "how one becomes what one is." Accordingly, *Ecce Cyborg* does not consider the cyborg as some catastrophic crisis that has recently come to threaten humanity in the form of technology. It merely points out a necessary monstrosity that is always and already afflicting and deconstructing the concepts of the human and technology. Therefore, it merely locates and indicates this.

Conclusion

Hackers are not sloganeers. They are doers, take-things-in-handers. They are the opposite of philosophers: They don't wait for language to catch up to them. Their arguments are their actions.

Harper's **Forum 1999, 141**

Cyberspace constitutes what is arguably one of the noisiest and most contested words in contemporary culture. Its terminological equivocation is not the product of lexical drift or polysemia but is the result of a fundamental and irreducible indetermination. According to Gibson's (1993) own account, the word *cyberspace* was assembled from "small and readily available components of language. Neologic spasm: the primal act of pop poetics. Preceded any concept whatever. Slick hollow—awaiting received meaning" (27). Cyberspace is, from the moment of its fabrication, radically indeterminate. It constitutes an empty signifier that not only ante-dates any formal referent but readily and without significant resis-tance receives almost every meaning that comes to be assigned to it. For this reason, cyberspace has capitulated and continues to yield to the imposition of all kinds of determinations, most of which are not, technically speaking, matters of technology. They include, among others, metaphors of the new world and frontier, assurances about the significance and status of communication, representation, and language, metaphysical assumptions concern-ing the material of the body, and evaluative criteria derived from the philosophy of humanism.

Hacking introduces a method of analysis that targets and works on these various components. Unlike other critical endeavors, however, it does not seek either to confirm or to dispute them. In-stead, it constitutes a blasphemous form of intervention that learns how to manipulate and exploit necessary lacunae that are constitutive of but generally unacknowledged by that which is in-vestigated. Hacking does so not to be mischievous or clever, but to locate, demonstrate, and reprogram the systems of rationality that not only determine cyberspace but generally escape critical investigation precisely because they are taken for granted and as-sumed to be infallible. *Hacking Cyberspace*, therefore, does not take sides in the conventional debates and arguments that compose cyberspace. It does not, for example, either advocate or dispute the various positions espoused by techno-utopians, techno-dystopians, or the various hybrids that attempt synthetic coali-tions between these dialectical opposites. Instead it endeavors to understand and to manipulate the cultural programs and social values that dictate and direct this and every other dialectic by which cyberspace is constructed, debated, and evaluated. In do-ing so, hacking exposes cyberspace to alternative configurations and eccentric possibilities that do not conform to usual expecta-tions, behave according to accepted criteria, or register on con-ventional scales of value. Consequently, the outcome of *Hacking*

Cyberspace is neither good or bad, positive or negative, nor constructive or destructive but constitutes a general strategy by which to explore and manipulate the systems of rationality by which these modes of assessment become possible, function, and make sense.

Notes

1. Philes are the primary means by which hacker activity is reported and archived. Written by hackers for hackers, philes are either posted online in discussion forums like *Phrack.com* or distributed in hacker publications like *2600* (cf. note 3). Philes are not literal recipes for hacking but constitute résumés of recent hacker operations, sets of basic instructions, and open invitations to additional hacking.

2. This may be one reason why publications addressing hacking and hackers take the form not of theoretical treatises but of individual case studies that examine particular hacks or hackers. The seminal text on the subject, Levy's (1984) *Hackers: Heroes of the Computer Revolution*, for example, chronicles the people, technology, and events involved in what he defines as the three distinct phases of computer hacking: "The true hackers of the MIT artificial intelligence lab in the fifties and sixties; the populist, less sequestered hardware hackers in California in the seventies; and the young game hackers who made their mark in the personal computer age of the eighties" (*x*). Similar chronicles of specific people and events are provided in the accounts of phreakers, a neologism that names the illegal appropriation and manipulation of the telephone system, and what Rosenbaum (1971) initially called "computer phreakers," the prototype of what would become the "outlaw hacker" that is so prevalent in recent literature on the subject. These texts provide biographies of individual phreakers or hackers like Captain Crunch, the Mad Hacker, Kevin Mitnick, and Mark Abene; narrative accounts of the exploits of hacker gangs like the Legion of Doom, the Masters of Deception, and NuPrometheus League; and detailed treatment of particular hacks and law enforcement responses like the 1989 crack of Apple software, the 1990 Martin Luther King Day Crash of the AT&T long distance network, and the Secret Service and Chicago Task Force raids. The specificity of these various texts is immediately evident in their titles: *Cyberpunk: Outlaws and Hackers on the Computer Frontier* (Hafner and Markoff 1991), *The Hacker Crackdown: Law and Disorder on the Electronic Frontier* (Sterling 1992), *Approaching Zero: The Extraordinary Underworld of Hackers, Phreakers, Virus Writers, and Keyboard Criminals* (Mungo and Clough 1992), *Masters of Deception: The Gang That Ruled Cyberspace* (Slatalla and Quittner 1996), *The Fugitive Game: On-line with Kevin Mitnick* (Littman 1996), *The Watchman: The Twisted Life and Crimes of Serial Hacker Kevin Poulsen* (Littman 1997), *@Large: The Strange Case of the World's Biggest Internet Invasion* (Freedman and Mann 1997), *Cyberwars: Espionage on the Internet* (Guisnel 1997), and *Hackers: Crime in the Digital Sublime* (Taylor 1999).

3. *2600* has long been recognized as the "hacker's quarterly." The magazine's name comes from the 2600-cycle tone that had been used by Bell Telephone for switching long-distance phone calls in the late 1960s and early 1970s. Phreakers, like John Draper (a.k.a. Captain Crunch), discovered and exploited this feature to hack the Bell system's network.

4. On the difference between catastrophe and monstrosity, cf. Derrida (1974) and Gunkel (1997b).

5. On the strategy and intricacies of deconstruction, cf. the Appendix.

1

TERRA NOVA: THE NEW WORLDS OF CYBERSPACE

> Today another frontier yawns before us, far more fog-obscured and inscrutable in its opportunities than the Yukon. It consists not of unmapped physical space in which to assert one's ambitious body, but unmappable, infinitely expansible cerebral space. Cyberspace. And we are going there whether we want to or not.
>
> **Barlow 1994, 1**

> If a new world were discovered today, would we be able to see it? Would we be able to clear from our minds the images we habitually associate with our expectations of a different world to grasp the real difference that lay before our eyes?
>
> **Calvino 1994, 1**

If a *new world* were discovered today would its contours conform to our understanding of "world" and "discovery"? Would it take place as a taking of place? Would it supervene as an uncovering and drawing into appearance of that which had been covered, hidden, or withdrawn? Would this new geographic possibility conform to these determinations that are as much a part of the

Columbian voyage as the modern scientific enterprise? And could this *conformity* be anything other than the trace of a certain violence that endeavors to uncover everything through the illumination of enlightenment and seeks to establish every different domain as a new world that is determined as the opposite and other of an old world?

This chapter embarks upon an exploration of what recent technical and popular discourses have called "the new world of cyberspace." It will investigate the legacy, logic, and consequences of this complex metaphor that appears to connect cyberspace to the Columbian voyages of discovery and the larger network of European expansionism.[1] Employing this particular metaphor to describe the significance of cyberspace is not without utility. The association designates the encounter with a previously unknown environment where little has been determined and the opportunities and perils appear to be immeasurable. This understanding hardwires cyberspace into a network of available meanings, which render it somewhat familiar and approachable. The metaphor, however, is not without significant limitations and consequences. "New world" not only links cyberspace to the Columbian adventure but communicates the exercise of power that is implied in the seemingly neutral act of discovery. This comparison, therefore, is not innocent but establishes a complex interaction between new communication and information technologies and the cultural systems of Western colonialism and European expansionism.

NewWorld@metaphor.org

All words, in every language, are metaphors.

McLuhan and McLuhan 1988, 120

The employment of the metaphor "new world" in order to designate and explain advances in communication and information technology does not commence with cyberspace or the Internet. At the beginning of this century, for instance, Charles Horton Cooley (1962 [1901]) had proclaimed a new world in the wake of late-nineteenth-century electric communication (i.e., telegraph and telephone): "We understand nothing rightly unless we perceive the manner in which the revolution in communication has made a new world for us" (65). Sixty-one years later, Marshall McLuhan (1962) generalized Cooley's perception, arguing that all communication technologies, "whether it be alphabet or radio . . . present men with a surprising new world" (23). The recent extension of this concept to the various technologies that compose what is called cyberspace is manifest in the discursive gestures that have been employed by researchers, theorists, and journalists. "In the rhetoric of the virtual realists," concludes Benjamin Woolley (1992), "this 'nonspace' was not simply a mathematical space nor a fictional metaphor but a new frontier, a very real one that was open to exploration and, ultimately, settlement" (122). The popularity and general acceptance of this frontier rhetoric is evident in the appointed subtitle to a special edition of *Time* magazine (25 July 1994), "The Strange New World of the Internet: Battles on the Frontier of Cyberspace." This title not only employs the imagery of "new world" and "frontier" but in doing so demonstrates the extent to which these concepts have become common and colloquial. In designating its edition in this fashion, *Time* was not introducing a nomenclature. The periodical was capitalizing on a discursive trope that had already been established and deployed in the field of telecommunications technology and information systems since the introduction of the telegraph.

The majority of publications employing the metaphor of the "new world" in order to explain and describe cyberspace do so uncritically. Timothy Leary (1999), for example, identifies Christopher Columbus as the first cyberpunk. Although Leary recognizes contemporary efforts to reevaluate the implications of the Columbian voyages of discovery, he quickly dismisses them as the dictates of the "Political Correction Department" (371). For Leary, as for many cyberspace enthusiasts and researchers, Columbus remains unproblematically one of the essential role models for technological discovery, invention, and exploration. This association informs all kinds of discussions and writings about cyberspace. John Perry Barlow (1990), cofounder of the appropriately named

Electronic Frontier Foundation, has situated the Columbian encounter with the American continent as the immediate precursor
to the experience and exploration of cyberspace: "Columbus was
probably the last person to behold so much usable and unclaimed
real estate (or unreal estate) as these cybernauts have discovered"
(37). And "The Magna Carta for the Knowledge Age," a publication of the Progress and Freedom Foundation that bears the signa-
tures of some of the most influential of the digerati, projects this
Columbian lineage both backward and forward in time, encom-
passing not only the seafaring exploits of ancient Greek mariners
but also the conquest of the American West and outer space: "The
bioelectric *frontier* is an appropriate metaphor for what is happening in cyberspace, calling to mind as it does the spirit of invention
and discovery that led ancient mariners to explore the world, gen-
erations of pioneers to tame the American continent, and, more recently, to man's first explorations of outer space" (Dyson et al.
1996, 297; italics in original). In these and a large number of similar cases, the metaphors of the frontier and the new world are employed to name and describe not only the vast potential of cyberspace but the experience of exploration and discovery. For this
reason, they are unquestionably seductive, especially for American audiences. They connect the nebulous concept of cyberspace
to a number of familiar and generally celebrated images concerning discovery, boundless exploration, and national identity. These
same metaphors, however, are also undeniably problematic. At
the same time that they have been circulated in writings in and
about cyberspace, they have been, in other parts of contemporary
culture, submitted to a wholesale reevaluation and critique. As
Mary Fuller and Henry Jenkins (1995) point out, "one has to wonder why these heroic metaphors of discovery have been adopted
by popularizers of the new technologies just as these metaphors
are undergoing sustained critique in other areas of culture, a critique that hardly anyone can be unaware of in the year after the
quincentenary of Columbus' first American landfall" (59).

Woolley's *Virtual Worlds* (1992) is one text that approaches these
heroic metaphors of discovery with some skepticism. In a consid-

eration of the origin of virtual reality technology, Woolley makes the following comment concerning the mythology of cyberspace research: "Its creation myth is filled with the rhetoric of invention and discovery, of 'founding fathers' and 'pioneers.' Technologists, being mostly American, are fond of titles that evoke their New World heritage" (40). Although Woolley explicitly marks the association of cyberspace and its enabling technologies with the rhetoric of exploration and frontierism, his brief statement remains nothing but an indication of the affiliation. He does not probe either the rationale or the significance of this fondness of the technologist for titles that evoke new world imagery. The logic that informs and animates the curious association between cyberspace and frontierism, however, has been submitted to examination in Simon Penny's "Virtual Reality As the Completion of the Enlightenment Project" (1994). In a brief subsection, entitled "VR and Colonialism," Penny not only connects cyberspace to the history of European expansionism but situates technology as the defining principle of the Euro-American frontier:

> Technological development has always defined the location of frontiers. Medieval principalities were limited in scale by the speed of communication and the rate at which troops could be deployed. The Atlantic coast of Europe remained the edge of the world (to Europeans) until explorers were liberated from coast-hugging travel by accurate navigational technologies and robust ships. The American West was claimed and held only once the steam locomotive, the telegraph, and the conoidal bullet combined into one technological complex. More recently, the space race advanced as soon as the technology was available. With geography filled up and the dream of space colonization less viable every day, the drive to the frontier has collapsed on itself. The space remaining for colonization is the space of technology itself. No longer the tool by which the frontier is defined, the body of technology is now itself under exploration. (237)

Although Penny suggests intriguing historical connections that situate cyberspace within the context of the European and American colonization of space, he does not pursue an analysis of the significance or repercussions of this genealogy. In other words, Penny argues that the colonialist project extends to cyberspace but does not investigate the general implications or significance of this extension.

One text that does take the next step, engaging in a critical examination of the consequences and repercussions of the collapse of the Euro-American concept of the frontier into the very material of technology, is Fuller and Jenkins's "Nintendo® and New World Travel Writing: A Dialogue" (1995). This discussion not only traces structural similarities between the navigation of video-game cyberspace[2] and the exploration and colonization of the Americas but attempts to develop modes of inquiry that address the general significance and consequences of this curious and pregnant confluence. The object of their analysis, however, is not technology per se but *metaphor*: "We felt it might be productive to take seriously for a moment these metaphors of 'new world' and 'colonization'" (59). Metaphor, as it is commonly understood, is a *figure of speech* in which a word or phrase literally denoting one kind of object or idea is used in place of another to suggest a likeness or analogy between them. Taking metaphor seriously, as demonstrated by the dialogue between Fuller and Jenkins, means locating, tracing, and critiquing the transference of meaning initially developed in New World Travel writing (i.e., the *Diario* of Columbus, Walter Raleigh's *Discoverie of the Large, Rich and Beautiful Empier of Guiana*, and John Smith's *True Relation of Such Occurances and Accidents of Noate As Hath Happened in Virginia*) to the narrative techniques and technologies of cyberspace. For Fuller and Jenkins (1995), therefore, the metaphors of the new world do not constitute mere figures of speech but are a potent mechanism for the production of meaning and the ongoing struggle over significance. A similar analysis is espoused by Ziauddin Sardar's "alt.civilizations.faq: Cyberspace As the Darker Side of the West" (1996). This essay, which proposes to examine the association between cyberspace and "Europe's imperial past of political and cultural conquest" (Sardar and Ravetz 1996, 5), not only critiques the employment of "colonial metaphors" but argues that "cyberspace is the newly discovered Other of Western civilisation, and it will be subjected to the same treatment that the West handed out to all other non-Western cultures" (Sardar and Ravetz 1996, 6). Like Fuller and Jenkins, Sardar takes seriously the metaphors of the new world and frontier, demonstrating that such metaphors import into cyberspace various information and assumptions about space, conquest, and power that are not without problematic historical precedents. In this way, Sardar's text takes a traditional and accepted approach to the critique of metaphor, demonstrating not only the limitations of the metaphor's configuration but exhibiting its often unacknowledged connotations.

Despite this unique attention to the implications and ramifications of the metaphors of new world and colonialism, the texts of Fuller and Jenkins and Sardar inevitably encounter structural difficulties that threaten to undermine their procedures and conclusions. Although both texts identify and critique the new world metaphors circulating in and around cyberspace, they do so by employing the very metaphors they question. For example, Fuller and Jenkins (1995) state the following concerning the status of their own dialogue: "This work is a confessedly *exploratory* attempt at *charting* some possibilities of dialogue and communication" (58, italics added). Fuller and Jenkins's (1995) discussion, according to their own descriptions, examines the metaphors of new world and colonialism, which includes, among other things, the concepts of exploration (59) and chartmaking or mapmaking (66–67). The investigation of these concepts, however, is accomplished through a dialogue that readily confesses that it employs the concepts of "exploration" and "cartography" as descriptions of its own methodology. Consequently, what Fuller and Jenkins address in their discussion is also a constituent of the way they discuss it. In other words, they employ in their discursive practice the very metaphors they endeavor to critique and submit to questioning. A similar complication is manifest in the subtitle to Sardar's text, which employs the very imagery the text investigates and contends. Nominating the essay the "Darker Side of the West" puts in play the conceptual oppositions of white and black and light and dark that are not only part and parcel of Western ideology but inform the racist assumptions that Sardar critiques in the traditions of European colonial conquest and cultural domination. Consequently, Sardar, on the one hand, critiques the metaphors of lightness and darkness that are appropriated from a specific European tradition and uploaded into cyberspace and, on the other hand, is somehow compelled to use these very metaphors to describe the significance of this critique. There is, therefore, a crucial gap or apparent self-contradiction between the what and how of the analysis, between what the text manifestly means to say and how it is nonetheless constrained to mean (Norris 1982, 3).

It is tempting to explain and account for these difficulties by calling them "practical contradictions." Doing so, however, would have the general effect of neutralizing the texts' analyses and undermining their timely and insightful conclusions. The situation, however, may be more complex and nuanced than it first appears. For designating these occurrences with the name "practical contradiction" already assumes that the metaphors of the new world and the frontier can and must be surpassed through the discursive practices of the texts that compose and coordinate their investigation and critique. In other words, such a decision presumes that there already exists something like a purified form of literal or nonfigurative discourse that is able to communicate the implications of metaphor without having to employ metaphor, especially the metaphor that is submitted to critical evaluation. Recent work in rhetoric and the philosophy of language, however, suggests that the situation may be otherwise. Mark Johnson and George Lakoff's *Metaphors We Live By* (1980), for example, argues that metaphors are not merely figures of speech or discursive decorations but the very mechanism of all possible conceptual thought: "Our ordinary conceptual system . . . is metaphorical in nature" (3). If Johnson and Lakoff are correct, and recent publications in rhetoric and philosophy tend to affirm their general position,[3] then not only is the operative difference between the literal and metaphorical critically suspended, but, as Derrida (1976) formulates it, "there is nothing that does not happen with metaphor and by metaphor" (8). Through the mobilization of this insight, the analyses of Fuller and Jenkins and Sardar do not immediately resolve into practical contradiction but demonstrate the fact that the examination of metaphor cannot take place or be produced without metaphor. This alternative conceptualization, however, implies several consequences for this and any subsequent analysis that endeavors to take seriously the role and function of metaphor.

If there is indeed nothing that does not happen with and by metaphor, then any statement concerning metaphor necessarily takes place by metaphor. In this way, any critique of metaphor is immediately and inextricably involved in a circular configuration wherein the mode of investigation cannot avoid or escape what is investigated. What is necessary in these circumstances is not to break out of this circular figure by deploying or developing some form of "literal discourse" or "proper meaning" but, as Briankle Chang (1996) argues following the precedent supplied by Heidegger, to enter into the circle in the right way (x). Entering the circle of metaphor in the right way involves, on the one hand, affirming that nothing happens without metaphor and, in doing so, recognizing that the analysis of metaphor must already use and cannot avoid employing what is analyzed. It means, therefore, a mode of inquiry that would, as Chang (1996) describes it, "replace the naïve empiricist picture of the inquiring mind as a tabula rasa, or empty receptacle, with the hermeneutical principle of interpretive embeddedness" (x). On the other hand, entering this circle also involves taking seriously the metaphors by which the analysis is produced, permitting the procedure and results of the investigation to impinge upon and affect the mode by which the investigation is developed and presented. In other words, the method of the investigation cannot be restricted to or quarantined from the object of its investigation. The examination of metaphor, therefore, not only does not escape the space of metaphor but must make space for a reflective, performative recoil in which the conclusions made about metaphor come to be introduced into the manner by which these conclusions have been generated.

The following examination both follows and extends the precedent established in the work of Fuller and Jenkins and Sardar. That is, it endeavors to take seriously the metaphors of the frontier and new world that have been employed in the discourses and discussions of cyberspace. Taking metaphor seriously entails, as Fuller and Jenkins demonstrate, that these rhetorical elements be investi-gated not as mere figures of speech but as potent mechanisms that not only participate in generating what cyberspace is but also as-sist in determining how it might develop. In this way, the investi-gation employs and tests one of the hypotheses proposed by John-son and Lakoff (1980): "In all aspects of life, not just politics or in love, we define our reality in terms of metaphors and then proceed to act on the basis of the metaphors. We draw inferences, set goals, make commitments, and execute plans, all on the basis of how we in part structure our experience, consciously and unconsciously, by means of metaphor" (158). Accordingly, cyberspace may be as much a product of technical innovation in hardware and software as it is the result of the discursive techniques by which it comes to be articulated, described, and debated. However, unlike the inves-tigations of Fuller and Jenkins and Sardar, which, for whatever reason, do not take seriously the metaphors of their own discur-sive production, this chapter learns to extend its earnestness about metaphor to the rhetorical material that necessarily comprises its own investigative methodology and textual presentation. That is, the text does not presume to be able to extract itself from the situ-ation it submits to critique but endeavors to understand how its critical activity already resides within and necessarily remains de-limited by the field of metaphor. In this way, the analysis proposes to develop a sophisticated critique that not only extends the inves-tigation of the new world metaphor but also traces and examines the necessary limits (or frontiers) of such critical activity.

Ethnocentrism@reality.edu

No selection process is value-free, by definition. Software projects are shaped by the worldview of their makers; their value systems are (often un-knowingly) incorporated into the work.

Penny 1994, 237

Cyberspace, like the Americas, has been proclaimed the "new world." A new world, however, is always posed as the correlate and other of an old world. In this way, the new world is situated under the conceptual domination of the old. In the new world, one finds only what s/he wanted to find and discovers only what one, in advance, already desired to procure. Columbus, for example, discovers only what he has come prepared to find. He is confronted only with what he thinks he should encounter. Throughout the *Diario* (1989) recounting the first voyage, Columbus provides numerous entries indicating that he was certain that his fleet was situated just off the coast of China. For this reason, he records his encounters with people he called "Indians," anticipates the discovery of valuable oriental spices, and anxiously awaits the moment when he will meet the Grand Khan. His comprehension is limited to a distinct cultural frame of reference erected by Eurocentric orientalism.[4] This concept gathers the new world under the logic of old world hegemony. The apparent formlessness of the new frontier does not resist this operation. The new world, its vegetation, and its inhabitants are made to yield to the force of European determination.

The same is true in cyberspace. Consider the following declaration made by Michael Benedikt (1993b), editor of *Cyberspace: First Steps*: "We are contemplating the arising shape of a new world, a world that must, in a multitude of ways, *begin*, at least, as both an extension and a transcription of the world as we know it and have built it thus far" (23). According to Benedikt, the new world of cyberspace must be formed by extending and transcribing principles derived from the old, so-called real, world. This beginning is understood precisely as the place of initiation. It is something that not only can be altered but is expected to change over time. The alterations, however, as described by Benedikt (1993a) in his essay "Cyberspace: Some Proposals," are still ruled (this word understood in its twofold sense as marked out and controlled) by the position from which he began. The alterations, therefore, remain variations on a theme: "A central preoccupation of this essay will be the sorting out of which axioms and laws of nature ought to be retained in cyberspace, on the grounds that humans have successfully evolved on a planet where these are fixed and conditioning of all phenomena (including human intelligence), and which axioms and laws can be adjusted or jettisoned for the sake of empowerment. Before dedicating significant resources to creating cyberspace, however, we should want to know how it might look, how might we get around in it, and, most importantly, what might we usefully do there" (119). With this explanation, Benedikt universalizes a particular understanding of reality under the title "laws of nature" and delimits all possible operations according to their prescription. He justifies the extension of particular experiences and interpretations of the real into cyberspace by naturalizing these perspectives and making them a universal condition for all phenomena, including the human intellect. In this way, Benedikt duplicates the gesture enacted by Columbus and all subsequent colonial administrators. He posits his own circumstance as natural and extends it to universal applicability. From this proclaimed "universal and natural" position, one begins to make decisions concerning what might be done usefully in this new locale. The apparent necessity for determining cyberspace in this way, however, is not natural. It must be seen for what it in fact is—an imposition and an exercise of cultural power. In beginning to determine cyberspace in accordance with a particular conception of reality, Benedikt perpetuates a trope of European expansionism that justifies its ethnocentrism by naturalizing and universalizing its own epistemology.[5]

A particularly instructive example of this operation and its consequences can be found in the fundamental structure and definition of cyberspace. The neologism *cyberspace* was coined by novelist William Gibson and publicized in his proto-cyberpunk novel, *Neuromancer* (1984). Although this self-proclaimed computer illiterate[6] was not involved in the myriad of technological experiments taking place in telecommunications, computer networking, and virtual reality (i.e., Bulletin Board Systems; computer animation; the early virtual reality projects of Scott Fisher, Ivan Sutherland, and Tom Furness; ARPA's experimental network that eventually became the prototype of the Internet; etc.), Gibson provided the proper name around which these different endeavors were organized, understood, and properly identified. Early on, theorists and researchers at the first conference on Cyberspace (University of Texas at Austin, 4–5 May 1990) recognized, as reported in the words of David Tomas (1993), that "Gibson's powerful vision is now beginning to influence the way virtual reality and cyberspace researchers are structuring their research agendas and problematics" (46).

Gibson assembled the word "cyberspace" from *cybernetics*, a neologism devised by Norbert Wiener to name the science of communication and control, and *space*. Although the inherent ambiguity of the word "space" leaves some room for interpretation, the spatiality of cyberspace has been described and determined in accordance with a particular understanding. The initial source of this determination can be found in *Neuromancer*. In the descriptions offered in this narrative, the cyberspatial environment not only displays data as three-dimensional, geometric objects but projects this information onto a Cartesian grid. For example: "People jacked in so they could hustle. Put the trodes on and they were out there, all the data in the world stacked up like one big neon city, so you could cruise around and have a kind of grip on it, visually anyway, because if you didn't, it was too complicated, trying to find your way to a particular piece of data you needed" (Gibson 1984, 13). Cyberspace is understood geometrically, and this understanding is particularly Cartesian. Theorists and designers have, for the most part, remained within these nominal determinations. The developers of virtual reality equipment, like the head mounted displays (HMD) of Ivan Sutherland and Thomas Furness, endeavor to create presentation systems that appear to surround and envelop the user. The HMD creates the illusion of objects in three-dimensional space through stereographic projections of wireframe or solid polygon models. The HMD provides a window into what Sutherland called a "mathematical wonderland" (Rheingold 1991, 13) that is programmed and displayed according to the principles of Cartesian geometry. Even text-based virtual realities, like multi-user dungeons/domains (MUDs) and object-oriented MUDs (MOOs), describe their environments in accordance with the properties of modern geometry. In a

MUD/MOO, users explore different rooms or locales and interact with each other by navigating through a textually described three-dimensional space. Characters enter rooms, look under sofas, take the elevator to the second floor, and even fall off dangerous precipices.

Consequently, the general goal of both HMD VR and text-based cyberspace is, according to Scott Fisher (1981), to simulate or "duplicate the viewer's act of confronting a real scene" (94). This "real scene," however, is always already an interpretation that is guided by a particular understanding of the real. "Reality," in the words of Barlow (1999), "is an edit" (330).

Cyberspace readily receives the X-Y-Z of the Cartesian coordinate system. It accepts the inscription and delimitation of the three-dimensional grid. It is, therefore, subject to the modern logic of space and spatiality. This determination, however, is neither natural nor necessary.[7] It is culturally determined and as such may be understood otherwise. Penny marks this at the beginning of his essay "Virtual Reality As the Completion of the Enlightenment Project" (1994): "But the Cartesian grid is built into our culture and our perception as an integral and structuring part of the rationalist determinism with which we have been inculcated. To propose an alternative to Cartesian space is to propose an alternative to the philosophical and technical legacy of the Enlightenment" (232). Cyberspace has the potential to interrupt the very structure, substance, and control of modern epistemology. This alternative, which Penny poses as a virtual impossibility, has been articulated by several discourses addressed to the aftermath of Enlightenment science. Cyberspatial theorists, such as Nicole Stenger (1993), describe this alternative by relying on the discursive tropes created in the hallucinatory poems of Henri Michaux: "Perception would change, and with it, the sense of reality, of time, of life and death. We would, as Michaux puts it, 'enter the world of Fluids,' it would be 'over with the solid, over with the continuous and with the calm,' some dance quality would invade everything, and Cartesian philosophers would go through a trance, floating on history like chops on gravy" (50). To begin to determine cyberspace from the perspective of the real (which is already a particular interpretation of what is called reality) is to limit our understanding to old world preconceptions and (mis)perceptions. Cyberspace has the potential to dissolve the solid monuments of Enlightenment science. In the face of this dissolution, there are two opportunities. Either this dangerous potential is controlled by submitting its formless otherness to familiar structures, insisting from the beginning that it behave according to protocols imposed by and from the established order. Or it will undermine the very means by which this control could be exercised, thereby reversing the flow of invasion and domestication. As Stenger (1993) suggests, "I felt that this hallucination behind a screen was just the first stage in a development, a rehearsal for a D-Day when this substance would finally escape and invade what we call reality" (49).

Commercialism@wealth.com

Cyberspace is the surrogate for old colonies, the "new continent" artificially created to satisfy Western man's insatiable desire to acquire new wealth and riches.

Sardar and Ravetz 1996, 6

Columbus seeks gold. In his *Diario* of the first voyage (1989), he indicates that he not only actively sought gold but, at every encounter, endeavored to ask the native peoples directions to stockpiles of such wealth. In his proposal submitted to Queen Isabella, Columbus (1993) promises that this new world would bring forth gold and riches beyond compare. And when the islands do not immediately supply the wealth originally promised, he fudges the account. Although the *Diario* indicates that he found only a few pieces of gold represented by decorations (earrings, rings, etc.), he assures the queen that "in the island Española, there are many spices and great mines of gold and of other metals" (Columbus 1993, 16).

The new world is always posited as a world of riches waiting to be exploited. The frontiers of the American West and Alaska were organized and articulated around the concept of gold and the gold rush. Justifications for the American space program, which set out to explore the "final frontier," were often couched in the discourse of wealth. This wealth consisted of a particular cold-war commodity—scientific knowledge and national identity (Web 1967). Cyberspace is also formulated as a world saturated with the potential for commercial gain. In *Neuromancer*, the matrix is dominated by the Zaibatsus, multinational organizations that employ the cyberspatial net for the enrichment of their information capital. In this way, cyberspace comprises a virtual mall of commercial operations and consumerism. In the published fragment "Academy Leader," Gibson (1993) offers the following description of the cyberspatial environment: "The architecture of virtual reality imagined as an accretion of dreams: tattoo parlors, shooting galleries, pinball arcades, dimly lit stalls stacked with damp-stained years of men's magazines, chili joints, premises of unlicensed denturists, of fireworks and cut bait, betting shops, sushi bars, purveyors of sexual appliances, pawnbrokers, wonton counters, love hotels, hotdog stands, tortilla factories, Chinese greengrocers, liquor stores, herbalists, chiropractors, barbers, bars. . . . These are the dreams of commerce" (28).

According to Gibson, cyberspace is predominantly composed of data that is brokered, traded, accumulated, and consumed. Commercialism is also the promise of the would-be nonfictional cyberspace. A caricature of this promise can be found in LucasFilm's Habitat, an early virtual environment designed by Chip Morningstar and Randall Farmer for a tele-network of Commodore 64s. Habitat consists of an inhabitable social space represented by a two-dimensional cartoonlike frame. The virtual persona, or avatar, who is the user's delegated agent, is represented by a cartoonlike figure, and his/her "speaking" is indicated by a speech balloon that appears over the character's head (Stone 1993, 94). In their published study, "The Lessons of LucasFilm's Habitat," Morningstar and Farmer (1993) offer only one frame as an illustration of "a typical Habitat scene." This frame depicts a suburban street with two houses in the background. The foreground is occupied by two characters engaged in the following exchange:

Cathy: Hi Terry.
Terry: Hi Cathy.
Cathy: Nice day for a quest!
Terry: It's always a nice day for treasure hunting. (275)

The illustration provided by Morningstar and Farmer suggests that the typical scene of cyberspatial interaction still falls under the purview of new world adventure, namely, the quest for discovery thinly veiling a search for gold. In this way, cyberspace is already conceptualized as a locale for the pursuit of treasure. Contemporary corporations have wasted no time in positioning themselves to capitalize on these new commercial possibilities. International Business Machines (IBM) (1996a), for example, has been optimistic about the possible riches to be netted in cyberspace. "The networked world is already arriving—in a hurry. Consider the Internet: hundreds of millions of people, perhaps billions, connected by the year 2000. Already we're seeing how people and organizations use these networks. They're moving from browsing to buying, from surfing to working. People are doing real work. They're seeing results. That's why our major thrust in network-centric computing is to help our customers get their valuable content to the right people and to new people—both within and outside of their organizations: to employees, to suppliers, and, of course, to customers" (1). Organizations like IBM conceive of cyberspace as a new domain for commercial transactions. Because of the recent proliferation in e-commerce, automated teller machines (ATMs), and electronic trading of stocks, bonds, and futures, cyberspace has become, in the words of Woolley (1992), "literally where the money is" (133).

In *Neuromancer*, cyberspace is dominated by the commercial. Any noncommercial entity, anyone loitering in the neon-laced mall of information is considered an unauthorized and dangerous presence. For this reason, *Neuromancer* describes cyberspace as the site of struggle between the multinational Zaibatsus and lone ICE hackers, which Gibson names (in a gesture that is not without consequence to this investigation) *cowboys*. However accurate this description, commercialism is not the only goal. Commercial exploitation is always recoded by reference to the social and cultural. European colonial commerce, for example, had been justified in terms of its presumed humanizing effects. In Joseph Conrad's *Heart of Darkness* (1988), the company boss offers the following comment on the presence of Europeans in the Congo: "Each station should be like a beacon on the road toward better things, a centre for trade of course but also for humanizing, improving, instructing" (34). A similar promise has been suggested for online commerce. Once again, IBM (1996b) provides a particularly insightful articulation: "IBM's view of a 'network centric' future is driven by the desire of people and enterprises to connect to other people and enterprises around the world and leverage information using powerful new technologies that transcend distance and time, lower boundaries between markets, cultures and individuals, and actually deliver solutions that fulfills the promise of universal connectivity" (1). IBM's vision of the "network centric" future recodes global commerce and commercialism under the millennial aspirations of intercultural communication and global communion. It's a global village after all, and IBM has already positioned itself to provided the necessary "solutions for a small planet." (IBM 1997). One should, however, approach such utopian statements with skepticism. As Penny (1994) warns, "we have no reason to delude ourselves that any new technology, as such, promises any sort of sociocultural liberation. History is against us here. We must assume that the forces of large-scale commodity capitalism will attempt to capitalize fully on the phenomenon in terms of financial profit" (247). Despite this warning, cyberspace is inundated with utopian projects and aspirations. Indeed, for many theorists and researchers, like Tomas (1993), cyberspace would be nothing more than a "waste of space" if it did not become the site of new communities that offer significant cultural promise:

If cyberspace represents, at the very least, the birth of a new postindustrial, metasocial spatial operator, it will remain for the most part still born if its parameters are engineered primarily to function, following Gibson's dystopic vision, as a virtual world of contestatory economic activity. In order to counter this vision, one must actively and strategically seek alternative spatial and creative logics, social and cultural configurations. If such creative flexibility is critically foregrounded in current research agendas, cyberspace will indeed become a site of considerable cultural promise. (46)

Utopianism@community.gov

You might think of cyberspace as a utopian vision for postmodern times. Utopia is nowhere (*outopia*) and, at the same time, it is also somewhere good (*eutopia*). Cyberspace is projected as the same kind of "nowhere-somewhere."

Robins 1995, 135

The "considerable cultural promise" that Tomas (1993) proposes in opposition to the dystopic commercialism envisioned by Gibson necessarily pulls in the direction of utopia. For the new world is always the place of utopia. The people that Columbus encounters on the islands of the Caribbean are described as living in an idyllic paradise. According to Columbus's (1989) unreliable reports, they do not have governments, engage in work, practice religion, have monetary systems, or wage war. For the European, the new world is paradise found. It already is utopian, serves as the physical location for the fictional *Utopia* of Thomas More, and eventually provides the site for numerous European experiments with alternative communities. The first of these utopian polities was instituted by Vasco de Quiroga as early as 1535. Similar utopian experiments occur throughout the history of the Americas. According to Carlos Fuentes (1993), "utopia persisted as one of the central stains of the culture of the Americas. We were condemned to utopia by the old world" (4).

Neuromancer is often criticized for its dystopic vision. According to Benedikt (1993b), Gibson's is a world of "corporate hegemony and urban decay, of neural implants, of a life in paranoia and pain" (1). Despite this vision and in direct opposition to it, theorists, practitioners, and advertisers have positioned cyberspace as the realm of cultural liberation and millennial aspirations. Cyberspace enthusiasts, as Sardar (1996) points out, "are latter-day Utopians, the counter-part of Sir Thomas More, Francis Bacon, Tommaso Campanella, and other European Utopians who cannibalised the ideas and cultures of the 'New World' to construct their redeeming fantasies" (34). Examples abound; let's recall two early and particularly interesting formulations. The first is found in Bruce Schuman's web-published "Utopian Computer Networking: America's New Central Project" (1988), which was originally posted and circulated within the virtual community of the WELL in response to Willis Harman and Howard Rheingold's *Higher Creativity*. The second comprises the conclusion to Nicole Stenger's 1993 paper, "Mind Is a Leaking Rainbow," which was presented at the first conference on cyberspace and subsequently published in *Cyberspace: First Steps*.

A powerful, central technology for achieving common vision and joint understanding must eventually emerge, and this technology, its primary underlying message perhaps the fundamental basic truths of the "Perennial Philosophy," must reach out to the entire human community, through a massive and unitary linkage of the entire body of humankind, creating as it were one giant living organism. The international telecommunications network, with its thousands of computers and millions of sophisticated users, is certainly the medium for the realization of this linkage and unification. . . . Through well-programmed international networking, we have the potential to make our world divine. (Schuman 1988, 6)

According to Sartre, the atomic bomb was what humanity had found to commit collective suicide. It seems, by contrast, that cyberspace, though born of a war technology, opens up a space for collective restoration, and for peace. As screens are dissolving, our future can only take on a luminous dimension! Welcome to the new world. (Stenger 1993, 58)

One should not be too quick to forget that this global "unitary linkage" and "collective restoration" had also been the promise of virtually every other form of communication technology. Electric telegraphy, for example, entered nineteenth-century discourses "not as a mundane fact but as divinely inspired for the purposes of spreading the Christian message farther and faster, eclipsing time and transcending space, saving the heathen, bringing closer and making more probable the day of salvation" (Carey 1989, 17). Similar millennial promises, in both religious and secular forms, were circulated in the popular and technical rhetoric of electricity (Marvin 1988), radio (Spinelli 1996), and television (McLuhan 1995). The general contours of this techno-utopian rhetoric had been articulated as early as 1852 in a work entitled *The Silent Revolution*, which predicted the attainment of a new social harmony due to "a perfect network of electric filaments" (Mattelart 1994, 33).

Despite these seductive utopian proclamations, the development and experience of both the European age of exploration and the history of telecommunications technology has demonstrated something quite the contrary. The European encounter with the new world of the Americas, although situated and promoted as redemptive, has been all too often experienced as a form of invasion, oppression, and genocide. One generation after Columbus's first landfall, for example, the people and cultures that he called *Indians* had all but disappeared through the importation of disease, armed conflict, and systematic deportation. Although the new world served as a resource for European utopian fantasies, these dreams had a considerable price. Consequently, one culture's utopia has often constituted another's enslavement and annihilation. Why then, if this is the case, is cyberspace continually and unabashedly connected to this lineage? Why isn't cyberspace haunted and complicated by what Sardar (1996) calls the "darkside" of the European (mis)adventure of discovery? Fuller and Jenkins (1995, 59) provide a compelling explanation. "I would speculate that part of the drive behind the rhetoric of virtual reality as a New World or new frontier is the desire to recreate the Renaissance encounter with America without guilt: This time, if there are others present, they really won't be human, or if they are, they will be other players, like ourselves, whose bodies are not jeopardized by the virtual weapons we wield."

The *terra nova* of cyberspace is assumed to be disengaged from and unencumbered by the legacy of European colonialism, because cyberspace is determined to be innocent and guiltless. What distinguishes and differentiates the utopian dreams of cyberspace from that of the new world is that cyberspace, unlike the Americas, is assumed to be victimless. This assurance, however, is naïve and deceptive. "Cyberspace," as Sardar (1996) points out, "does have real victims" (19). Although the virtual *terra nova* contains no "indigenous peoples" who are conquered, deported, or subjugated, the concept and technology of cyberspace does already exclude a good number of people from participating in its magnificent techno-utopia. As both a concept originating in a particular genre of Western literature and an ensemble of technologies developed for and demonstrated in video games and computer simulation and internetworking, cyberspace has been limited to a highly specific demographic. Recent studies of Internet usage and telecommunications infrastructure (Anderson et al. 1995; Hoffman, Novak, and Chatterjee 1996; Wresch 1996; Katz 1997; Novak and Hoffman 1998), for example, have found that the majority of cybernauts or netizens are, not surprisingly, Caucasian, upper-middle or upper class, and male. Data associated with video games and cyberpunk science fiction, both of which have been criticized for their recirculation of adolescent male fantasies (Pfeil 1990, 89; Ross 1991a, 145), reveal demographic percentages that are at least commensurate with those studies if not significantly higher. As a result, cyberspace has been and continues to be the privileged realm of white European culture. In this matter Barlow (Gans and Sirius 1991) did not know to what extent he was right, with what exactitude he had accurately described the demographics of cyberspace: "Cyberspace is presently inhabited almost exclusively by mountain men, desperadoes and vigilantes, kind of a rough bunch" (49). Consequently, the same group that had excluded indigenous peoples from the utopian fantasies of the new world now effectively exclude others from participating in the techno-utopia of cyberspace. Although this virtual exclusion is admittedly bloodless and seemingly sanitized of the stigma of colonial conquest, it is no less problematic or hegemonic. What is especially disturbing is that this particular cultural privilege is not recognized as such but has been concealed and legitimated by the utopian rhetoric of sociopolitical emancipation, universal human equality, and global unity.

Similar forms of cultural violence are associated with and have been the experience of most other forms of telecommunications technology. Despite initial utopian promises organized around the telegraphic network, the actual employment and development of this technology came to serve other purposes. "The messages that passed through these far-flung communications links were," as Steven Lubar (1993) points out, "messages not of peace and unity but of unprecedented technological warfare" (89). Similar complications have been recorded in the history of the telephone, television, and radio. Martin Spinelli (1996), for example, argues that "the utopian rhetoric that surrounded the emergent medium of radio functioned largely to obscure a profit motive" (8). There is, therefore, significant dissonance between a particular technology's utopian promises and its actual deployment and development. If the utopian ideals, which were previously predicated of the telegraph, telephone, radio, and television, were never fully attained by these technologies, what is it that leads contemporary researchers, theorists, and engineers to believe that the fate of cyberspace will be otherwise? Why, despite the warnings like those provided by Penny (1994, 247), have we ignored the fact that history is against us here, that no new technology, as such, can provide any form of sociocultural liberation? How is it that the well-documented history of communication technology fails to inform contemporary discussions and discourses of cyberspace, virtual reality, and the Internet?

There are at least two, related reasons for this blind optimism. First, computer technology, like the new world of the Americas, has traditionally been determined to be radically ahistorical. As Penny (1994) describes it, "new technologies are often heralded by a rhetoric that locates them as futuristic, without history, or at best arising from a scientific-technical lineage quite separate from cultural history" (231). Just as the new world of the Americas was formed out of the European desire to forget history and to establish a new beginning unencumbered by old world prejudices, computer technology has been situated as futuristic and disconnected from specific historical circumstances and precedents. This form of historical amnesia, however, is not only a kind of deliberate self-deception but ironically constitutes a practice that is culturally specific and has its own complex history. Cyberspace, despite its futuristic rhetoric, is not ahistorical. It has a history, and this history is directly connected to some problematic precedents. As N. Katherine Hayles (1996b) points out, cyberspace "did not spring, like Athena from the forehead of Zeus, full-blown from the mind of William Gibson. It has encoded within it a complex history of technological innovations, conceptual developments, and metaphorical linkages that are crucially important in determining how it will develop and what it is taken to signify" (11). The metaphor of the new world, rather than enabling and supporting historical amnesia, should empower this historical sense and complicate these all too simple utopian assurances and proclamations.

Second, even when the concepts and technologies that comprise cyberspace are situated in historical context, they are all too often located at the apex of a simple, linear path of technological progress. Benedikt (1993b) contextualizes cyberspace by following what he calls four intertwining threads: "the history of narrative" (5), "the history of media technology" (7), "the history of architecture" (13), and "the history of mathematics" (18). In all four cases, cyberspace is situated at the zenith of a linear progression that develops and evolves through the course of time. This limited, one-dimensional progression, which is entirely commensurate with Western formulations of history, traces a narrative trajectory that locates cyberspace as the eventual perfection and proper end of a specific historical development. In this way, cyberspace is both part of a historical progression and the fulfillment and completion of its *telos*. Similar progressive accounts are provided in Jay David Bolter's (1991) and George Landow's (1992) account of hypertext, which situate electronic textuality, now familiar from the experience of the World Wide Web and CD-ROMs, as the next stage in the development and eventual perfection of writing technology. Likewise, the study of virtual reality (VR) in Biocca, Kim, and Levy (1995) begins by situating the technology of VR within the history of the "2000-year search for the ultimate display" (7). Predictably, this historical introduction traces a straight line that begins with painting, progresses through photography and television, and concludes with the promise of VR.[8] Although these various attempts to historicize computer technology appear to move beyond the simple ahistoricism criticized by Penny, they do so by following a simple and specific form of history as progress. This formula, which is distinctly European, not only situates cyberspace as the proper end of a historical progression but, in doing so, makes cyberspace the perfection and fulfillment of whatever difficulties and problems have been situated in the historical narrative. Consequently, cyberspace is often unencumbered by the manifest failures of earlier forms of communication technology to deliver on their fantastic promises, precisely because cyberspace has been situated as the one technology that finally fulfills these various dreams and utopian proposals.

From its inception, the "nonspace of cyberspace" (Gibson 1987, 15) has been informed and influenced by utopian rhetoric. The new world has always been the location of utopias, and cyberspace, already disengaged from the problematic constraints of physical geography, promises to provide a virtually limitless resource for utopian fantasies. This utopian tendency, however, no matter how attractive and seductive, already entails significant complications and difficulties. On the one hand, cyberspace, like the new world of the Americas, is a privileged domain that has been granted to a particular segment of Western culture. Consequently, cyberspace not only has victims but these victims are all too often effaced by a techno-utopian rhetoric that both occludes and legitimates this exclusivity. Just as the numerous forms of utopia situated in the new world of the Americas excluded indigenous peoples, the new world of cyberspace already disenfranchises a majority of the world's population from participation in the global utopia of computer technology. On the other hand, cyberspace cannot and should not be quarantined from the actual experiences of other forms of communication and information technology. If the initial techno-utopian dreams of telegraphy, telephone, radio, and television have led to disappointing conclusions, there is good reason to be skeptical and critical of similar promises now circulating within the networks of cyberculture. Cyberspace certainly is not ahistorical. But its relationship to the history of technology is complicated by approaches that employ, without question, a specific form of history as linear progress. As a result, cyberspace is all too often situated as the *telos* of dreams and aspirations that are, in a curious form of retrospect, determined to be two thousand years old. Although one cannot simply forget that cyberspace is always located in a specific context, one should also not forget that the delimitation of this context is itself subject to various articulations, interpretations, and manipulations.

Conclusions: Decolonizing Cyberspace

Just when we thought that the age of European colonialism has finally come to an end, suddenly we are copied into the second age of virtual colonialism.

Kroker and Weinstein 1994, 11

The meaning of *cyberspace* has been open to considerable interpretation. Gibson (1993) has provided an account of this matter in the fragment "Academy Leader": "Assembled word *cyberspace* from small and readily available components of language. Neologic spasm: the primal act of pop poetics. Preceded any concept whatever. Slick hollow—awaiting received meaning" (27). According to Gibson, the only determinations properly belonging to cyberspace are formless, hollow, passive, and receptive. Gibson's cyberspace, therefore, is bestowed with all the characteristics attributed to χώρα, the protometaphysical concept usually translated as space and initially described by Timaeus in the Platonic dialogue that bears his name. It is precisely this *choric* (in)determination that has permitted the seemingly endless chatter in and about cyberspace. Cyberspace has become the receptacle of all sorts of determinations that seek to leave their imprint in the malleable material of Gibson's neologism.

One determination that has left a considerable impression is the metaphor *terra nova*. We have only begun to trace the consequences and implications of this complex designation. Initially, the concept of the new world was most certainly employed to help explain new forms of information and communication technology and the opportunities they apparently engender. And "new world" does, indeed, provide some compelling explanations and conceptualizations. Its employment, however, has not been without significant consequences, which, although not necessarily intended, have had a definite effect on what cyberspace is and how it has been understood. Under this sign, cyberspace has already been made to yield to a particular conception of geometry, which effaces its ethnocentrism under the universal concept "law of nature." Its resources have already been surveyed, partitioned, and allocated for contemporary treasure hunters and marketing executives. And all this is recoded and justified through the promise of sociocultural emancipation, which turns out to be nothing more than a luxury belonging to the majority who continually efface or recode the history of their privileged position. In this way, the "new world" of cyberspace offers nothing new but is already appropriated into a specific lineage and tradition. Five hundred years after Columbus, the process of discovery begins anew but discovers little, if anything, new.

One may be tempted to disregard these conclusions as the unfortunate side effects of taxonomy or the noise of imprecise language. But the activity of naming is never a matter of mere words. It remains one of the primary mechanisms of appropriation and control. The power that is exercised through such nominal operations is evident in the Columbian encounter with the Americas. Prior to the counter-Eurocentric critique initiated in the latter half of the twentieth century, mainstream America said that Columbus *discovered* the new world. The manner of discovery, however, did not constitute the mere unveiling of something already available. Instead, the new world took form through the various descriptions inscribed in the reports and journals issued by the admiral. It was this nominal activity that eventually dictated what was discovered and what became possible within the space of this new frontier. As suggested by Fuentes (1993), "to discover is to invent is to name" (2).

The nominal act is always an exercise of power and must, therefore, be taken seriously. The words that are employed to describe a technological innovation are never mere reports of the state-of-the-art but constitute sites for the production of and struggle over significance. Describing cyberspace through the words *frontier* and *new world* have had definite and often disturbing implications and consequences. The crucial task, it appears, would be to escape this kind of metaphorical thinking *tout court*, avoiding any and all problematic associations and comparisons whatsoever. This fantastic ideal is at least impractical if not impossible. Whether one accepts or rejects Johnson and Lakoff's (1980) proposal that "our ordinary conceptual system . . . is metaphorical in nature" (3), the fact remains, as is evident in the analysis of Sardar (1996) and the discussion of Fuller and Jenkins (1995), that the critique of metaphor cannot be presented without employing, in practice, metaphors. What is required, therefore, is not a naïve rejection of metaphor for some kind of perfected and noiseless form of communication but an active and critical approach to their seemingly inescapable application and significance. This critical treatment entails, in the first place, the realization that metaphor cannot be submitted to investigation without participating in and employing what is questioned. If "there is nothing that does not happen with metaphor and by metaphor" (Derrida 1976, 8), then the investigation of metaphor cannot extract itself from what it seeks to examine. The critique of metaphor, therefore, necessarily takes place in an unavoidable circular configuration. This complex circularity, which is not merely reducible to a debilitating form of "circular reasoning" (Chang 1996, x) or an ironic practical contradiction, has at least two general implications for this and future investigations of cyberspace.

First, metaphors are always more than mere words. They are mechanisms of real social and political hegemony that have the capacity to determine the current and future shape of what they seem merely to designate. As a result of this, current and future configurations of cyberspace will be determined not only through innovations in hardware and software but also, and perhaps more so, through the various metaphors that have been circulated and are employed to describe their significance. The ongoing struggle over the meaning of cyberspace, therefore, is a conflict that must be waged as much in the material of microprocessors, network protocols, and visual display technologies as in the language and rhetoric that have been and are used to introduce, discuss, and describe these technical innovations. As a result, the decolonization of cyberspace cannot, as it has often been suggested, be reduced to a matter of telecommunications infrastructure, local access to high-tech equipment, computer literacy, or the bridging of the digital divide.[9] Because cyberspace has already been submitted to a kind of colonization through the metaphors of the new world and the electronic frontier, its decolonization is a task that, if it ever transpires, must take place in and by engaging the material and legacy of these particular rhetorical configurations.[10] For decolonization, as postcolonial literature has often demonstrated, is a conflict situated not only in extant social and political systems but in the material of the language one is already compelled to employ (Aschcroft, Griffiths, and Tiffin 1995, 284).

Second, if "there is nothing that does not happen with metaphor and by metaphor," then any decolonizing effort or critical position that contests the hegemony of the "new world" metaphor is itself already constrained to employ metaphors and is implicated in their circulation. These metaphors are not necessarily different from or an improvement over the ones they endeavor to criticize and contend. As demonstrated by the discussion of Fuller and Jenkins (1995) and the analysis of Sardar (1996), one is often in the curious position of having to employ in the texture of critique the very metaphors that are the subject of that critique. In addition, alternative descriptions and conceptualizations of cyberspace, like the "information superhighway" and "the virtual community," are no less metaphoric or problematic. For they all channel, in one way or another, various forms of discursive power. This means that any and all alternative formulations of cyberspace cannot be simply disengaged from the complications and difficulties that have been demonstrated in the examination of the new world metaphor. Consequently, there neither is nor can be a protected and uncontaminated outside from which one could or would be able to provide an adequate critique of metaphor, whether it be the metaphors of the new world and electronic frontier or an alternative that would oppose and contend these various configurations. As a result, one is, from the beginning, always and already operating on and from the terrain that one wishes to submit to questioning. In this curious situation there are no prior assurances, easy answers, or simple solutions. But, as postcolonial practices have demonstrated, there is only an interminable struggle that must continually learn to submit to questioning the implications and outcome of its own movements and innovations.

Notes

1. On recent reevaluations of Columbus and the Columbian encounter, see Todorov (1984), Hulme (1986), Fuentes (1988), Lopez (1992), *Rethinking Columbus* (1991), Momaday (1992), and Fusco and Gómez-Peña's "Radio Pirata: Colón Go Home!" in Fusco (1995). For critical examinations of travel, exploration, and geography, see Harvey (1969); Helm (1988); Enloe (1990); Leed (1991); Clifford (1992); Unwin (1992); Dathorne (1994), especially chapter 1, "Europe Invents a New World"; Godlewska and Smith (1994); and Appadurai (1996). For an examination of similar issues in the "geography" of cyberspace, see Morse (1996) and Hillis (1996).

2. Although Fuller and Jenkins trace interesting parallels between the virtual geography of Nintendo® and the accounts of travels to and within the Americas, a more literal connection between the rhetoric of the New World and video gaming has been enacted by a recent release from Sunflower Interactive Entertainment Software, GmbH. The object of this game, titled *Anno 1602: Erschaffung einer Neuen Welt* [Year 1602: Creation of a New World], is to discover a new world, take control of its resources, and administer a colony.

3. This proposal, despite initial appearances, is actually nothing revolutionary. It merely psychologizes a suspicion already articulated by Nietzsche in an often-quoted passage from "On Truth and Falsity in an Extra-Moral Sense": "What then is truth? A mobile army of metaphors, metonymics, anthropomorphisms: in short, a sum of human relations which became poetically and rhetorically intensified, metamorphosed, adorned, and after long usage, seem to a nation fixed, canonic and binding; truths are illusions of which one has forgotten they are illusions; worn out metaphors which have become powerless to affect the senses" (Quoted in Derrida 1982, 217).

4. Cf. Said (1978).

5. On colonialism and European expansion, see Anzaldua (1987), Morris (1988), Chakravorty Spivak (1988), Trinh T. Minh-ha (1989), Giroux (1992), Bhabha (1994), and Fusco (1995). A good introduction to and survey of issues in postcolonial studies can be found in Ashcroft, Griffiths, and Tiffin's *Post-Colonial Studies Reader* (1995). A good introduction to issues surrounding ethnocentrism and marginal cultures can be found in Ferguson et al.'s *Out There: Marginalization and Contemporary Cultures* (1990).

6. Gibson not only did not own or know how to operate a personal computer, but wrote the entire text of *Neuromancer* on a manual typewriter.

7. For a comprehensive examination of the cultural politics of mathematics and geometry, see Bishop (1995).

8. A sustained examination of this approach to VR is provided in Chapter 3.

9. Vice President Al Gore (1999), for example, has simplified the problem of *technological privilege* to a matter of access to telecommunications equipment and services. This reduction is immediately evident in the first article of his "Digital Declaration of Independence": "We must improve access to technology so that everyone on the planet is within walking distance of voice and data telecommunications services within the next decade. Right now, sixty-five per cent of the world's households have no phone service. Half of the world's population has never made a phone call" (14). Although unequal access is a considerable problem, it is not the only source of technological privilege. For more on this issue, see Chapter 5.

10. For examples of alternative, postcolonial employments of cyberspace and information technology, see Haraway (1991b), Nelson (1994), Sandoval (1995), Todd (1996), and Gómez-Peña (1997).

2

ARS METAPHORICA: THE COMPUTER AS A DEVICE OF COMMUNICATION

Computing and communication are becoming one.

Pool 1990, 8

Although the Internet is generally considered to be a technology of communication, computer networks have not always been interpreted and understood in this manner. As its name indicates, the computer was initially designed to provide for rapid and automatic computation. Computer networks, by extension, were devised as means to facilitate telecomputing or time-shared access to powerful computational machines from any number of dispersed locations. The shift from an understanding of the computer as a device of computation to a device of communication was first publicized and explicated in J.C.R. Licklider and Robert W. Taylor's 1968 publication, "The Computer As a Communication Device." In this article, Licklider and Taylor not only introduced the term "computer-aided communication" (29) but announced the development of a "network of networks" (38) to facilitate a kind of telecommunication that is "as natural an extension of individual work as face-to-face communication" (40). One year after the publication of this influential and remarkable article, ARPAnet, the precursor to the Internet, began operation. As if to fulfill Licklider and Taylor's thesis, the actual use of this network "did not support remote computing. The network evolved instead to become primarily a medium for interpersonal communication" (Dutton 1995, 95).

With "The Computer As a Communication Device," the computer network was no longer limited to the discipline of computer science and the activities of remote computing but, for better or worse, entered the purview of communication studies. As a result, there is now a complex of texts, discussions, and debates that address the communicative potential and consequences of the computer and the network. These discourses run from sober assessments that find the Net to be nothing more than "an instantaneous telegraph with a prodigious memory" (Marvin 1988, 3) to inflated exaltations that announce a "communications revolution" (Pool 1990; Brunn and Leinbach 1991; Gore 1993; Dyson et al. 1996; Negroponte 1995; Biocca and Levy 1995b; USAC-NII 1996; Cairncross 1997; Dizard 1997). The following does not, at least directly, enter into the texture of these discussions and debates. It steps behind it, as it were, and undertakes an investigation of the common understanding of communication that not only makes these discussions possible but enables debate by establishing communication between them. Consequently, the subtitle to this chapter may require some qualification. What is pursued in this investigation is not, strictly speaking, an examination of the communicative potential and consequences of the computer and cyberspace but a critical inquiry into the fundamental principles of communication by which these examinations first become possible and develop.

Although "the temptation to define communication," as Briankle Chang (1996) points out, "is as persistent as it is notoriously difficult" (x), scholars have traditionally recognized and operated with two competing general characterizations. In his now seminal work on communication and culture, James Carey (1989) argues that intellectual work on communication, at least in Western traditions, is grounded in two heterogeneous viewpoints or "metaphors of communication" (41): "Two alternative conceptions of communication have been alive in American culture since the term entered common discourse in the nineteenth century. . . . We might label these descriptions, if only to provide handy pegs upon which to hang our thought, a transmission view of communication and a ritual view of communication" (14–15). A similar distinction was proffered by Raymond Williams (1976), who in *Keywords* points out that the word *communication* has an unresolved double valence, which vacillates between what he calls transmission and mutual sharing (63). According to both Carey and Williams, these two viewpoints not only have substantially distinct consequences but "derive from differing problematics; that is the basic questions of the one tradition do not connect with the basic questions of the other" (Carey 1989, 43). Although Carey recognizes that this generalization does not necessarily exhaust all possible alternatives, it does, he argues, "express preponderant tendencies of thought" (42). This preponderance is especially evident in and definitive of the field of computer-mediated communication (CMC). As Steve Jones (1995) argues in the introduction to *CyberSociety: Computer-Mediated Communication and Community*, "the distinction between the two views of communication Carey draws are critical to understanding the full range and scope of CMC" (12). Consequently, in order to understand the computer as a device of communication, one would need to take an account of how these two metaphors of communication structure the field of CMC and regulate its current discussions, debates, and controversies.

Transmission

By communication is here meant the mechanism through which human relations exist and develop—all the symbols of the mind, together with the means of conveying them through space and preserving them in time. It in-

cludes the expression of the face, attitudes and gestures, the tones of the
voice, words, writing, printing, railways, telegraphs, telephones, and whatever else may be the latest achievement in the conquest of time and space.

Cooley 1962 [1901], 61

To write anything about communication is, it appears, to be immediately involved in what is addressed. Derrida (1993), for example, begins "Signature Event Context" by questioning the significance of the word *communication*, the polysemia[1] of which
appears to impede its being communicated effectively. In order to
formulate this question, however, he realizes that he has already
been compelled to prescribe communication as kind of transportation. "Even to articulate and to propose this question I have
had to anticipate the meaning of the word *communication*: I have
been constrained to predetermine communication as a vehicle, a
means of transport" (1). To write about communication is, it
seems, to participate in a practice that has already determined
communication as a kind of information transmission. "What do
we mean by communication?" asks Williams (1967) at the beginning of *Communications*. "The oldest meaning of the word, in English, can be summarized as the passing of ideas, information,
and attitudes from person to person. . . . [Thus] I mean by communication the process of transmission and reception" (17). This
characterization of communication, what Carey (1989) calls the
"transmission or transportation view" (43), has occupied a privileged position in the traditions of the West. "The transmission
view of communication," Carey (1989) points out, "is the com-
monest in our culture—perhaps in all industrial cultures—and
dominates contemporary dictionary entries under the term. It is
defined by terms such as 'imparting,' 'sending,' 'transmitting,' or
'giving information to others'" (15). The transmission view is invoked and operative in any approach to the study of communication that emphasizes the passage of messages and information
from one point to another. As such, it applies to a wide range of
activities from the interaction of neurons within an organism to

linguistic exchanges between human interlocutors and the operation of microprocessors engaged in the transference of digital data.

The transmission view of communication, Carey (1989) argues, is derived from a metaphor of geography or transportation that is rooted in an original identification between two forms of interchange. "In the nineteenth century but to a lesser extent today, the movement of goods or people and the movement of information were seen as essentially identical processes and both were described by the common noun 'communication.' From the time upper and lower Egypt were unified under the First Dynasty down through the invention of the telegraph, transportation and communication were inseparably linked" (15). According to Carey's account, the movement of goods and people and the propagation of information were, at one time, identical in both function and name. Functionally, both information and material goods were distributed in the form of physical objects, or what Negroponte (1995) has called "atoms." Nominally, one finds that the word *communication* was employed in the eighteenth and nineteenth centuries to describe not only the circulation of printed material and letters but also the development of "roads, canals, and railways" (Williams 1976, 62).[2]

It is the telegraph, Carey (1989) suggests, that dissolves this immediate functional and nominal identity. With the telegraph, the exchange of information was no longer connected to the physical movement of objects but "allowed for symbols to be moved independent of and faster than transportation" (204). Consequently, some time in the late nineteenth and early twentieth centuries the term *transportation* was reserved to name the physical conveyance of people and goods while *communication* became limited to the exchange of information and ideas (Williams 1976, 63). Although the telegraph ended the identity between what are now called communication and transportation, it did not, Carey (1989) maintains, "destroy the metaphor" (15). In fact, if we were to adhere strictly to Carey's formulation, one would have to admit that the "transportation metaphor" first becomes a *metaphor* with the advent of the electric telegraph. In other words, telegraphy did not simply not destroy the metaphor of transportation but actually inaugurated it by both instituting the conceptual distance between the two terms and maintaining a common, analogical connection that permitted *communication* across this difference. As a result, even though the identification between "the movement of goods or people and the movement of information" (Carey 1989, 15) was dissolved by the technology of telegraphy, communication remained understood as a *form of movement*. Perceived in this fashion, the metaphor of transportation does not constitute one metaphor among others, but it describes the function and operation of metaphor in general. "Metaphor," states Aristotle (1982) in an often quoted passage from the *Poetics*, "is the application of a strange term transferred ἐπιφορὰ (*epiphora*); either from genus and applied to the species or from the species to genus, or from one species to another, or else by analogy" (1457b7–9). According to the Aristotelian characterization, metaphor constitutes a form of transportation. In fact, the words "meta-phora and epi-phora have the same root, from the Greek φέρειν, to carry, to transport" (Derrida 1982, 231). Consequently, transportation is constitutive of the concept of metaphor with which one claims to comprehend the semantic movement from communication understood as physical conveyance to communication understood as the transmittal of information. As a result, whatever comes to be determined about the metaphor of transportation will have also been constitutive of metaphor in general.

Understood as a mode of transportation, the general purpose of communication is determined to be effective teleaction. "The center of this view of communication," Carey (1989) argues, "is the transmission of signals or messages over distance for the purpose of control. This view of communication derives from one of the most ancient of human dreams: the desire to increase the speed and effect of messages as they travel in space" (15). Communication, therefore, is primarily understood as a means of effective control over distance, whether that distance be semantic, interpersonal, or geophysical. This formulation engenders two important consequences. First, this understanding is not only evident in but permits communication between the oldest and most recent articulations of the art and science of communication—rhetoric and cybernetics. Rhetoric is traditionally defined as the art of persuasion or, as Aristotle (1991) formulates it, "the function of rhetoric is not so much to persuade, as to find out in each case the existing means of persuasion" (1355b.14). From Aristotle's *On Rhetoric* to John Austin's (1957) *How to Do Things with Words*, the emphasis has been on effective speech—speech that moves the audience by argument, entreaty, or expostulation to a belief, position, or course of action. Consequently, "the archetypal case of communication," Carey (1989) argues, "is persuasion; attitude change; behavior modification; socialization through the transmission of information, influence, or conditioning." (42–43). Cybernetics, as initially formulated by Norbert Wiener, comprises the universal science of control and communication in both organic and mechanical systems. As the title to Wiener's seminal text attests, *Cybernetics; or, Control and Communication in the Animal and the Machine* (1961), the science of cybernetics conjoins communication to control. Wiener explicates this conjunction in the sequel to *Cybernetics, The Human Use of Human Beings: Cybernetics and Society* (1988): "In giving the definition of Cybernetics in the original book, I classed communication and control together. Why did I do this? When I communicate with another person, I impart a message to him, and when he communicates back to me he returns a related message which contains information primarily accessible to him and not to me. When I control the actions of another person, I communicate a message to him, and although the message is in the imperative mood, the technique of communication does not differ from that of a message of fact" (16). Cybernetics, like the tradition of classical rhetoric, conceives of communication, whether in interpersonal interaction or through the various modes of telecommunications media, as an effective process wherein messages are transmitted by a sender for the purpose of determining the disposition and/or actions of the receiver(s).

Second, as long as communication is understood as a means of effective teleaction, examinations of the technique and technology of communication are framed by issues derived from this specific, transportation problematic. As Mark Poster (1995) explains, "the question to ask is how much information with how little noise may be transmitted at what speed and over what distance to how many locations?" (25). The study of communication, therefore, usually consists in inquiries that focus on measuring the amount, speed, and extent of information flow. Carey (1989) illustrates this method of scholarship through the example of what is considered to be a traditional form of mass communication: "If one examines a newspaper under a transmission view of communication, one sees the medium as an instrument for disseminating news and knowledge, sometimes *divertissement*, in larger and larger packages over greater distances. Questions arise as to the effects of this on audiences: news as enlightening or obscuring reality, as changing or hardening attitudes, as breeding credibility or doubt" (20). The transportation metaphor conducts investigations of communication to specific problematics concerning the movement and effect of information.[3] Such inquiries, which focus on the quantity and quality of information, have the appearance of an empirical science and constitute a good deal of what is usually considered communication studies whether that be framed in the tradition of the social sciences or in that of the humanities. By explicating this position, one does not aim to cast a disparaging shadow on traditional forms of communication scholarship. Indeed, such inquiries have, Carey (1989) argues, produced "solid achievement" (23). The goal of such explication is simply to demonstrate that the customary mode of research is itself framed and delimited by a highly specific understanding of communication that is neither natural, exclusive, nor beyond critical inquiry.

If, as Carolyn Marvin (1988) suggests, the computer is only a telegraph with a prodigious memory (3), one would expect the transportation metaphor to be present in the rhetoric of the Internet, cyberspace, and computer-mediated communication. And this has been the case. A prime example is the figure of the information superhighway, which is formed by associating data-communication networks, such as the Internet and the developing National and Global Information Infrastructures (NII and GII),[4] with the system of interstate roadways.[5] Vice President Al Gore (1993), who is often credited with having coined the term,[6] introduced the concept to the National Press Club in the following manner:

> One helpful way is to think of the National Information Infrastructure as a network of highways, much like the Interstates of the 1950's. These are highways carrying information rather than people or goods. And it's not just one eight-lane turnpike, but a collection of Interstates and feeder roads made of different materials in the same way that highways are concrete or macadam or gravel. Some highways will be made of fiberoptics, others of coaxial cable, others will be wireless. But this is a key point: They must and will be two-way highways so that each person will be able to send information in video form as well as just words, as well as receive information." (6)

Gore's description not only employs but exploits the transportation metaphor that comprises the transmission view of communication. Whereas the interstate highway system facilitates the movement of people and goods, the information superhighway is, as Negroponte (1995) asserts, "about the global movement of weightless bits at the speed of light" (12). Gore's description, therefore, not only situates the network as a mode of transportation but initiates a comparison that extends experiences with the network of interstate highways to the developing National Information Infrastructure. In the remarks the vice president delivered to the National Press Club, this comparison is limited to technical issues such as differences in network infrastructure, bandwidth, and the direction of information traffic flow. In a policy initiative issued the same year, *Technology for America's Economic Growth* (1993), the comparison includes economic and social development: "Just as the interstate highway system marked a historical turning point in our commerce, today 'information superhighways'—able to move ideas, data, and images around the country and around the globe—are critical to American competitiveness and economic strength" (18). The rhetoric of the information superhighway not only associates the network of computers with a system of interstate transportation but uses that association to predict the impact and significance of investment in and development of computer networks.

Because the transportation metaphor contained in a phrase like the "information superhighway" is, as Frank Biocca and Mark Levy (1995b) point out, "a root metaphor in communication" (21–22), the comparison also determines the content and form of many of the critiques of and alternatives to the information superhighway. Frank Hartmann (1999), for example, argues that the information superhighway functions differently in different social and political contexts. For U.S. users, the interstate highway has been experienced and is mythologized as an element of postwar prosperity. In Europe, however, the situation is otherwise. There the highway is tied to propaganda surrounding the *Reichsautobahn*[7] and the experience of prewar, nationalist expansion (14). This critique, although a compelling criticism of the cultural specificity of the information superhighway, does not question the transportation paradigm that underlies it but employs it as the basis for generating critique. A similar situation is evident in Mark Stefik's (1996) *Internet Dreams*, one of the only texts to take seriously the function of metaphor in shaping technological development. Following the work of Mark Johnson and George Lakoff (1980), Stefik argues that metaphorical language is not a mere description or rhetorical embellishment: "Because metaphors can guide our imagination about a new invention, they influence what it can be even before it exists" (*xvi*). Stefik not only identifies the importance and function of the "most celebrated metaphor" for the Internet, the information superhighway or what he terms the I-way, but calls for a thorough analysis of its role in organizing thoughts about the current status and future potential of the network. His investigation, however, postpones direct examination of the metaphor of the I-way. Instead he directs his critical work toward a derivative, second-order set of metaphors or what he calls, without any sense of irony, *"metaphors for the I-way"* (*xx*). Stefik considers, according to his own descriptions, "the I-way *as* publishing and community memory," "the I-way *as* a communications medium," "the I-way *as* a place for selling goods and services" and "the I-way *as* a gateway to experience" (*xx*; emphasis added). In all four scenarios, Stefik's "critical investigation" accepts without question and works within the framework of the information superhighway metaphor, limiting his inquiries to second-order metaphors for this metaphor of transportation. In this way, Stefik's approach necessarily falls prey to his own criticism. He absorbs the metaphor of transportation so quickly that he does not notice it, making much of his investigation "completely unconscious" (*xvi*).

Even apparently direct examinations of the figure of the information superhighway eschew questioning the transportation paradigm and limit themselves to a kind of metaphorical cost/benefit analysis. Stefik provides an excellent example of this kind of endeavor: "Mathew Miller, a Connecticut technology consultant, has a list of the ways regular highways differ from information highways. Miller uses these contrasts to help his clients avoid carrying over assumptions about highways to their thinking about information highways" (*xix*). This comparative list is bounded by and operates within the transportation metaphor by facilitating a critique of the information that is usually carried over from highways to information superhighways. As such, it does not criticize the transportation metaphor per se but employs the transportation paradigm, in both form and content, to identify and help others to avoid transporting the "wrong information." Similar problems are encountered by critiques that propose alternative figures for the technology in question. This is particularly manifest in a publication of the conservative think-tank Progress and Freedom Foundation (PFF) written by Esther Dyson, George Gilder, George Keyworth, and Alvin Toffler (1996). This document, following the PFF's penchant to oppose anything proffered by the Clinton administration, strongly objects to the concept of the information superhighway: "The one metaphor that is perhaps the least helpful in thinking about cyberspace is—unhappily—the one that has gained the most currency: the Information Superhighway. Can you imagine a phrase less descriptive of the nature of cyberspace, or more misleading in thinking about its implications?" (297). Dyson et al. demonstrate this thesis by providing a list contrasting the figures of the information superhighway and cyberspace. The third item distinguishes the highway's "moving on a grid" from the cyberspatial "moving in space" (Dyson et al. 1996, 297). Although Dyson et al. endeavor to distinguish the image of cyberspace from that of the information superhighway, both are conceptualized as forms of movement, just different kinds of movement in different environments. Because the transportation metaphor formally constitutes the dominant understanding of communication in Western traditions, it is inevitably employed by both advocates and critics of the information superhighway metaphor. For this reason, "the debate about the Information Superhighway," as George Gerbner (1997) suggests, "is not only highly specific but perhaps not even a debate at all."

Understood as a form of transportation, computer-mediated communication, like other forms of telecommunication, has been proposed as a replacement for physical travel. This proposition is immediately evident in and conveyed by the marketing discourse of hardware and software manufacturers. Throughout 1997, for example, IBM ran a series of print and television advertisements under the moniker "solutions for a small planet." Each ad consisted of a vignette in which the Internet was situated as the means to solve problems of geophysical distance and transportation. In one piece addressing distance education, a vintner in Europe describes how he completed his degree in agriculture at Indiana University without ever leaving his Mediterranean vineyard. And in a 1998–1999 advertisement addressing e-commerce, a small, family-run olive-oil business effectively competes in the evolving global market without *bambino* having to leave his *nonna* or take one step outside his family's provincial village. In each case, the argument is not simply that networked communication is comparable to transportation but that it constitutes a form of transport that can ostensibly replace physical travel. Also beginning in 1997, Microsoft introduced a campaign for the Microsoft Network that was organized around a refrain offered in the form of a rhetorical question: "Where do you want to go today?" Like IBM's "solutions for a small planet," this question does not simply associate computer-mediated communication with transportation but suggests that CMC is itself a mode of transportation, the PC becoming what Paul Virilio (1993) has called "the ultimate vehicle, the *static audiovisual vehicle*" (5; italics in original). In doing so, the Microsoft campaign employs and exploits a common perception that is expressed in colloquialisms describing network usage. On the World Wide Web, for example, one does not access data, place a call, or exchange information; one is said to be visiting a site and traveling to different locations.

In marketing their products and services in this fashion, IBM and Microsoft have not introduced a new idea into the currents of cyberculture. They have merely situated their commodities under a common assumption that is not only constitutive of the rhetoric of cyberspace but is definitive of the project of telecommunications in general. William Gibson's *Neuromancer* (1984), for example, not only introduced the neologism *cyberspace* but also determined the general function and operation of cyberspace under the rubric of transportation. Case, the protagonist of the novel, jacks his consciousness into the matrix and, through the mediation of the "cyberspace deck," is able to "reach the Freeside banks as easily as he could reach Atlanta" (77). In the rhetoric of *Neuromancer*, cyberspace comprises a complex data environment through which console cowboys like Case transport their entire sensorium. For this reason, Case not only denigrates the body[8] as meat but regards any form of physical travel as an obsolete "meat thing" (Gibson 1984, 70). This fictionalized account of the computer matrix has been reproduced in virtual reality (VR) interface systems for computer-mediated communication. As Tom Furness (1993) described it in his remarks to the first IEEE Virtual Reality Annual Symposium, "advanced interfaces will provide an incredible new mobility for the human race. We are building transportation systems for the senses ... the remarkable promise that we can be in another place or space without moving our bodies into that space" (*i*). According to the rhetoric employed by the pioneers of both the fictitious and "real" cyberspaces, computer-mediated communication technology is not simply analogous to but is understood and experienced as a form of transportation capable of replacing physical movement through geophysical space/time. This form of transportation, therefore, does not just mediate spatial extension but also overcomes temporal duration. As Virilio (1993) explains: "today we are beginning to realize that systems of telecommunication do not merely confine *extension*, but that in the transmission of messages and images, they also eradicate *duration* or delay" (3; italics in original).

Because computer-mediated communication technology is determined to provide forms of instantaneous transportation that overcome geophysical distance and temporal duration, the circulation of information in cyberspace is determined to surpass the problems and hazardous byproducts of physical transportation. Indicative of this promise is Michael Benedikt's (1993b) prophetic description of cyberspace:

> Cyberspace: The realm of pure information, filling like a lake, siphoning the jangle of messages transfiguring the physical world, decontaminating the natural and urban landscapes, redeeming them, saving them from the chain-dragging bulldozers of the paper industry, from the diesel smoke of courier and post office trucks, from the jet fuel fumes and clogged airports, from billboards, trashy and pretentious architecture, hour-long freeway commutes, ticket lines, and choked subways ... from all the inefficiencies, pollutions (chemical and informational), and corruptions attendant to the process of moving information attached to *things*—from paper to brains— across, over, and under the vast and bumpy surface of the earth rather than letting it fly free in the soft hail of electrons that is cyberspace. (3; italics in original)

For Benedikt, the transmission of immaterial bits in cyberspace not only replaces physical travel but in doing so promises to redeem the physical world, overcoming the hazardous byproducts of information transmittal attached to things.[9] Similar claims are made for telepresence and telecommuting. For example, Jack M. Nille et al. (1976) ask the following questions: "Can telecommunications and computer technology be substituted for some portion of urban commuter traffic? Can such a substitution reduce commuter congestion and mitigate the major economic impacts of new commuter-oriented transportation systems?" (5). Dyson et al. (1996) answer these questions in the affirmative: "Socially, putting advanced computing power in the hands of entire populations will alleviate pressure on highways, reduce air pollution, allow people to live further away from crowded or dangerous urban areas, and expand family time" (302). Understood as a form of transportation, therefore, the computer network and cyberspace are wired into and informed by a kind of utopian optimism that promises not only transcendence of space and time but a general restoration and redemption of real, physical spaces.[10]

The promise of the "death of distance" (Cairncross 1997) and the eradication of delay (Virilio 1993), although prevalent in the discourses of cyberspace and computer networking, does not originate with the technology of the computer or the data communications network. It is an artifact of the general project of telecommunications, which, as George Oslin (1992) describes it, "is the story of man's rebellion against the barriers of time and space, and his success in overcoming them" (1). No matter who narrates this story, the plot follows a well-known and simple trajectory. That is, each new development in the evolution of telecommunications technology is understood as providing for an increase in the quantity, quality, and speed of information that can be transmitted over distance and, as a result, contributes to a progressive contraction of geophysical separation.[11] Indicative of this kind of narrative is Pierre Teilhard de Chardin's assessment of communication technology in the *Phenomenon of Man* (1959): "What, in fact, do we see happening in the modern paroxysm? It has been stated over and over again. Through the discovery yesterday of the railway, the motor car, and the aeroplane, the physical influence of each man, formerly restricted to a few miles, now extends to hundreds of leagues or more. Better still: thanks to the prodigious biological event represented by the discovery of electro-magnetic waves, each individual finds himself henceforth (actively and passively) simultaneously present, over land and sea, in every corner of the earth" (240). Teilhard's explanation not only conjoins the technologies of transportation and communication but does so in terms of a general project that aims at the overcoming of time and space. Consequently, as Martin Heidegger (1971) points out, "all distances in time and space are shrinking. Man now reaches overnight, by plane, places which formerly took weeks and months of travel. He now receives instant information, by radio, of events which he formerly learned about only years later, if at all. . . . The peak of this abolition of every possibility of remoteness [Ferne] is reached by television [Fernsehapparatur], which will soon pervade and dominate the whole mechanism and drive of communication" (165). This general movement toward the ultimate eradication of distance is also evident in Marshall McLuhan's (1995) description of the development of media technology: "After three thousand years of explosion, by means of fragmentary and mechanical technologies, the Western world is imploding. During the mechanical ages we had extended our bodies in space. Today, after more than a century of electric technology, we have extended our central nervous system itself in a global embrace, abolishing both space and time as far as our planet is concerned. Rapidly, we approach the final phase of the extensions of man—the technological simulation of consciousness, when the creative process of knowing will be collectively and corporately extended to the whole of human society" (3–4). For McLuhan, as for Teilhard and Heidegger, electronic telecommunications technology promises to reduce the size of the planet by collapsing spatial and temporal distance.[12]

The ultimate goal of this contraction is the eventual eradication of distance that separates human beings. Consequently, the result of the telecommunications explosion, or implosion as McLuhan describes it, is the creation of a progressively smaller international community or "global village." "As electrically contracted," McLuhan (1995) argues, "the globe is no more than a village" (5). Or as Negroponte (1995) describes it in the context of digital technology, "the digital planet will look and feel like the head of a pin" (6). The contraction of geophysical space/time facilitated through communication technology promises new forms of social and political association. "Until now," wrote Ithiel de Sola Pool (1990),

> the fact that interacting over a distance cost very much more than interacting with those close at hand meant that we lived our lives in communities, and most activity was within these confines. For almost any activity, one could draw a curve of frequency of interactions by distance, and the shape of the curve would show a rapid falling off with distance. Increasingly now at least one of the causal factors behind that curve—namely, cost of long-distance communication—is vanishing." (39)

With the advent of telecommunications technology, there has been an increase in the discussion of expanded and global communities, ranging from Teilhard's (1959) telematic "noosphere" and Licklider and Taylor's (1968) proposal for the creation of "online communities" (35) to Howard Rheingold's (1993) "virtual communities" and Dyson et al.'s "'electronic neighborhoods' bound together not by geography but by shared interests" (302). This expansion of community via telecommunication systems not only marks a point of intersection between the transmission and ritual viewpoints (which will be examined in a moment) but also constitutes one of the fundamental principles of the social application of cybernetics. "Properly speaking," wrote Wiener (1961), "the community extends only so far as there extends an effectual transmission of information" (157–158). Understood in this way, community is a function of communication so that one extends community by extending the means of communication. For this reason, the transmission approach is not only oriented toward controlling the activities of the receiver but also aims at establishing connections that regulate the distances that separate human beings.

Although a principle of cybernetics, this extension of community through enhanced forms of information transmission has specific religious roots and as such demonstrates the insight provided by Armand Mattelart (1996) that "a straight line has been traced between communication and religion" (*xvi*). Carey (1989) explains this affiliation in the following way:

> In its modern dress the transmission view of communication arises, as the *Oxford English Dictionary* will attest, at the onset of the age of exploration and discovery. . . . Transportation, particularly when it brought the Christian community of Europe into contact with the heathen community of the Americas, was seen as a form of communication with profoundly religious implications. This movement in space was an attempt to establish and extend the kingdom of God, to create the conditions under which godly understanding might be realized, to produce a heavenly though still terrestrial city. (15–16)[13]

Although this religious information is usually suppressed in contemporary considerations of technology, it has, Carey (1989) argues, "never been eliminated from our thought" (18). Consequently, communication technology, from the printing press through the railroad and telegraph to the Internet, is situated, at least in Western traditions, in a religious context that renders the machine nothing less than a kind of *deus ex machina*. Carey (1989), quoting Miller's *Life of Mind in America*, traces this situation in the railroad and telegraph:

> In 1848 James L. Batchelder could declare that the Almighty himself had constructed the railroad for missionary purposes and, as Samuel Morse prophesied with the first telegraphic message, the purpose of the invention was not to spread the price of pork but to ask the question "What hath God wrought?" This new technology entered American discussions not as a mundane fact but as divinely inspired for the purposes of spreading the Christian message farther and faster, eclipsing time and transcending space, saving the heathen, bringing closer and making more probable the day of salvation. (16–17)

Similarly, the computer network has been positioned as a *deus ex machina* or talisman of contemporary social problems, and it is the figure of the superhighway that has functioned as the major conduit of this religious and moral subtext. As Stefik (1996) describes it,

> highways connect civilization together. They are so important for moving people, goods, and services that they are usually funded as part of the infrastructure that serves a broad social good. . . . Some of the most important roads being built today are the information highways. These highways are entering our lives; they connect us to each other and reduce the distance between us. We can use them to create electronic communities and to discover our place in communities larger than our physical neighborhoods. (*xxiv*)

This optimistic assessment is also evident in the marketing and advertising rhetoric of computer technology. A 1997 IBM television commercial, for example, made the following proclamation: "Something magical is happening to our planet. Our world is growing smaller. Each day the global web of computers weaves us closer together."[14]

Given these conclusions and complex implications, one may wish to question whether the transportation view is indeed an accurate characterization of the process and operation of communication. Such skepticism, however, is itself already regulated by the concept that would be scrutinized. In order to propose or articulate any criticism of the assumptions, processes, or implications of information transmission, one is already, in practice, involved in some kind of message transmittal. Indeed, what is the foregoing if not an attempt to transmit accurately and efficiently information concerning the transmission view? Consequently, any investigation of communication already finds itself in what Chang (1996) calls an unavoidable epistemological circularity: "Any such attempt to make public my skepticism about communication can be realized only by and through communication (for example, in writing)—a fact that seems to nullify the basis of my inquiry, if only because the very subject matter I interrogate is employed as the medium of the interrogation" (*ix*). As a result, any examination

or criticism of the transportation paradigm risks becoming rein-
scribed in the very object it endeavors to investigate. This seemingly paradoxical situation, however, is not necessarily some defi-
cient circular reasoning that would either neutralize the
investigation in advance or be at odds with what is usually called
"objective science." For, as Chang (1996) points out, "such a
predicament . . . is not unique to those who problematize communication; in fact, it characterizes the epistemic quandary of writers
from diverse fields in which the act of the investigation is itself implicated in the object of inquiry as its condition of possibility"
(ix–x). What is required, therefore, is not acceptance or rejection of
the transmission viewpoint but a decisive understanding of the
complexity and necessary consequences of this highly specific understanding of communication.

What is necessary, in this particular case, is explicit recognition
that any investigation of the metaphor of transportation cannot escape what is questioned but must proceed by situating its inquiry
within the space delimited by the transportation paradigm. Such
an undertaking requires nothing less than a purposeful and deliberate redoubling of the transmission viewpoint, and this is precisely what Carey (1989) proposes: "The transmission view of
communication has dominated American thought since the 1920's.
When I first came into this field I felt that this view of communication, expressed in behavioral and functional terms, was exhausted. It had become academic: a repetition of past achievement, a demonstration of the indubitable. Although it led to solid
achievement, it could no longer go forward without disastrous intellectual and social consequences" (23). Carey's conclusion,
which employs a kind of apocalyptic rhetoric, is derived from applying the evaluative criteria of transmission to the transmission
view of communication. In other words, he turns the transmission
paradigm on itself. According to the transmission view, communication concerns the transmittal of information and is evaluated on
the basis of the quantity, quality, and speed of transmission. The
transmission view, however, when evaluated in this fashion, actually supplies little or no new information about communication.

Consequently, the transmission viewpoint, when assessed from the perspective of transmission, comprises nothing less than a seemingly endless repetition of a predictable, redundant, and somewhat uninteresting set of possibilities. Perhaps the best example of this insight is the first part of this chapter. According to Carey's and Williams's analyses, the transmission view of communication constitutes the most common understanding of communication within the traditions of the West. If this is indeed an accurate characterization, then pointing it out is, from the perspective of the transmission viewpoint, redundant to the point of being superfluous. In other words, if the transmission metaphor is the most common understanding of communication, then its explicit demonstration actually conveys little or no information about the process and purpose of communication. It merely repeats and reconfirms what is already considered to be common knowledge. For this reason, the foregoing has either communicated very little information or its function as communication must be understood otherwise.

Ritual and Beyond

If *communication* possessed several meanings and if this plurality should prove to be irreducible, it would not be justified to define communication a priori as the transmission of *meaning*.

Derrida 1993, 1; italics in original

It is with an eye on this kind of alternative understanding, that Carey (1989) proposes the ritual view: "A ritual view of communication is directed not toward the extension of messages in space but toward the maintenance of society in time; not the act of imparting information but the representation of shared beliefs" (18). A ritual view of communication, unlike that of transportation, emphasizes and exploits the shared etymological root of the words "communication," "community," and "commonness," a common etymology that lies in the very concept of the common and commonality. Consequently, the ritual understanding of communication is directed not toward the transmittal of information for the purpose of controlling people and distance. It is concerned with the way in which communicative events function to create a common understanding that is definitive of a specific community. As John Dewey (1916) explains it, "there is more than a verbal tie between the words common, community, and communication. Men live in a community by virtue of the things which they have in common; and communication is the way in which they come to possess things in common" (5). It could be said, therefore, that the previous section, although apparently concerned with conveying information about the transmission metaphor, demonstrates in practice the ritual view. In addressing transmission, the section did not necessarily convey new information but joined in communion with the common understanding of communication that is constitutive of a particular community of scholars, educators, and practitioners. Within the ritual paradigm, communication is comprehended as an intentionally redundant activity or infinitely repeatable practice that does not necessarily seek to provide new insight or to convey information but endeavors to establish and maintain the common tenets that compose and define a specific social organization and/or tradition.

The ritual view of communication, although articulated and addressed subsequently, actually predates the dominant understanding of communication as the transportation of information. Evidence of this precedence is manifest not only in dictionary definitions, which designate the ritual view as archaic (Carey 1989, 18), but also behind the scenes, as it were, in approaches organized under the transportation paradigm. In order for a message to be conveyed from one point to another, from a sender to a receiver as Shannon and Weaver's (1963) mathematical model describes it, there must first be a common element, most notably a shared language or code, that serves as the condition for the possibility of any information transfer whatsoever. As Chang (1996) describes it, "such a display of communication . . . implies that before the message in question is sent, and certainly before that message can be properly received, the act of communication must communicate its communicability as the very foundation of message transfer" (*xii*). It is only because the sender and receiver already share and participate in a common linguistic community or mutual set of data protocols that it becomes possible to transmit any information between them. Understood and formulated as information transmittal, the process of communication necessarily presupposes and is founded upon a prior, general communication, which is nothing less than the common precondition of communicability in general. As Heidegger (1962) describes it: "'Communication' in which one makes assertions—giving information, for instance—is a special case of that communication which is grasped in principle existentially. In this more general kind of communication, the Articulation of Being with one another understandingly is constituted. Through it a co-state of mind gets 'shared.' . . . Communication is never anything like a transportation of experience, such as opinions or wishes, from the interior of one subject into the interior of another. *Dasein*-with is already essentially manifest in a co-state-of-mind and a co-understanding" (205). The ritual view of communication, therefore, focuses attention on this fundamental and common substructure that, although constituting the condition for the possibility of information transfer, is often taken for granted or simply ignored by the almost exclusive concern with the more specialized, instrumental aspects of data transmission, flow rate, and effective outcome.

"The ritual view of communication," Carey (1989) admits, "has not been a dominant motif in American scholarship" (19). Therefore, it forms what he calls a "minor thread" (18). This assessment has at least two consequences. First, in order to find works that emphasizes the ritual aspect, one would need to look outside the frame of mainstream American communication scholarship. Carey suggests that such literature can be found in the writings of European theorists and Americans influenced by Continental thought. As evidence of this, one could point out that the demonstration of the ritual view undertaken here has proceeded by employing works derived from distinctly European traditions, namely, the

phenomenology of Heidegger and the solicitation of this tradition
in Chang (1996) as well as the work of Dewey, indebted as it is to
the innovations of European sociologists such as Max Weber and
Émile Durkheim. Although this division, which is based on and derived from what could be called "an accident of geography," appears to be an oversimplification, it is continually reinforced in
contemporary debates about computer networking and communication. In an official policy statement issued by the European
Union, for example, the E.U. distinguished its general position on
computer networking by differentiating the American preoccupation with the metaphor of transportation from the distinctly European concern with community: "The general preference in the
United States until recently was for the term 'information superhighways,' implying a more limited, technology-based apprecia-
tion for what is happening. By contrast, 'information society'
reflects European concerns with the broader social and organizational changes which flow from the information and communication revolution" (Hartmann 1999, 74). Second, as a "minor thread,"
the ritual approach is necessarily articulated, within the tradition
that takes information transmission as the dominant understanding of communication, as the counterpoint to and negation of
transmission. Carey (1989), for example, introduces the ritual mode
through explicit negation of the transportation metaphor: "A ritual
view of communication is directed *not* toward the extension of
messages in space but toward the maintenance of society in time;
not the act of imparting information but the representation of
shared beliefs" (18; emphasis added). This negative characterization is not a semantic accident; it is a necessary effect and artifact of
the dominance enjoyed by the transmission paradigm. Consequently, even a text that proffers an alternative to transmission is
constrained to work within the context of transmission, introducing the alternative as the negative and opposite of the assumed
positivism already granted to the transmission viewpoint.

Because the ritual view provides a fundamentally different understanding of the origin and purpose of communication, it directs

attention and scholarship to a different set of problems and possible solutions. "It will, for example, view reading a newspaper less as sending or gaining information and more as attending a mass, a situation in which nothing new is learned but in which a particular view of the world is portrayed and confirmed. News reading, and writing, is a ritual act and moreover a dramatic one. What is arrayed before the reader is not pure information but a portrayal of the contending forces in the world" (Carey 1989, 20). Whereas the transmission view is concerned with the movement of information and endeavors to measure and maximize its effectiveness, the ritual approach focuses attention on the way in which communication participates in and defines common social practices. The ritual view, therefore, is not concerned with how much information may be sent over what channels to how many people for what effect. It is interested in the way in which communicative events are employed to create, sustain, and transform specific social traditions and affiliations. As a result, the ritual approach provides for an understanding of communication that is not so much concerned with the traditional issues of clarity, speed, and efficiency but is interested in intentionally repetitious, highly inefficient, and at times noisy performances that produce and reproduce specific communal structures. This is not to say, however, that the ritual view simply negates or invalidates that of transmission. It only provides an alternative perspective for looking at and studying the technique and technology of communication. Carey is emphatic on this point:

> Neither of these counterposed views of communication necessarily denies what the other affirms. A ritual view does not exclude the processes of information transmission or attitude change. It merely contends that one cannot understand these processes aright except insofar as they are cast within an essentially ritualistic view of communication and social order. Similarly, even writers indissolubly wedded to the transmission view of communication must include some notion . . . to attest however tardily to the place of ritual in social life. (21–22)

Although the two approaches frame and advocate opposing view-points, they are not necessarily mutually exclusive.

The ritual approach, although remaining a minority position in communication scholarship, has recently been taken up and championed by researchers who study cyberspace and computer-mediated communication. According to Jones (1995), for example, the transportation approach has been unduly privileged in the study of computer systems: "Much of our energy has been directed toward understanding the speed and volume with which computers can be used as communication tools. Conspicuously absent is an understanding of how computers are used as tools for connection and community" (12). For Jones, Carey's work not only provides insight into this problem but supplies an alternative for reformulating communication research and scholarship:

> Media technologies that have largely been tied to the "transportation" view of communication . . . were developed to overcome space and time. The computer, in particular, is an "efficiency" machine, purporting to ever increasing speed. But unlike those technologies, the computer used for communication is a technology to be understood from the "ritual" view of communication, once time and space have been overcome (or at least rendered surmountable) the spur for development is connection, linkage. Once we can surmount time and space and "be" anywhere, we must choose a "where" at which to be. (32)

Jones's work in computer-mediated communication and virtual community, which includes two anthologies (Jones 1995; Jones 1997a) and a number of articles (Jones 1997b; Jones 1998), not only identifies the limitation of the transmission approach but advocates and pursues a general shift in scholarship to a ritual paradigm, which emphasizes, according to Jones's reading, not information transmittal but community formation and connection.[15] Similar alterations in perspective have been proposed and practiced by Rheingold (1993), Dibbell (1994), Mitchell (1995), Slouka (1995), Stone (1995), Bromberg (1996), Doheny-Farina (1996), Wilbur (1997), Foster (1997), and Tepper (1997).

Carey, however, is not interested in simply shifting emphasis from the transmission paradigm to that of ritual. What makes communication compelling, in Carey's estimation, is not the one or the other point of view but the essential tension between these two counterpoised, but not mutually exclusive, configurations. Consequently, Carey is not concerned with promoting the ritual viewpoint over and against that of transmission.[16] He is interested in restoring the conceptual tension between the transmission and ritual views that has all but been eliminated in American communication scholarship due to a privileging of the transportation metaphor. The principal task, then, is not simply to restore the meaning of ritual as an alternative to transmission but to return the word *communication* to its proper ambiguity and essential polysemia. Carey, therefore, does not propose a mere return to the ritual view of communication, which would be nothing less than a kind of simple nostalgia for the depreciated term. Instead, he advocates restoring conceptual tension to communication in order to render it "a far more problematic activity than it ordinarily seems" (25).

Carey's restoration of the essential and irreducible polysemia of communication begins by recollecting and reestablishing the ritual view not to replace or to oppose transmission but merely to rehabilitate, within the concept of communication, the indeterminate tension between transmission and ritual. In doing this, Carey introduces what he calls a "fresh perspective on communication" (23). This "fresh perspective," which is formulated by returning to a number of European and American works in the sociology of communication that predate the exclusive transportation orientation, is introduced as follows: "From such sources one can draw a definition of communication of disarming simplicity yet, I think, of some intellectual power and scope: communication is a symbolic process whereby reality is produced, maintained, repaired, and transformed" (Carey 1989, 23). This formulation, which constitutes nothing less than a kind of "symbolic production of reality" (Carey 1989, 23), does not simply install the ritual view in place of the dominant transportation paradigm. It intervenes in

the shared commonsense realism that underlies traditional conceptualizations of communication whether understood as transmission or ritual. As Carey (1989) describes it, "our common sense
and scientific realism attest to the fact that there is, first, a real
world of objects, events, and processes that we observe. Second,
there is language or symbols that name these events in the real
world and create more or less adequate descriptions of them.
There is reality and then, after the fact, our accounts of it" (25).

Carey's "fresh perspective on communication" intervenes in this
pretense of realism. This intervention is best illustrated through
the employment of religious imagery, which constitutes a kind of
playful parody of the religious origins of both the transmission
and ritual views. "I want to suggest," Carey (1989) writes, "to play
on the Gospel of St. John, that in the beginning was the word;
words are not the names for things but, to steal a line from Kenneth Burke (1966), things are the signs of words. Reality is not
given, not humanly existent, independent of language and toward
which language stands as a pale refraction. Reality is brought into
existence, is produced by communication—by, in short, the construction, apprehension, and utilization of symbolic forms" (25).
In this manner, Carey deliberately alters the assumed relationship
between words and things. Words, it is suggested, are not derivative signs that convey information about things; they comprise potent mechanisms that first produce the things they appear to represent. Consequently, the real does not necessarily precede or
become reflected in language, but it is language that precedes, creates, and produces what is called reality. This does not mean, however, that words, images, and other means of communication
simply cease serviceability as representations. Carey (1989) complicates this form of simple inversion, situating in the symbolic a
dual capacity. Symbols, he argues, have the "ability to be both representations 'of' and 'for' reality . . . as 'symbols of' they present
reality; as 'symbols for' they create the very reality they represent"
(26).[17] Consequently, Carey's "fresh perspective on communication" involves a double gesture. On the one hand, he inverts, following the precedent established in Burke (1966), commonsense

realism by emphasizing the symbolic over and against the real. On the other hand, he complicates this simple inversion by situating within the material of symbolism a dual capacity with respect to the "real."

Although the title to Carey's essay (see note 16) suggests that this "reordering of the relation of communication to reality" (Carey 1989, 25) should be termed "a cultural approach," Carey admits (in a brief parenthetical aside) that he is tempted to apply to it the word *ritual*: "All human activity is such an exercise (can one resist the word "ritual"?) in squaring the circle. We first produce the world by symbolic work and then take up residence in the world we have produced. Alas, there is magic in our self-deceptions" (30). In questioning (even parenthetically) the retention of the name "ritual," Carey's analysis engages in a curious and potentially dangerous paleonymy. Although his "fresh perspective on communication" does not simply install the ritual view over and against that of transmission, Carey is still tempted to call it by a name that is derived from one of the two terms in question.[18] Such a procedure seems, at first glance, to be counterproductive and contrary to his proposal. This difficulty, however, is unavoidable and absolutely necessary, for in doing so Carey's analysis takes the form of deconstruction. Deconstruction, despite Carey's misunderstanding and misuse of the term elsewhere (Carey 1990, 20), does not constitute the mere antithesis of construction; it does not signify "to take apart" or "to un-construct." Instead, deconstruction, as a general practice, always operates within a structural field of conceptual pairs, one of which has traditionally not only had the upper hand but has determined the other as and through negation.[19] Deconstruction, therefore, entails an irreducible double gesture that overturns the traditional hierarchy at a certain point by momentarily privileging the depreciated term in the pair and, while retaining its name, introduces "the irruptive emergence of a new 'concept,' a concept that can no longer be, and never could be, included in the previous regime" (Derrida 1981a, 42). The ritual view, as Carey points out, comprises the depreciated term of the two views of communication. By engaging in a paleonymic gesture and naming the fresh perspective on communication "ritual," Carey not only overturns the hierarchy that has reigned in communication studies, granting privilege to the depreciated term, but also introduces a new concept or model of communication, one that was not and could not be included in the traditional schema. Consequently, it is with this brief and remarkable parenthetical aside that Carey releases into his work the play of deconstruction, although it is doubtful that he would recognize it as such.

The cultural approach to communication is concerned not simply with the transmission of information or the relationship between communication and community but concentrates on how the common understanding of reality, which underlies both viewpoints, is first produced, developed, and maintained. This alternative conceptualization, which understands all communicative activities as creative and fosters not one reality but a multiplicity of possible and competing realities (Carey 1989, 35), is precisely what Licklider and Taylor had in mind when they first proposed that the computer be treated as a communication device. According to Licklider and Taylor (1968), communication is not necessarily about the transference of information but involves something more: "A communication engineer thinks of communication as transferring information from one point to another in codes and signals. But to communicate is more than to send and to receive. . . . We want to emphasize something beyond its one-way transfer: the increasing significance of the jointly constructive, the mutually reinforcing aspect of communication" (21). This "jointly constructive, mutually reinforcing" aspect of communication involves what Licklider and Taylor call modeling. "For modeling, we believe, is basic and central to communication. Any communication between people about the same thing is a common revelatory experience about informational models of that thing. Each model is a conceptual structure of abstractions formulated initially in the mind of one of the persons who would communicate, and if the concepts in the mind of one would-be communicator are very different from those in the mind of another, there is no common model and no communication" (22). Licklider and Taylor were not interested in the engineering problems of effective information transmission. They were primarily concerned with the ways in which the computer participated in the common activity of creating, developing, and maintaining models. It was this capacity to construct and maintain a common reality that comprised, for Licklider and Taylor, the real potential of computer-aided communication. The computer did not necessarily facilitate the transmission of greater quantities of high-quality information but provided a "plastic or moldable medium" that enables "cooperative modeling" (Licklider and Taylor 1968, 22).

If one adheres to these proposals, the study of computer-mediated communication will necessarily take an entirely different tack than it has in recent years. Accordingly, CMC will not be limited either to examinations of the technical capabilities of information transmission or investigations of the possibility and extent of virtual communities. It will be researched for its capacity to construct, sustain, and contend competing models of reality. As Carey (1989) characterizes it:

> To study communication is to examine the actual social process wherein significant symbolic forms are created, apprehended, and used. Our attempts to construct, maintain, repair, and transform reality are publicly observable activities that occur in historical time. We create, express, and convey our knowledge of and attitudes toward reality through the construction of a variety of symbol systems: art, science, journalism, religion, common sense, mythology. How do we do this? What are the differences between these forms? What are the historical and comparative variations in them? How do changes in communication technology influence what we can concretely create and apprehend? How do groups in society struggle over the definition of what is real? These are some of the questions, rather too simply put, that communication studies must answer. (30)

Considered in this fashion, the technology of CMC will come to be examined as an element of and a technique involved in the ongoing construction and maintenance of the real. It will take its place alongside other forms of communication technology not as the next step in the evolution of mediated communication, promising either improved capacity for information transmission or restoration of fractured communities, but as one more technique participating in the ceaseless process of cooperative modeling or symbolic construction. This approach, although deviating from the established trajectory of contemporary research in communication technology, actually constitutes a return to the initial understanding of cyberspace as it is presented in the novels of William Gibson. According to Gibson's (1984) characterizations, cyberspace is "a consensual hallucination" (51). That is, it consists in a shared construct that, like fiction itself, comprises a mythic plane in which a common understanding of the real is produced, maintained, and even contested. As Benedikt (1993b) points out, in a sentence that echoes Carey's (1989) essay, "myth both reflects the 'human condition' and creates it" (5). Consequently, the technology of CMC, like other means of producing fiction and consensual hallucination, constitutes a site for the construction, maintenance, and contestation of the real. To study CMC in this fashion is to research how the technology does this, what realities it produces, and what their implications can and will be.

This alternative approach to the process and technology of communication, however, engenders an ironic twist wherein the subject matter doubles back on itself. As Carey (1989) describes it: "We understand communication insofar as we are able to build models or representations of this process. But our models of communication, like all models have this dual aspect—an 'of' aspect and a 'for' aspect. In one mode communication models tell us what the process is; in their second mode they produce the behavior they have described" (31). The transmission, ritual, and cultural views, therefore, constitute models of communication. As such, they not only do not escape "symbolic construction" but are always and already implicated in this process. In other words, these different approaches to the study of communication are not mere neutral descriptions of a process that is "revealed in nature through some objective method free from the corruption of culture" (Carey 1989, 31) but constitute models that determine the proper form and function of communication. Like maps, they do not simply represent the territory, but "they constitute nature itself" (Carey 1989,

28). Carey exemplifies this insight, which exhibits important affinities with Baudrillard's (1983) concept of simulation,[20] by returning to and reviewing his own consideration of the transmission paradigm: "In describing the root of the transmission view of communication in nineteenth-century American religious thought I meant to imply the following: religious thought not only described communication; it also presented a model for the appropriate use of language, the permissible forms of human contact, the ends communication should serve, the motives it should manifest. It taught what it meant to display" (31). Consequently, Carey's proposal for an alternative model of communication does not escape the system of symbolic construction it describes. It is also a model that determines the reality that it appears to represent. What distinguishes the cultural approach, therefore, is not that it constitutes the one true, transparent representation of the reality of communication (which would be nothing less than a criterion derived from the transmission viewpoint), but that it explicitly conceptualizes the process of symbolic construction in which it and all other models of communication necessarily participate. What distinguishes the cultural approach, therefore, is not that it is a better description of the "nature of communication" but that it constitutes the one model of communication that explicitly conceptualizes its own performance and significance as a model.

Conclusion

We can say with genuine and strong conviction that a particular form of digital computer organization, with its programs and its data, constitutes the dynamic, moldable medium that can revolutionize the art of modeling and that in so doing can improve the effectiveness of communication among people so much as perhaps to revolutionize that also.

Licklider and Taylor 1968, 27

Although the study of computer-mediated communication can be traced back to Licklider and Taylor (1968), their unique approach to the subject matter has been either forgotten, misunderstood, or simply ignored. Consequently, research in CMC has taken rather predictable forms that have been simply appropriated, with little or no critical self-reflection, from the traditions of communication studies. Investigations of CMC have been framed by either a transmission view, which directs research to technical issues concerning the quantity, quality, and speed of information transmittal, or a ritual view, which envisions the computer network as a means of social integration that participates in the organization and development of virtual communities. Although these two approaches incorporate new and unfamiliar technology into established methods of inquiry, they also involve various metaphysical perspectives and epistemological strategies that remain unacknowledged. To continue to organize research under these two viewpoints is not only to restrict inquiry to highly specific problematics that have limited and predictable sets of possible outcomes but, more important, to perpetuate unquestioned assumptions concerning the general operation and function of communication. Licklider and Taylor's article not only anticipates these complications but provides the theoretical framework for an alternative mode of inquiry, one which demonstrates affinity with Carey's proposal for a cultural approach to communication.

This alternative has the potential to reprogram the rules of the game and, as is to be expected, entails a number of important consequences that need to be explicitly demarcated. First, this approach challenges the customary understanding of the role and function of communication. Communication does not simply consist in either the transmission of information or the means of producing connections that sustain community. It constitutes a powerful creative and productive undertaking that has extensive metaphysical and epistemological repercussions. Specifically, communication is a form of symbolic construction that provides models both of and for reality. This alternative conceptualization, however, does not simply negate the traditional understanding of communication as either transmission or ritual. It provides for a more fundamental articulation that not only explains but substantiates these two, seemingly contrary, viewpoints—transmission and ritual are themselves nothing other than models of and for communication. As Carey (1989) summarizes it, "our models of communication consequently create what we disingenuously pretend they merely describe. As a result our science is, to use a term of Alvin Gouldner's, a reflexive one. We not only describe behavior; we create a particular corner of culture—culture that determines, in part, the kind of communicative world we inhabit" (32). Although Carey recognizes that such an approach may be perceived by some scholars as less than scientific, he maintains the opposite, arguing that it is only through this reflective method that scholarship becomes sufficiently attentive to the complexities of · communication and culture.

Second, this reconfiguration of the role and function of communication will necessarily affect and transform the customary relationship situated between computer technology and the texts that supposedly represent and report on it. If one affirms the cultural approach to communication, then the various words, images, and discourses addressing technology cannot be understood and employed as mere representations of some independent and extant object. On the contrary, they constitute models of and for the object in question, producing the various things they are said merely to represent. As a result, the textual maneuvers and discursive elements that are used to describe, discuss, and debate technology can no longer be treated as mere conduits for communicating information about something but comprise potent mechanisms by which different versions of technological reality are prototyped, maintained, and even contended. The metaphors of transmission and ritual, for example, do not merely represent the process, operation, and significance of computer-mediated communication. They are already involved in manufacturing the reality of communication one will want to say they merely signify. Metaphor, therefore, is not a mere verbal embellishment or illustration. It constitutes a mechanism of significant epistemological and ontological power. It can, for instance, determine the relevant problems that come to be assigned to a technology, dictate the kind of questions that can be asked of it, and delimit the type of answers that will count as significant. Critical approaches to technology, therefore, cannot simply ignore these potent rhetorical techniques or write them off as superfluous and unimportant aspects of language. They must learn how to situate their investigations in this material and how to wage their struggles within its context.

Finally, everything that is presented here must be applied to the form of the presentation. For this text, as a text, is not outside the speculative mirror-space that it identifies, explicates, and reflects. Consequently, one cannot claim for this discourse some kind of "objective truth" that would be independent of or disengaged from the scene it describes. It too, as a form and technology of communication, is always already involved in the process of creating models of and for reality. Indeed, it must be admitted that Carey's particular brand of symbolic constructivism is itself, strictly speaking, a symbolic construction. This is, however, neither a pointless tautology nor a temporary dilemma that can be ultimately resolved or overcome. It constitutes the necessary condition, as Chang (1996) points out, of any reflection on communication. That is, to articulate anything about communication is always and already to be entangled in what is addressed. The examination of communication, therefore, can never proceed in a naïve fashion. The critical task is not to avoid, repress, or divert this "epistemological circle" but to enter it at the correct angle, fostering a kind of interminable analysis that continually permits the stated outcome to recoil and bend back upon the very means of producing such an analysis. Consequently, one cannot, without engaging in a contradiction that would undermine everything that has been presented, claim that the cultural approach to the study of computer-mediated communication is a more truthful or a more accurate description of the subject matter. Such an argument would already be regulated by a set of criteria that is determined by a traditional understanding of the role and function of communication and shared by and definitive of a specific community of scholars. What can be argued is that this alternative understanding explicitly acknowledges and theorizes its own practice as a model of and for communication. Such an approach not only lends a certain sophistication to scholarship and research in computer networking, which has proceeded by adopting traditional modes of investigation, but also provides a method of inquiry that adheres to the insights initially introduced by the text that first proposed the subject of computer-aided communication and the system of computer networking we now call the Internet.

Notes

1. In mentioning this polysemia, Derrida is not arguing for any new understanding of communication but merely repeating an insight that had been available since the mid-eighteenth century. Denis Diderot, for example, provides the following definition in the *Encyclopedia*: "Communication: a term with a great number of meanings" (Mattelart 1996, *xiii*).

2. Although the original, double meaning of the word *communication* has generally been forgotten by users of the English language, it does persist in cognates of the word in other languages. In Polish, for example, the noun *komunikacja* indicates both communication as understood in contemporary English usage and modes of transportation, including roadways, the railroad, and systems of mass transit.

3. One would have to admit that a similar evaluative criteria is always and already evident in the traditional consideration of metaphor. Because metaphors are also formulated as a kind of transportation, they are usually evaluated for their ability to convey accurate information about something with little or no noise. Consequently, the demonstration/evaluation of the transportation metaphor, like this one here, concerns measuring the relative effectiveness of the metaphor to convey accurate information about the process and function of communication while minimizing the introduction of noise, which has the potential to distort the message and understanding.

4. Strictly speaking, it is a mistake to identify the information superhighway with the Internet. According to a January 1996 study published by the United States Advisory Council on the National Information Infrastructure (USAC-NII), "the Information Superhighway is more than the Internet. It is a series of components, including the collection of public and private high-speed, interactive, narrow, and broadband networks that exist today and will emerge tomorrow" (13). Consequently, the information superhighway, although including the Internet, is a broader and more comprehensive concept. Despite this clarification, the popular and academic presses have, almost without exception, continued to use the name "information superhighway" as a synonym for the Internet.

5. It should be noted that this association follows a well-established precedent. Nineteenth-century electrical engineers, for example, often compared the power

grid and telegraphic networks to the system of railroads (Marvin 1988). A similar comparison was employed to describe early forms of computer networking based on the mainframe. A good illustration of this comparison can be found in Patton's (1986) criticism of the railroad network in his examination of the American highway system: "The relationship of the car to the road can be understood by turning around a comparison tossed about in the world of electronics. The mainframe computer, this analogy holds, is like the railroad: it is centralized, controlled by large companies that own both hardware and software. The individual can use it only by acceding to a fixed schedule—timesharing—and is often subjected to being 'folded, spindled, and mutilated' by its operation" (15).

6. The term *information superhighway* is commonly credited to Al Gore, who claims to have invented the phrase sometime in 1979 (Gore 1994a, 8). This claim is most often justified and explained by way of paternity. As Stefik (1996) describes it, "the Vice President is the son of Albert Gore, Sr., who served as senator from Tennessee from 1959 through 1971 and was a force behind Federal Aid to Highways Acts. . . . Creating highways is in the Gore family tradition" (*xvii*). The origin of the phrase, however, like any influential and popular idea, is not without contention. Stefik (1996), for example, suggests that the concept first entered common currency with Robert Kahn, who in 1988 "proposed building a high-speed national computer network he often likened to the interstate highway system" (*xvii*). However, earlier employment of the highway metaphor can be found in Martin (1978), the second chapter of which is entitled "New Highways," and Smith (1972), which proposed the construction of an "electronic highway system to facilitate the exchange of information and ideas" (83). Whatever its genesis, the information superhighway has become a powerful discursive model in technical, critical, and popular literature for explaining the function and significance of computer networking. As Dillon (1996) points out, "the information superhighway metaphor has attained remarkable status in the minds of people far beyond the fairly limited confines of academic researchers and software developers, being referenced almost daily in the news media, in political presentations, in advertisements, and so on" (336).

7. For a critical history of the Autobahn and its complex associations with Nazi politics and ideology, see Hartmut Bitomsky's documentary, *Reichsautobahn*.

8. For an examination of the denigration of the body in writings in and about cyberspace, see Chapter 5.

9. This convergence is also evident in the work of Al Gore during the tenure of his vice presidency. The two projects with which the vice president was associated during the era of the Clinton administration were the information superhighway and various efforts to address the problems of global warming. The convergence of these two issues is not an empirical accidental. It is systemic and dictated by the very issues involved. For a detailed examination of the logic of corporeal redemption through the technology of cyberspace, see Chapter 5.

10. The redemption promised by the network takes aim at and endeavors to repair the damage caused by another system of transportation—the automobile and the superhighway. Ironically, the liberatory promises currently associated with the computer network had, at one time, also been ascribed to the automobile and the interstate highway. Rose (1979, 1) provides a useful recollection:

> By 1960, a recorded voice promised visitors to General Motors' Futurama exhibit at the 1939 New York World's Fair, fourteen-lane express roads would accommodate 'traffic at designated speeds of 50, 75, and 100 miles an hour.' Spectators, six hundred at a time, rode around GM's 35,738 square foot mock-up of future America while the synchronized recording in each chair continued. Automobiles from farm and feeder roads would 'join the Motorway at the same speed as cars traveling in the lane they enter,' and motorists would be able to 'make right and left turns at speeds up to 50 miles per hour.' In urban areas, express highways would be 'so routed as to displace outmoded business sections and undesirable slum areas.' In cities themselves, men would construct buildings of 'breathtaking architecture,' leaving space for 'sunshine, light, and air.' Great sections of farm land, 'drenched in blinding sunlight' according to an observer, were under cultivation and nearly in fruit. Traffic, whether in rural or urban areas, flowed along without delays and without hazards at intersections and railroad crossings. 'Who can say what new horizons lie before us . . . ?' asked the voice on the record, 'new horizons in many fields, leading to new benefits for everyone, everywhere.'"

Unfortunately, but not surprisingly, this irony has been lost on the majority of advocates of the information superhighway.

11. For a detailed examination of cultural and intellectual reactions to the compression of time and space in the modern era, see Kern (1986).

12. Similar promises for a technologically mediated eradication of time and space can be found in Brunn and Leinbach (1991), Dizard (1997), and Bakis and Roche (1997), the last of which begins with the following proclamation: "It is clear to most observers the world has shrunk astonishingly in evident size driven by rapid and sustained advances in transportation, telecommunications, and information technology" (1). The often unquestioned assumption that telecommunications will overcome distances in space and time not only constitutes one of the fundamental principles of contemporary research in communication technology but is itself a general effect of the transmission view of communication.

13. On the complex interaction between the history and rhetoric of the European "Age of Discovery" and the development of telecommunications systems, including CMC, see Chapter 1.

14. One of the principal myths directing and animating this desire for global reunification is the story of the Tower of Babel (Genesis 11:1–9). According to this narrative, human beings originally lived in immediate proximity and because of this were able to cooperate with each other on a massive building project. This undertaking is eventually destroyed by Yahweh, who not only confuses their language but disperses the participants over the face of the earth. It is at Babel, therefore, that geophysical distance is introduced as a principle of separation between human beings. Transportation and telecommunication comprise subsequent attempts to mediate this dispersion, drawing people together into community despite this distance. For this reason, the subject of telecommunication is, in the words of Maddox (1972), a project that is concerned with what happens beyond Babel. Discussions of computer internetworking, in particular, draw upon the Babelian *mythos* to explain and justify their general undertaking. A particularly instructive example has been provided by Gore (1993):

It is important in discussing the information age that we discuss not merely technology but the essence of communications. Because from communication comes community. For example, not long ago when travel was very difficult, communities were small and communication was personal and direct between families, neighbors, those doing business together. Then the means of travel improved, moving us all away from each other and making communication more difficult. Until recently, for example, if an immigrant came to the United States from England, France or China or Russia, it meant saying good-bye to one's family that stayed in the Old World and never having a conversation with them again. Now we see television advertisements from companies competing for the lucrative business of communicating—or providing the communications links between families that are separated by the oceans. I read a little while ago about a family that was scattered in many countries around the world, where in more than a hundred different members of the same family keep in touch through the Internet. They keep people informed of births and deaths and graduations, and children in dozens of countries who have never met each other feel as if they know each other and understand the bonds of family. Our world is being brought closer together. And it's important in focusing on what is ahead in communications to zero in, not just on technology, but on what we use the technology for. (2–3)

This remarkable statement requires at least three comments. First, Gore reiterates the Babelian narrative in a kind of American vernacular. The original, preindustrial communities so celebrated in American ideology since Thomas Jefferson eventually come to be dispersed in space as a result of developments in the technology of transportation. The systems of telecommunications, however, promise to repair this dispersion and to permit not only the feeling of family over distance but, as Gore (1994b) states elsewhere, "instant communication to the great human family" (12). Consequently, communication technology and especially the Internet, which constitutes for Gore a privileged example, promises through the mediation of one form of transportation technology to overcome the devastating fragmentation suffered by human communities and the great human family at the hand of another form of transportation technology. Second, the distance-shattering effect of telecommunications is, as Gore describes it, presented in television commercials, which constitute one of the mechanisms of this promised tele-mediated contraction. Consequently, the idea of a communication link that reconnects dispersed people is itself explicitly marked as part of the rhetoric used to sell and to narrate the story of telecommunications. Whether this marketing discourse ever delivers on its promises is a question that is skillfully not asked. Finally, communication technology is presented as a mechanism that is capable of bringing the world closer together. For Gore, the technology of telecommunications constitutes a global unifying force that, in a gesture reiterating Christian eschatology, promises to repair human fragmentation and difference. For a detailed examination and critique of the Babelian narrative that animates and informs this position, see Chapter 4.

15. For Jones, it should be noted, this shift remains evolutionary rather than revolutionary. The ritual viewpoint does not, according to his reading, constitute an alternative to that of transmission. It is understood as the necessary sequel and

supplement to the completion of information transmittal. In other words, the ritual view point is invoked "once time and space have been overcome" (Jones 1995, 32). In this way, the ritual viewpoint does not so much provide an alternative mode for understanding computer-mediated communication but is formulated as an accessory to be added onto the traditional, transportation-oriented approach. In Jones's analysis, therefore, the ritual viewpoint remains subservient to and attendant upon the transmission metaphor.

16. This position is necessarily at variance with and intentionally deviates from established interpretations of Carey's work as employed in the field of communication studies. Carey's *Communication As Culture* (1989) has traditionally been read as proposing two models of communication and advocating a shift in emphasis from a transmission model to that of ritual (Jones 1995; Calvert 1997; Lenert 1998). This interpretation, although not necessarily ineffectual for framing specific inquiries, is not, I would argue, attentive to the complexity of Carey's work, which presents not two but three models of communication. This thesis, which of necessity deviates from an established tradition, is explored and explicated in detail in the analysis provided above. However, one can perceive the contours of this demonstration by considering the structure of the essay that first identified and evaluated the transmission and ritual models. Carey's essay, "A Cultural Approach to Communication" (in Carey 1989), is divided into two main parts, indicated with Roman numerals. The first part (13–23), introduces and explicates the difference between the transmission and ritual views of communication. The second part (23–35), proposes what Carey terms a "fresh perspective on communication" (23). This "fresh perspective" is not simply reducible to the ritual view as it is presented in the first part of the essay. It comprises, as Carey (1989) articulates it, "a definition of communication of disarming simplicity yet . . . of some intellectual power and scope" (23). This alternative understanding of communication is not commensurate with either the ritual or the transmission viewpoints. It comprises a *third term* that is not so much distinguished from the dialectic of transmission and ritual but situated in such a way that it relocates within the concept of communication the essential tension between these two traditional understandings. Consequently, Carey's work is richer and more complex than is usually admitted. Although distinguishing between transmission and ritual, the text does not simply advocate two models of communication but intervenes in this traditional understanding of communication in a way that produces a third and far more interesting approach to the subject matter.

17. If Carey's alternative position simply inverted the customary relationship between words and things, he would not be justified in calling it "a fresh perspective." Indeed, such a proposal had been already espoused and circulated in Berger and Luckmann (1966) and Burke (1966). What makes Carey's approach "fresh," what makes his formulation of "symbolic constructivism" particularly new and interesting, is that he proposes a double operation: He not only advocates, in almost absolute proximity to Burke, an inversion of the causal relationship customarily situated between words and things but, at the same time, displaces this simple inversion by considering words to be both symbols of and for things.

18. This paleonymy may be the primary reason for the continued misreading of Carey's work. Because Carey, preserves an old name to identify a new defini-

tion of communication, it is understandable that one could simply conflate Carey's "fresh perspective on communication" with the ritual viewpoint. Such conflation, although understandable, is not attentive to the complexities and implications of the play of paleonymy in this context.

19. For a detailed explanation and demonstration of the procedure of deconstruction, see the Appendix.

20. Carey's (1989) "symbolic production of reality" (23) is situated in almost absolute proximity to Baudrillard's concept of "simulation." Both proposals not only seek to intervene in the commonsense realism established between representations and things but also employ the same illustration to demonstrate their position—maps. According to Baudrillard (1983), "the territory no longer precedes the map, nor survives it. Hence forth it is the map that precedes the territory—Precession of Simulacra—it is the map that engenders the territory" (2). And in the words of Carey (1989), "maps not only constitute the activity known as mapmaking; they constitute nature itself" (28). For an examination of the concept of simulation, see Chapter 3.

3

VERITATEM IMITARI: VIRTUAL REALITY AND THE DECONSTRUCTION OF THE IMAGE

> Grammarians complain about the oxymoron "virtual reality," but the semantic twist of the phrase tells us as much about our tenuous grasp on reality as it does about the computerization of everything we know and experience.
>
> **Heim 1995, 65**

In the initial essay in *Communication in the Age of Virtual Reality*,[1] Frank Biocca, Taeyong Kim, and Mark Levy (1995) situate VR in the larger context of what they call, in a gesture that alludes to Ivan Sutherland's (1965) seminal paper on image technology, the "2000 year search for the ultimate display" (7). According to the authors, "the dream of the 'ultimate display' accompanies the creation of almost every iconic communication medium ever invented" (7), which includes painting, photography, cinema, and most recently television. What makes VR so compelling, consequently, is that it not only participates in this rich tradition but seems to promise substantial developments toward the fulfillment and final realization of the ultimate visual display medium. In situating the issue in this fashion, VR is immediately and almost unconsciously subsumed under the concept and technique of representation. Even if, as Biocca and Levy (1995a) suggest, this new technology eventually "challenges our most deeply held notions of what communication is or can be" (*vii*), VR is still located within and assumed to be a form of iconic representation. This assumption not only makes examinations of VR possible by framing recognizable approaches and deploying well-established methodologies but, like any unexamined presupposition, also has the potential to restrict inquiry to a limited set of predetermined possibilities.

As long as the concept and technology of VR remain within the restricted horizon of iconic communication, we will miss the radical possibilities and fundamental challenges that virtual reality poses to our most deeply held ideas of what communication is or can be. For what is at stake in VR is not a new form of mediated representation, but a specific kind of computer-generated *simulation* that deconstructs the metaphysical system that institutes and regulates the very difference between representation and reality. I, therefore, agree with Biocca and Levy (1995a) that VR may become too important, too wondrous, and too powerful to permit disciplinary ignorance and passivity (*vii*). However, this chapter maintains that their general approach, considering VR as a medium of iconic communication, is itself part and parcel of this ignorance and passivity. In other words, to begin to understand the impact of VR on the art and science of communication, we cannot simply presume that it is a medium of representation but must consider how the concept and technology of VR also challenge our most deeply held convictions about communication media and mediated images.

The Metaphysics of Representation

"Could you tell me in general what imitation is? For neither do I myself quite apprehend what it would be." "It is likely, then," he said, "that I should apprehend!"

Plato 1987, 596e

The quest for the ultimate display, according to Biocca, Kim, and Levy (1995), is animated and underwritten by the desire for what Norman Bryson (1983) called the essential copy: "Seeking the *essential copy* is to search for a means to fool the senses—a display that provides a perfect illusory deception" (Biocca, Kim, and Levy 1995, 7; italics in original). By situating their investigation in this fashion, the authors not only position VR as a natural and inevitable outgrowth of the past, making connections to familiar values and ideology, but package the technology in familiar cultural wrapping, constructing a historical narrative where VR is the necessary outcome and conclusion (Chesher 1993, 2). In particular, the "essential copy" simultaneously connects the ultimate display of VR to the history and situates it as the fulfillment of a concept of imitation and reproduction that is at least as old as Plato.

According to a logic initially formalized in Book X of the *Republic*, the image has been understood as a kind of derived reproduction, the value of which is determined by proximity and similarity to the original or real. In the initial moments of this text, Socrates proposes an image by which to examine and explain the nature of imitation. This image consists of a three-stage hierarchy of artisans and their products, in this case, home furnishings (couches). At the apex, Socrates locates the εἶδος, the real and true form that is created by the deity. Subordinate to the singular εἶδος he situates a first-order replication, which is produced through the art of the craftsman. The craftsman, Socrates reasons, produces his creation by looking to and following the information provided by the original εἶδος (Plato 1987, 596b). The derived product of the craftsman is subsequently copied by the painter who creates not a couch per se but the appearance (φαινόμενα) of a couch (Plato 1987, 596e). Although the craftsman copies the εἶδος, the name imitator or copier is reserved for the painter, for as Glaucon, Socrates' interlocutor, argues, "he is the imitator of the thing which the others produce" (Plato 1987, 597e). For this reason, imitation is situated in the phenomenal product that is three removes from the reality of the εἶδος. According to this schema, the value of any copy comes to be assessed on the basis of its proximity and attention to the real, or its "realism." Relying on this illustration, Socrates eventually proposes two alternatives for dealing with the imitative practice. Either imitation is to be expelled from the city, for, as he proposes, "it is a deception and corruption of the mind" (Plato 1987, 595b), or imitation must be strategically employed as a tool capable of serving and representing the real and true nature of things. Indeed, Socrates cleverly deploys both alternatives in Book X. On the one hand, he reiterates the banishment of the imitative artists that had already been suggested in Book III, and on the other hand, he justifies this exile by employing an image in order to represent and explain the true nature of imitation.

The "essential copy" comprises a technique of imitation that attempts to close the distance separating the copy from its formal referent by producing an image or icon so accurate that it could be confused with the real thing. Indeed, the primary example provided by Biocca, Kim, and Levy (1995) to illustrate the essential copy entails this kind of confusion. The illustration is derived from a story that is recounted in Pliny's *Natural History*, and it concerns a contest of skill undertaken by two Greek painters.

> The contemporaries and rivals of Zeuxis were Timanthes, Androcydes, Eupompus, and Parrhasius. This last, it is recorded, entered into a competition with Zeuxis. Zeuxis produced a picture of grapes so dexterously represented that birds began to fly down to eat from the painted vine. Whereupon Parrhasius designed so lifelike a picture of a curtain that Zeuxis, proud of the verdict of the birds, requested that the curtain should now be drawn back and the picture displayed. When he realized his mistake, with a modesty that did him honor, he yielded up the palm, saying whereas he had managed to deceive only birds, Parrhasius had deceived an artist. (7–8)

What makes VR so compelling is that it promises to supply an even greater sense of realism and consequently confusion, for VR removes the frame that distinguishes and quarantines the space of imitation. As Simon Penny (1992) points out, VR endeavors to dissolve the proscenium: "Through painting, sculpture, drama, cinema, TV, the separation of audience from art was complete. VR effects a melding of experience and representation rather than the separation effected by the proscenium" (2). This dissolution of the enframing proscenium or paragon has been one of the distinctive characteristics of early VR development. As Jaron Lanier has pointed out on several occasions: "With a VR system you don't see the computer anymore—it's gone" (Lanier and Biocca 1992, 166). It is this "invisibility of the computer," as Brenda Laurel (1991, 143) calls it, that renders the representations of VR virtually indistinguishable from reality.

Under the conceptualization of the essential copy, VR does not challenge the Socratic formulation that distinguishes the real from its derivative imitations, but operates within its logic, striving to produce more accurate and nearly perfect reproductions. In this way, VR is understood as a technique of almost perfect imitation, a flawless and transparent medium through which one sees and comprehends the referent in its original presence. In VR, iconic representation is not experienced as such but as the delegate of something else to which the image defers and refers. As Marie-Laure Ryan (1994) points out, "the 'virtual reality effect' is the denial of the role of signs in the production of what the user experiences as unmediated presence" (3). VR, therefore, is often described as an "interface that disappears," opening a doorway to another world (Rheingold 1991, 131). Understood in this way, the fundamental difference between VR and the other iconic media (i.e., painting, photography, cinema, and television) would consist in effectiveness, which is usually defined as the degree of achieved "realism." A mark of quality in VR design, therefore, is the extent to which the experience of a representation disappears as such and the system "duplicates the viewer's act of confronting a real scene" (Fisher 1981, 94).[2] In this way, VR portends the creation of the ultimate communication medium, promising to provide images of the real so perfect that for all intents and purposes they are experienced *as* if they were the real thing.

The essential copy imaged through the "ultimate display" of VR has prompted two responses, both of which follow the contours of the Socratic assessment of imitation. On the one hand, VR can be a tool employed for the sake of and in the service of the real. For the scientific and engineering communities, VR is, in the words of Frederick Brooks (1988), primarily a means for "grasping reality through illusion" (1). As an illustration of this concept, Howard Rheingold (1991) describes the University of North Carolina's (UNC) molecular-docking simulation, a haptic-VR system that permits users to experience and to navigate complex chemical interactions intuitively, learning molecular bonding not by abstract formulas but through direct manipulation of the molecules. Similar applications have been proposed in the field of medical imaging to assist physicians in performing diagnosis and treatment planning (Pimentel and Teixeira 1993). In an interview with Rheingold, Stephen Pizer, a medical imaging researcher at UNC, provides the following imaginative account of the future possibilities of VR applications in the medical profession: "Once you are putting 3D virtual worlds in front of the surgeon or diagnostician, why not put them where they belong—namely, in the patient, superimposed on where the organs are located? One could imagine a situation where surgeons can see their surgical instruments, can see the real tissue of the patient as they operate, and can simultaneously see an augmented image that allows them to see behind the blood and opaque surfaces" (Rheingold 1991, 33–34).

Two proven applications of VR technology can be found in military training simulators, like SIMNET, and architectural design and walk-through systems. SIMNET comprises a network of tank and aircraft simulators scattered across the globe that can interact and perform maneuvers with each other: "In the computer-generated battlefield displayed on the simulator screen, other tanks and aircraft that appear are 'driven' by other crews in other simulators, the data on their movements and actions passed along the network so that all the simulated tanks and planes seem to be sharing the same space" (Woolley 1992, 192; Rheingold 1991, 360). Architectural walk-through software facilitates the evaluation of an edifice by placing designers and clients within a virtual representation of the building prior to construction (Negroponte 1970, 1975; Rheingold 1991; Aukstakalnis and Blatner 1992; Morgan and Zampi 1995; Bertol and Foell 1997; Spiller 1998). Similar instrumental applications have been proposed for education, entertainment, data visualization and management, and hazardous-environment telepresence. The logic animating these instrumental applications is in complete agreement with the Socratic tradition. Because the copy seeks to represent a real system, it can be employed as a way to get a grasp on and perceive reality. Like the Socratic representation that was employed to get a grasp on the reality of imitation, the technology of VR has been perceived as a tool by which to understand the intricacies and to manipulate the elements of reality.

On the other hand, no matter how useful or perfect the VR representation is, it is still an imitation and, as such, necessarily remains a counterfeit and illusion. Indeed, the degree of achieved realism in the imitation is directly proportional to its potential for deception. "As VR simulations grow more realistic," Rheingold (1991) points out, "their potential for being dangerously misleading also increases. No model can ever be as complex as the phenomena it models, no map can ever be as detailed as the territory it describes, and more importantly, as semanticist Korzybski noted, 'the map is not the territory'" (44). This "fact" has become the foundation not only of popular reactions to VR but of scholarly criticism and hesitation concerning the import and significance of imaging technologies. According to this assessment, VR, although a useful tool for some applications, is still a deceptive illusion and, therefore, "not really real." If used improperly or excessively, the argument concludes, one may be in danger of losing oneself in an artificial fantasy cut off from the real situation. This argument is in complete compliance with the Socratic denigration of imitation. Namely, a copy, no matter how useful or beneficial, is misleading and, therefore, essentially dangerous and potentially corrupt.

The netploitation film *Lawnmower Man* (1992), for instance, is a cautionary tale about the potent risks of VR. At the beginning of the narrative, VR is introduced as an instrument for enhancing education and accelerating learning. The film's climax, however, demonstrates the dangers implicit in this undertaking. At the apex of his "cyberlearning," Jobe, the film's protagonist, endeavors to upload his consciousness into the electronic matrix, leaving "reality" altogether and becoming virtually immortal. His virtual transcendence[3] is, however, interrupted:

> What prevents the virtual-entity Jobe from being completely divine—what preserves his humanity—is the memory of a person he loved as a child when in his former human body. Little Peter, Jobe's young friend, remains a remembered and valued human being in the *primary world*. With a bomb threatening the body of little Peter, Jobe suspends his omniscient tyranny and commands, "Go save Peter!" And so the bridge between the primary and the virtual world establishes once again the importance of existential care, of personal pain and loss, of limited lifetimes. (Heim 1993, 146)

The narrative trajectory traversed by Jobe illustrates the Socratic argument against imitation. Reiterating the Socratic dialogue, *Lawnmower Man* reminds us that representations are potentially dangerous and, for this reason, one must always return to and remain grounded in the real and the true.

This reaction to the dangerous "unreality of VR" is not limited to popular media. It has also been deployed within and has informed the texture of critical research. Michael Heim (1993), for example, like all good modern philosophers, always retreats to the real, the essential, and the true. At the end of his metaphysical investigation of the ontology of cyberspace, Heim recognizes the potential deceptions instituted within the virtual information system and, as a result, issues an imperative that once again privileges and exonerates the "primary world": "As we suit up for the exciting future in cyberspace, we must not lose touch with [William] Gibson's Zionites, the body people who remain rooted in the energies of the earth. They will nudge us out of our heady reverie in this new layer of reality. They will remind us of the living genesis of cyberspace, of the heartbeat behind the laboratory" (107). For

Heim, as well as for other VR theorists and critics, VR may be an exciting new medium of representation, but like all imitations, it must always be distinguished from and grounded in a clear sense of reality. A similar criticism is deployed by Michael Shapiro and Daniel McDonald (1995): "Obviously spending too much time in virtual reality could be damaging to those who need to confront reality and not escape it. It could be particularly damaging to children and adolescents. But in some cases living in a VR could be therapeutic" (342). The concern over excessive employment as opposed to restricted therapeutic usefulness, the potential dangers confronting children and adolescents, and the assumption that all this is somehow obvious is animated and substantiated by the Socratic assessment of imitation. It should be no surprise that similar arguments have been deployed against other media of representation from the novel to cinema and from photography to television (Lubar 1993; Marvin 1988).

Under these conceptualizations, VR not only resides within the metaphysical distinction that divides reality from derivative imitations but retains and validates the privilege that has been granted to the real. Imitation is either submitted to and made an instrument of the real, or it is distinguished from reality as a deception and, as such, constitutes a potential depravation. In this way, VR is restricted to a replication or imitation of Western metaphysics. Appropriately, Heim (1993) suggests that "cyberspace is Platonism as a working product" (89). VR designates a practice of imitation that is located at the zenith of iconic communication by creating copies that are so close to the original as to fool even the best metaphysicians. Understood in this way, VR is nothing new. It only reiterates and reinforces Platonic metaphysics. As Penny (1994) has pointed out, "while VR is technically advanced, like most computer graphics practices it is philosophically retrogressive" (231). It must be remembered, however, that the metaphysical formulation of imitation that informs and substantiates this evaluation of VR is itself introduced through an image initially created by Socrates. Consequently, the reality of imitation is itself only virtually real.

Simulation and the
Deconstruction of Representation

This call for a more "organic" representation in the digital realm may be regarded as a retrograde critical position.

Penny 1994, 234

The conception of VR as a medium of near-perfect representation, although certainly useful for scientific research, medical
procedures, military operations, education, and such, appears to
be rather limited. Theorists like Heim (1993) suggest that VR
should be able to do more than merely mirror reality. "It should,"
he writes, "evoke the imagination, not repeat the world. Virtual
reality could be a place for reflection, but the reflection should
make philosophy, not redundancy" (137). Myron Krueger (1977),
the artist-scientist who designed and constructed the virtual environments of GLOWFLOW, METAPLAY, and VIDEOPLACE,
has made a similar statement, distinguishing between the usual
instrumental understanding of technology and its transforming
ideological potential: "We are incredibly attuned to the idea that
the sole purpose of our technology is to solve problems. But it
also creates concepts and philosophy" (423). VR, therefore, may
be more than a medium of representation that is submitted to the
order and rule of the real. It also has the potential to become a
laboratory in which to challenge and investigate the metaphysics
of representation.

The majority of contemporary VR equipment originates in and
was created for simulator systems. For this reason, simulation has
been from the beginning intimately connected to the concept and
tools of VR. In fact, throughout the scientific community, the term
simulation has been routinely substituted for the more cryptic and
seemingly less scientific *virtual reality* (Biocca, Kim, and Levy 1995,
4). Etymologically, the word *simulate*, from the Latin verb *simulare*,
means to copy, to imitate, or to feign. In this way, simulation appears to be nothing more than another name for imitation and, as
a result, would be appropriated as an instrument of mimetic re-

production. Indeed, the techniques and technologies of computer simulation follow this formulation. "Simulation," as defined by Robert Shannon (1975), "is the process of designing a model of a real system and conducting experiments with this model for the purpose either of understanding the behavior of the system or of evaluating various strategies for the operation of the system" (2). Yet simulation somehow exceeds and is differentiated from what is understood as imitation. As Benjamin Woolley (1992) suggests, "the distinction between simulation and imitation is a difficult and not altogether clear one. Nevertheless, it is vitally important. It lies at the heart of virtual reality" (44).

Simulation is neither simply identical to nor the dialectical opposite of imitation. Although etymologically connected to and informed by the concept of imitation and the techniques of computer modeling, simulation is always more and less than what is meant by imitation. "Simulation," writes Baudrillard in his now famous essay *Simulations* (1983), "is no longer that of a territory, a referential being or a substance. It is the generation by models of a real without origin or reality" (1). This definition of simulation no longer reproduces the Socratic logic of imitation. Indeed, it inverts while it displaces the usual position and status granted the real and its mimetic delegate, creating a situation in which "neither image nor the world is 'first'" (Morse 1998, 21). Understood in this way, simulation deconstructs[4] imitation. Deconstruction, however, does not indicate "to break up" or "to un-construct." These endeavors are indicated by another name, analysis. Analysis (from the Greek ἀναλύω) connotes "to break apart" or "to loosen up." Deconstruction may include something like an analytical moment, but it will be nothing more than a moment. Analysis, therefore, does not exhaust deconstruction, which is always more and less than analysis. On the contrary, deconstruction is a kind of general operation by which to intervene in the closed field of metaphysical knowledge.

Metaphysics, which is not one region of knowledge among others but that upon which such distinctions have been founded, is animated and informed by a network of dualities. "The fundamental faith of the metaphysicians," wrote Nietzsche (1966), "is the faith in opposite values" (2). A sample of these "opposite values" that have been persistent in and constitutive of Western traditions has been collected in Donna Haraway (1991b). They include, among others, "self/other, mind/body, culture/nature, male/female, civilized/primitive, reality/appearance, whole/part, agent/resource, maker/made, active/passive, right/wrong, truth/illusion, totality/partiality" (177). Within the Western metaphysical tradition, these dualities are never situations of peaceful coexistence but constitute hierarchies. As Derrida (1982) explained, "an opposition of metaphysical concepts is never the face-to-face of two terms but a hierarchy and an order of subordination" (329). Deconstruction, therefore, constitutes a general strategy for intervening in these metaphysical dualities that avoids either simply neutralizing the hierarchical relationship or residing within its closed field and thereby confirming it. It entails, as Derrida (1982) succinctly describes it, both "an *overturning* of a classical opposition *and* a general *displacement* of the system" (329; italics in original). This abstract and rather schematic characterization is necessarily incomplete and insufficient. "We must," as Briankle Chang (1996) points out, "note that deconstruction cannot be adequately understood in the abstract. . . . What we ought to do, when trying to understand what deconstruction is all about, is to focus on the actual operation of deconstruction, on what happens when deconstruction takes place" (119). The proper way to characterize deconstruction, then, is by tracing its work on and within a specific context, say, for example, simulation. By placing emphasis on a term that is originally and etymologically associated with imitation, simulation effectively inverts the system that subjects imitation to the rule and order of the real. However, simulation, as Woolley is quick to point out, has never been simply identical to imitation. It is this almost imperceptible difference or dissonance that displaces simulation outside the metaphysical system, opening it to new and previously inconceivable possibilities. Simulation, therefore, consists in a double gesture that on the one hand inverts the duality real/imitation and on the other hand displaces the system that has been overturned.

At the beginning of *Simulations* (1983), Baudrillard provides an illustration of this necessary and irreducible double gesture by alluding to a fable about cartography written by Luis Jorge Borges. By beginning with a fable that problematizes the relationship between maps and territory, Baudrillard not only mocks the Socratic gesture that initiates the investigation of the nature of imitation through an image but also parodies the cartographic image Rheingold had appropriated from Korzybski in order to reiterate the potential dangers of imitation: "The territory no longer precedes the map, nor survives it. Hence forth it is the map that precedes the territory—Precession of Simulacra—it is the map that engenders the territory." (2). This formulation inverts the usual positions occupied by the real territory and the cartographic image, granting precedence to the imitation over and against the so-called real-world referent. As a result of this inversion, the territory is derived from and becomes the product of the map. This is precisely the situation that concerns Socrates and animates both his indictment of imitation in Book X of the *Republic* and all subsequent criticisms of representation that adhere to this Socratic precedent. This simple inversion, however, like all revolutionary operations, would do little or nothing to challenge the system in which it intervenes. In exchanging the positions of the two terms, one still maintains, albeit in an inverted form, the traditional relationship between imitation and reality. Mere inversion, therefore, does not dispute the essential structure of the system in question but only exchanges the relative positions occupied by the two terms.

Although simulation begins with a phase of inversion, inversion alone is not sufficient. In addition to reversing the positions customarily occupied by the territory and the map, simulation also displaces the relationship between these two terms. In this second phase of the deconstruction, the map does not simply take up the position once occupied by the territory, which is the case in all simple revolutions—the ruled becomes the ruler or the dominated becomes the dominator. With simulation, Baudrillard (1983) continues, "it is no longer a question of either maps or territories. Something has disappeared: the sovereign difference between them" (2). Simulation, therefore, not only inverts the relative positions of imitation and reality but also disperses or dissolves the very difference that would hold them in dialectical opposition. It "threatens the difference between 'true' and 'false,' between 'real' and 'imaginary'" (Baudrillard 1983, 5). Simulation, therefore, is neither map nor territory but an undecidable that exceeds and disturbs the very relationship that has been situated between the "real world" and its cartographic images. As Mark Taylor and Esa Saarinen (1994) suggest: "The point is not simply that truth and reality have been absorbed by illusion and appearance. Something far more subtle and unsettling is taking place. Somewhere Nietzsche suggests that when reality is effaced, appearance disappears as well. What emerges in the wake of the death of oppositions like truth/illusion and reality/appearance is something that is neither truth nor illusion, reality nor appearance but something else, something other" (15). Simulation, therefore, does not announce the mere substitution of images for reality, which is not only the object of the Socratic critique but the concern of all those who worry about and propose to resist the "virtual life" (Brook and Boal 1995; Slouka 1995). Rather, it designates a radical intervention that not only suspends the very difference that would oppose imitation to reality in the first place but results in an undecidable and irreducible alternative that is neither one nor the other.

Understanding VR under the concept of simulation requires not only a different perspective on the technology but researchers and research projects that are capable of perceiving VR systems differently, that are capable of perceiving the logic and limitations of imitation as such. Such an undertaking will depend less on those who have a vested interest in the "truth of iconic media" or the creation of an "essential copy," namely, scientists, engineers, philosophers, and imitative artists. Exploring this other possibility that is neither simply real nor mere representation will require a new kind of virtual art—the virtues of which lie beyond the metaphysical dualisms that have traditionally structured the practices and techniques of imitation. As a result, VR can no longer be understood as a technology to be evaluated or judged according to the criteria of *realism*. As Heim (1998) argues, "we no longer need to believe we are re-presenting the real world of nature. Virtual worlds do not re-present the primary world. They are not realistic in the sense of photo-realism" (47–48). Although a majority of VR technology and experimentation appear to affirm the "search for the essential copy" and the criteria of realism, there are a number of innovative projects that undermine and interrogate this purely imitative employment.

Architect Michael Benedikt (1993a), for example, finds in the constructed environments of cyberspace the potential to reprogram and experiment with reality for the sake of empowerment:

> Because virtual worlds—of which *cyberspace* will be one—are not real in the material sense, many of the axioms of topology and geometry so compellingly observed to be an integral part of nature can there be violated or re-invented, as can many of the laws of physics. A central preoccupation of this essay will be the sorting out of which axioms and laws of nature ought to be retained in cyberspace, on the grounds that humans have successfully evolved on a planet where these are fixed and conditioning of all phenomena (including human intelligence), and which axioms and laws can be adjusted or jettisoned for the sake of empowerment. (119)

Benedikt's proposal is situated on the threshold of simulation. On the one hand, he sees in the images of VR the opportunity to modify and redesign what has been called and understood as reality for the sake of empowerment. Understood in this way, VR constitutes not merely a technological innovation for "grasping reality through illusion" but, more important, a fundamental intervention that questions and revolutionizes what has been defined as real. On the other hand, Benedikt's particular approach remains at the first phase of deconstruction. In proposing that one employ VR to interrogate and redesign the real, Benedikt advocates overturning the traditional relationship that submits imitation to the rule and dictate of reality. Although potentially useful for new allocations of power, this inversion still operates within and leaves untouched the metaphysical system that distinguishes artificial images from the real. Indeed, Benedikt's proposal demonstrates the way in which inversion is always open to the risk of reinscription in the very system that it works against and proposes to overturn, for his particular approach to VR design is still limited and ruled by a restricted formulation of the real that remains beyond question by being elevated to the status of "natural law." According to this formulation, the adjustments and alterations that can be introduced in cyberspace, although potentially useful for empowerment, remain nothing more than strategic variations deployed from and delimited by what is already called and legislated as real.

Benedikt's approach remains limited to the first phase of deconstruction. Although he advocates employing VR to introduce potentially revolutionary alterations in the definition of the real, these modifications remain structured by a system that maintains the metaphysical opposition that distinguishes imitations from reality. Myron Krueger's (1991) experimentation in artificial reality pushes the operation one step further. Artificial reality (AR), a name that actually predates Lanier's "virtual reality" by some eighteen years, intervenes in and deconstructs the logic of imitation that has come to define and delimit VR systems. This radical intervention is not only designated by the curious moniker "artificial reality" but is explained in the introduction to the text that first described and developed the concept: "The promise of artificial realities is not to reproduce conventional reality or to act in the real world. It is precisely the opportunity to create synthetic realities, for which there are no real antecedents, that is exciting conceptually and ultimately important economically" (Krueger 1991, xiv). Artificial reality, according to Krueger, seeks neither to reproduce reality nor to facilitate operations in the so-called natural or real world. Unlike the "essential copy" proffered in the work of Biocca, Kim, and Levy, Krueger's AR comprises artificial constructions that not only do not seek to represent the real but, more important, have no real antecedent whatsoever. Artificial reality, therefore, participates in the deconstruction of imitation. It inverts the hierarchy real/imitation by privileging synthetic artificiality over the real and displaces the system that had been overturned by the additional qualification that this artificiality not only does not refer to a real referent but is utterly without any realistic attachments. Artificial reality, therefore, is neither image nor reality but something other, something that is neither/nor and either/or. It is another name for *simulation*. Similar employments of VR technology have recently been explored and promoted by the Banff Centre for the Arts (Moser and MacLeod 1996) and Penny (1994).

Simulation intervenes in the metaphysics of representation by deconstructing the binary opposition real/imitation. This deconstruction comprises a double gesture that inverts the relationship between representations and the "real world" and introduces a new and undecidable concept that is displaced outside the very system that had been inverted. As a result, simulation constitutes a significant challenge to the concept of the "essential copy" and the criteria of realism by which the technology of VR has been evaluated, understood, and explained. Understood as a technology of simulation, VR can no longer be restricted to the "2000 year search for the ultimate display" or delimited by the Socratic logic that has substantiated and informed this essentially metaphysical project. Consequently, VR is not necessarily a tool for grasping the real through illusion nor a potentially dangerous delusion. It is something other, something that is both more and less, and something that exceeds the metaphysical system that opposes reality and imitation. This does not mean, however, that the mimetic understanding of VR has somehow simply collapsed or been exhausted. Indeed, the representational employments of VR will continue to be valuable in physics, biomedicine, chemistry, applied mathematics, and such. What this does mean, however, is that the instrumental or representational employments of VR are not somehow natural, unavoidable, and beyond question. Although VR can be and has been employed to duplicate Western metaphysics, it also exceeds this employment and in doing so interrogates the hegemony of metaphysics by posing alternatives to its rather restricted set of binary possibilities. Simulation, therefore, does not constitute a competing theoretical position that opposes imitation. To do so would mean nothing less than a relapse into the metaphysical oppositions that simulation always and already deconstructs. Simulation, rather than simply being identical with or opposed to imitation, occupies a monstrous position that places the entire structure and system of metaphysics in question. As Baudrillard (1983) points out, "The representational imaginary, which both culminates in and is engulfed by the cartographer's mad project of an ideal coextensivity between map and the territory, disappears with simulation," and with this dissolution, he concludes, "goes all of metaphysics" (3).

Conclusion

The true world—we have abolished. What world has remained? The apparent one perhaps? But no! *With the true world we have also abolished the apparent one.*

Nietzsche 1983b, 486; italics in original

From the beginning, the concept and technology of VR has been incorporated into the metaphysics of representation and the two-thousand-year search for the ultimate communication medium. In pursuing this course, however, VR remains philosophically retrogressive, participating in distinctions and architectonics that have been in place at least since Plato. A new technology like VR always runs the risk of this kind of appropriation, for it is by this very gesture that a new medium can be said to make sense and have recognizable meaning. Under this formulation, VR has been comprehended as an illusion instrumental for perceiving and working in reality. Affirming this mode appears to be both understandable and necessary. It informs all those discourses that divide the virtual world from the real and argue either against its deceptive corruption or in favor of its instrumental benefits. Understood as simulation, however, VR exceeds this restricted formulation by deconstructing the metaphysical system that opposes imitation to reality. In this way, VR does not remain philosophically retrogressive or a mere application of Platonism. It constitutes a critical intervention in the history of thought affecting and infecting every aspect of what has been considered to be real or not. Consequently, VR is, as Krueger (1991) argues, "not just another technology; it is a powerful idea with possible implications for every human transaction" (*xv*). This conclusion engenders several consequences.

First, VR is not just a technological amusement, even if the majority of users still encounter it in the form of computer games. Like all imaging systems, VR is necessarily hardwired into politics. In fact, the duality opposing the real and the true to its other, the imitation or copy, is fundamentally a political matter. This facet is initially evident in the *Republic*. The opposition between the real and imitation is not only situated in the context of a work on the political (the title of the text in Greek is Πολιτεια), but the discussion of imitation that is instituted in Book X is itself framed by a political agenda. Socrates' discussion of imitation is undertaken in order to justify the expulsion of the imitative art of poetry from the well-governed city. Imitation, he argues, poses a threat to the *polis* (πόλις) because it deceives, posing illusory alternatives to the real. Plato's *Republic*, therefore, is a text that not only considers the reality of the political but, more important, the politics of the real. The imitative arts and media have always been recognized as posing alternatives that threaten and promise to alter the status quo. Today we speak of fiction that challenges or seeks to change social reality (Haraway 1991b) and struggle within communities that debate the banning of representations, literary, visual, or otherwise, that do not accord with a particular vision/version of reality (e.g., the controversy surrounding the funding of the Maplethorpe exhibition of supposedly homoerotic photographs by the National Endowment for the Arts). VR has been entwined in this political debate from the beginning. For example, Mark Slouka (1995) delivers the following warning concerning the dangers of virtual representation and the "politics of virtual reality": "By flooding the culture with digitally manipulated images, I'm saying, we risk devaluing *all* visual representations and, by extension, the reality they pretend to depict, which is no small thing. Al-

lowed to run unchecked, the crisis I am describing could come to
have a profound effect on Western democratic culture" (124). In
the end, VR is fundamentally a political matter. It, therefore, can
neither be contained behind the screen nor will its significance be
limited to technical discourses and research. Research and development in VR constitutes fundamental interventions in real politics and the politics of the real. Consequently, critical investigations of and practical experimentation with VR cannot and should
not avoid this fundamental political dimension.

Second, VR challenges not only "our most deeply held notions
of what communication is or can be" but the theoretical framework by which such a challenge would be formulated and recognized. For Biocca, Kim, and Levy, the "challenge" posed by VR is
delimited by Western metaphysics and restricted to its binary possibilities. Under this conceptualization, VR constitutes the fulfillment of the metaphysics of representation, portending the
achievement of the essential copy and the completion of the two-
thousand-year search for the ultimate medium of imitation. This
formulation does not, strictly speaking, challenge our most deeply
held notions of what communication is or can be but situates the
technology of VR within a two-thousand-year-old tradition that is
firmly anchored in and informed by Platonism. For Biocca, Kim,
and Levy, the "challenge" VR introduces into communication is in
complete compliance with the metaphysical system from which
our most deeply held notions of what communication is or can be
has been derived and regulated. As long as communication research remains within the restricted parameters of the quest for
the ultimate medium or the desire for the essential copy, we essentially blind ourselves to the radical possibilities that VR presents to the theory and practice of communication. Understood as
simulation, however, VR poses a significant challenge to this tradition. As simulation, VR critiques the very foundation of mediated representation and iconic communication by deconstructing
the metaphysical system that opposes imitation to reality. This
fundamental intervention in the field of metaphysics exceeds mere
revolutionary possibilities, for it not only inverts the causal rela-

tionship situated between imitation and reality but suspends the very difference that would hold them in binary opposition. This deconstruction not only has repercussions for future work in communication technology but effects the very history of the concept of representation and mediated communication. In this way, the *challenge* posed by simulation to the theory and practice of communication cannot be contained within or limited to the present technology of VR. Rather, it affects and infects the entire history and future prospects of the mediated image and iconic communication. Consequently, the simulated environments of VR do not portend the completion of the two-thousand-year search for the essential copy but deconstruct this tradition by inverting and displacing its very metaphysical foundation. Tracing the effects of this deconstruction constitutes the ongoing task of communication in the age of VR.

Finally, although it is tempting to credit or even blame the technology of VR for instituting this deconstruction, it would be a mistake or at least an exaggeration to do so. For deconstruction is neither a "voluntary decision" (Derrida 1981a, 82) nor an accidental occurrence. Deconstruction, therefore, is not something that, at a certain point, is done or happens to a previously well-established and pure concept. Instead, deconstruction has always and already been underway within the texture of the metaphysical system in which and on which it operates. For this reason, deconstruction has been characterized not as an activity in which one voluntarily or coercively engages but "as the vigilant seeking-out of those 'aporias,' blind spots or moments of self-contradiction where a text involuntarily betrays the tension between rhetoric and logic, between what it manifestly *means to say* and what it is nonetheless *constrained to mean*" (Chang 1996, 119). Such an *aporia* is already evident in the *Republic*, the text that not only introduces and delimits the critical difference between imitation and reality but organizes the entire metaphysical system by which iconic media have been understood and evaluated. As indicated, the Socratic argument against imitation situated in this text is made possible through the employment of an image. This inconsistency between

what the Platonic text means to say and what it is nonetheless constrained to mean, an inconsistency which Derrida demonstrates in
a number of other places in the Platonic corpus, opens the space
for and already releases the play of deconstruction within the tradition of metaphysics. The deconstruction of the image, therefore,
is not something that is caused by or limited to VR. Rather, VR
participates in a general movement of deconstruction that is always and already underway within the tradition of Western metaphysics and, as such, constitutes nothing more than a technique by
which to identify, articulate, and participate in this operation.

Notes

1. Although numerous texts have been published on the subject of VR and cyberspace, Biocca and Levy's book is privileged here because it constitutes the first
monograph explicitly connecting virtual reality to the discipline of communication.

2. This disappearance of the interface and immediate experience of another
world is also one of the attributes of fiction according to recent work in literary
theory; see Ryan (1994).

3. According to Biocca, Kim, and Levy (1995), the "desire for physical transcendence" (7) is one of the fundamental ideologies animating the development
of VR. For a sustained examination of technological transcendentalism, see Chapter 5.

4. For an extended treatment of deconstruction, see the Appendix.

4

LINGUA EX MACHINA: COMPUTER–MEDIATED COMMUNICATION AND THE TOWER OF BABEL

We've finally reversed the damage done by the
Tower of Babel, and God, no doubt, is wondering
what we're going to do for an encore.

Stratton 1996, 1

The "Tower of Babel" (Genesis 11:1–9) provides an account of the plurality of languages as issued from an original and apparently universal tongue. The first line of the fable reads: "And all the earth was one lip and there was one language to all." The mythic loss of an original, linguistic universality as well as subsequent attempts to reestablish it by overcoming the *confusio linguarum* already constitute a kind of universal idiom. According to Umberto Eco (1995), "the story of the confusion of tongues, and of the attempt to redeem its loss through the rediscovery or invention of a language common to all humanity, can be found in every culture" (1). The computer and the technologies of computer-mediated communication manifest the most recent version of this supposedly universal endeavor. According to numerous popular and

technical discourses, the computer promises to supply a technological solution to the linguistic cacophony that has been the
legacy of Babel. In this manner, computer technology participates
in an old and apparently universal obsession, one that situates
universality as both its origin and purpose.

This chapter undertakes an examination of the Babelian information currently circulating through cyberspace and determining the general significance of networked computer systems. It
traces the origin and purpose of the desire for universal under-
standability, locates the computer within this tradition, and asks
about the underlying assumptions and consequences of this project. The inquiry is directed toward not only computer technology but also the various discourses that have reflected on and
shaped the meaning of this technology. In short, the examination
attempts to understand the rather cacophonous babble concerning Babel as it has been deployed within the networks of cyberspace. Whether this babble derives from and is reducible to a single and univocal meaning cannot be answered in advance—for
this question constitutes the very issue that is at stake in the
"Tower of Babel."

The Universal Machine

> In the popular mythology the computer is a mathematics machine; it is de-
> signed to do numerical calculations. Yet it is really a language machine; its
> fundamental power lies in its ability to manipulate linguistic tokens—sym-
> bols to which meaning has been assigned.
>
> **Winograd 1984, 131**

Although its taxonomy is derived from a mathematical concept,
the computer is not primarily a computational apparatus. Its
substance and genealogy have been determined to be otherwise.
Michael Heim (1993), the self-proclaimed metaphysician of cyberspace technology, traces the genesis of the computer to the
universal language movement. "Underneath the computer's cal-

culating power lies an inner core sprung from a seed planted two centuries ago. . . . That initial germ for the birth of computers started with the rationalist philosophers of the seventeenth century who were passionate in their efforts to design a world language" (36). Seventeenth-century Europe saw the development of several projects related to the creation of a universal idiom. In a 1657 publication, for example, Cave Beck proposed a *Universal Character, by which all the nations of the world may understand one another's conceptions, reading out of one common writing their own mother tongues.* A similar pasigraphic endeavor was undertaken by Athanasius Kircher in the *Polygraphia nova et universalis ex-combinatoria arte detecta* (1663), which proposed a system of writing in which "all languages are reduced to one." Eleven years earlier, Francis Lodwick published *The Groundwork or Foundation Laid (or So Intended) for the Framing of a New Perfect Language and a Universal Common Writing.* This text not only proposed a universal idiom to which everyone would have equal access but also a perfected language that was "capable of mirroring the true nature of objects" (Eco 1995, 73). Similar systems were introduced by the *Via lucis* (1668) of Comenius, George Dalgarno's *Ars Signorium* (1661), and John Wilkins's *Essay Toward a Real Character, and a Philosophical Language* (1668).

The seventeenth-century philosopher to which the computer makes particular reference, however, is Gottfried Wilhelm von Leibniz. According to Heim (1993), "Leibniz's general outlook on language became the ideological basis for computer-mediated telecommunications" (93). This privileged status was canonized by Norbert Wiener (1961) in the introduction to the text that originated the science of cybernetics. "If I were to choose a patron saint for cybernetics out of the history of science, I should have to choose Leibniz. The philosophy of Leibniz centers about two closely related concepts—that of a universal symbolism and that of a calculus of reasoning" (12). The significance and interrelationship of these two concepts had been summarized by Leibniz in a 1679 missive to the Duke of Hanover, which addressed the invention of an artificial, philosophical language: "For my invention uses reason in its entirety and is, in addition, a judge of controversies, an interpreter of notions, a balance of probabilities, a compass which will guide us over the ocean of experiences, an inventory of all things, a table of thoughts, a microscope for scrutinizing present things, a telescope for predicting distant things, a general calculus, an innocent magic, a non-chimerical Kabal, a script which all will read in their own language; and even a language which one will be able to learn in a few weeks, and which will soon be accepted amidst the world" (Eco 1995, *xii*). The proposed invention would accomplish two goals: it would provide a thoroughly rational protocol whereby all debate and controversy would be resolved through calculation, and it would establish a universal writing that would be acceptable to all nations and cultures. These two operations are necessarily interrelated. The rational perfection of the idiom ensured that the new system of writing was not arbitrary and ambiguous like the "natural languages." Instead, this *characteristica universalis* was substantiated by, and resided in perfect concord with, reason. It was therefore appropriately suited to all particular members of that genus that European philosophy had defined as *animale rationale*. Leibniz's rational calculus would thus be capable of overcoming the *confusio linguarum* once and for all, for it "would compile all human culture, bringing every natural language into a single shared database" (Heim 1993, 94).

In canonizing Leibniz as the patron of the new science of communication and control, Wiener (1961) encoded this dream of a universal and perfect language in the fundamental program (or operating system) of computer technology. According to Wiener's estimations, "Leibniz's *calculus ratiocinator* contained the seed of the *machina ratiocinatrix*"—the reasoning machine or computer (12). Universal language, then, is not a project to which the computer has been applied but constitutes the very genetic structure and fundamental program of the technology itself. For this reason, information technologies, as such, have been determined to supply a universal idiom that restores the earth to the millennial conditions that were allegedly ruined at Babel. Bruce Schuman (1988) provides a rather explicit articulation of this promise:

The fabulous resources of human knowledge and wisdom can be combined through modern information science technology to create the most authoritative voice for spiritual truth and insight which has ever existed on this planet. The vast resources of illumination and enlightenment which have been released to the human community in a flood of valuable and unquestionably authentic but somewhat diverse and competing metaphysical, philosophic, theological, and religious literature from all corners of the world, East and West, can be gathered up by methods of systematic scholarship, organized by underlying thematic invariants, conceptually recoded into a uniform and unified analytic/conceptual language—and made into a single towering "lighthouse of hope" that can illuminate for the entire world the true spiritual path back to harmony and freedom and love. (6)

The computer is understood as a machine of language. Not only does its fundamental power reside in its ability to manipulate linguistic tokens, but its very substance has been shaped by the Babelian dream of linguistic universality. The computer, therefore, constitutes a "universal machine" not only because it is capable of simulating the function of any machine, but also because it promises to provide the very means of universal communication and concourse. For this reason, the computer has served as the platform for applications that promise to deliver practical solutions to the *confusio linguarum* that is the legacy of Babel—applications that include efforts at machine translation and postlinguistic communication.

Machine Translation

Students of languages and of the structure of languages, the logicians who design computers, the electronic engineers who build and run them—and specifically the rare individuals who share all of these talents and insights—are now engaged in erecting a new Tower of Anti-Babel. This new tower is not intended to reach to Heaven. But it is hoped that it will build part of the way back to that mythical situation of simplicity and power when men could communicate freely together.

Weaver 1955a, *vii*

In narrating the beginnings of linguistic difference, the story of the Tower of Babel provides an account of the origin of translation—literally the carrying across from one language into another. Mechanized translation seeks to automate this process by designing technologies that translate one language into another with little or no human interaction. The prospect of immediate, automated translation is as old as the first electronic data processors, and efforts to produce computerized translators has led to the development of a distinct discipline called machine translation (MT).[1] According to Muriel Vasconcellos (1993), president of the Association of Machine Translation in the Americas, the discipline of MT has been developed in direct response to the Babelian legacy: "If you can't conquer Babel, at least, thanks to MT, you can have a better idea of the knowledge that's available in the world and how you can tap into it" (152). Machine translation endeavors to design software, or what is called "Babelware" (Miller 1993, 177), that provides automatic, interlingual translation. The first-text based systems were developed in the early 1950s and employed the processing and memory power of the mainframe. In the early 1980s, MT systems began to migrate to the desktop PC and are now routinely available on the World Wide Web through the various search engines and portals.

Although many MT systems are organized around restricted language sets, the ultimate goal has always been *universal translation* of unrestricted language, or what Erwin Reifler (1951) called *general* MT (1). The universal translator would do more than mitigate the disparity between two (or even multiple) languages. It would overcome the confusion instituted at Babel by translating any language into and out of every other language, automatically and simultaneously. The universal translator, then, aspires to nothing less than a technologically enabled Pentecost. This objective has been articulated by the "patron saint" of the telematic world, Marshall McLuhan (1995):[2] "Language as the technology of human extension, whose powers of separation we know so well, may have been the 'Tower of Babel' by which men sought to scale the highest heavens. Today computers hold out the promise of a means of instant translation of any code or language into any other code or language. The computer promises by technology a Pentecostal condition of universal understanding and unity" (80). For McLuhan, the Tower of Babel is correlative with the technology of language itself. Language embodies the promise of universal connectivity and cooperation but has been experienced as an agent of separation. The apocalypse of this linguistic segregation is achieved at Pentecost, which is described in the second chapter of the Acts of the Apostles. After receiving the gift of the holy spirit, the apostles quit their room and began speaking in the streets. As they spoke, everyone heard the word of God in his/her native language. "And the people were amazed and marveled saying: 'Are not all these men who are speaking Galileans? How is it that each of us hears them in our own language to which we were born?'" (2:7–8). Pentecost alleviates Babelian confusion through real-time, interlingual translations. The apostles, while speaking their own native language, are immediately understood by everyone in whatever language constitutes their native tongue. In this way, Pentecost reestablishes universal understanding between human agents despite differences in their means of communication.

The computer promises to become the technological equivalent of this miracle, providing the "means of instant translation of any code or language into any other code or language." Although this Pentecostal operation remains beyond the scope of contemporary MT efforts, it constitutes the goal and has determined the general trajectory of the discipline. According to Vasconcellos (1993), "the dream is to build the equivalent of the babblefish [sic][3] of Douglas Adams' [1979] book *The Hitchhiker's Guide to the Galaxy*—a wearable device that simultaneously interprets from and into any language of the world" (152). According to *The Hitchhiker's Guide*, a title that names both a novel by Douglas Adams and an encyclopedic text cited within Adams's novel, the Babel fish is a small, leech-like parasite that resides in the auditory canal of the ear. "The practical upshot of all this is that if you stick a Babel fish in your ear you can instantly understand anything said to you in any form of language" (Adams 1979, 59–60). The Babel fish, therefore, reproduces the miracle of Pentecost for its host by providing flawless, real-time translations from any and all languages.[4] This form of universal translation was recently validated and popularized by Al Gore during his tenure as vice president of the United States. In "The Digital Declaration of Independence," which was initially delivered as a speech before the Telecommunications Union on 12 October 1998, the vice president presented the following challenge to the telecommunications and computer industries: "We must overcome our language barriers and develop technology with real-time digital translation so that anyone on the planet can talk to anyone else. Just imagine what it would be like to pick up a phone, call anywhere in the world and have your voice translated instantly so you could have a conversation without language being a barrier. I can see a day when we have a true digital dialogue around the world—when a universal translator can instantly shatter the language barriers that so often prevent true collaboration" (Gore 1999, 14–15).

General translation systems, although currently associated with computer technology, had been proposed as early as the seventeenth century. In many of the pasigraphic projects of the 1600s, the proposed *characteristica universalis* constituted not a universal language per se, but a translation protocol into which and from which any natural language could be translated. Athanasius Kircher's *Polygraphy* (1663), for instance, proposed a technique of writing whereby "anyone, even someone who knows nothing other than his own vernacular, will be able to correspond and exchange letters with anybody else, of whatever their nationality" (Eco 1995, 197). In order to accomplish this task, Kircher proposed two translation tools: dictionary A, by which one was able to *write* in any language even though one only knows his/her own vernacular, and dictionary B, by which one could *understand* a text written in an unknown language (Eco 1995, 199). Strictly speaking, Kircher's *Polygraphy* is not a universal language but a technique of general translation capable of negotiating the difference between languages. Similar translation systems were proposed in Cave

Beck's *Universal Character, by which all the nations of the world may understand one another's conceptions, reading out of one common writing their own mother tongues* (1657), Joachim Becher's *Character pro notitia linguarum universali* (1661), and Gaspar Schott's *Technica curiosa* (1664). Recent studies in MT, like Luigi Heilmann's "J. J. Becker: Un Precursore della Traduzione Meccanica" (1963) and W. John Hutchins's *Machine Translation: Past, Present, Future* (1986), have recognized these seventeenth-century projects as the precursors to contemporary efforts in MT.

Despite the ambitious aspiration of universal translation, most contemporary MT products have been developed around language pairs and are limited, therefore, to mediating between two or more predetermined languages—for example, Systran (English/Russian, English/French, English/German), Météo (English/French), CITEC (Chinese/English), and PENSEE (Japanese/English). In these systems, which Reifler (1951) termed *specific* MT (1), translation is accomplished through a transfer module that directly links the two languages through a series of steps specific to that language pair. Specific translation systems, although capable of providing acceptable output, experience significant complications when applied to more than two languages. For n languages, this systems architecture requires $n(n - 1)$ transfer modules; consequently, a MT system for the nine official languages of the European Community would require seventy-two separate translation modules. To address this limitation, which affects not only translation efficiency but, more important, its expense, several multilingual systems have been designed employing a third, intermediate language, or interlingua. As Klaus Schubert (1992) explains: "the $n(n-1)$ formula is based on the assumption that every source language is linked directly with every target language. If these direct links can be given up in favour of a single, central representation, the combinatorial problem is removed" (81). For n languages, this alternative systems-architecture requires only $2n$ translation modules; consequently, a translation system for the nine official languages of the European Community would require eighteen transfer modules, each language having

its own protocols for translating into and out of the interlingua. In-
terlinguas consist in both natural languages that have been chosen
for convenience as an intermediary or artificial languages that
have been invented for the purposes of mediating linguistic difference. Booth, Brandwood, and Cleave (1958), for example, advocate
the use of a natural language such as English, arguing, on the basis of economics, that such translation systems would require not
$2n$ transfer modules but $2n-2$. Ivan Guzmán de Rosas has suggested the use of Aymara, which Emeterio Villamil de Rada in
1860 argued was the proto-language spoken by Adam (Eco 1995,
346–347). BSO's (*Buro voor Systeemontwikkeling*) DLT (*Distributa
Lingvo-Tradukado*) system employs the artificial language of Esperanto, arguing that this idiom combines the expressiveness necessary for translating natural languages with the extreme clarity of
an artificial symbolic system necessary for automated processing.
Other artificial-language-based systems have been proposed by
Carnegie-Mellon University's Center for Machine Translation
(1996), Bell Labs, and NEC. And some rather speculative schemes
have suggested employing Klingon, the fictional language developed for *Star Trek* and the most popular artificial language currently in use (Edwards 1996).

Although the use of an interlingua overcomes the limitations of
combination in multilanguage MT systems, these intermediaries
have a distinct limitation. In relying on either a specific natural
language or an artificial one, the intermediary is set up *a posteriori*.
That is, the language that is supposed to mediate between all other
languages is either one of those languages or an artificial idiom
that is derived from empirical research on a specific natural language or set of natural languages. In either case, the interlingua is
neither universal nor equally accessible to everyone. The translation system would privilege certain users, restricting all possible
expressions to concepts and logics that are germane to that particular idiom. Esperanto, for example, although formulated as a universal, international language, privileges native speakers of European languages from which Esperanto has derived its grammar,
vocabulary, and alphabet. The *a posteriori* interlingua, whether it is
composed of a natural or artificial language, is limited by the eth-

nocentrism of the specific language(s) from which it is derived. Although universal translation or general MT could be based on such a systems architecture, these systems would be neither universal nor general.

General or universal translation, in order to be truly general and universal, would require an interlingua that is not derived empirically from one or more natural languages, but that is instead an *a priori* intermediary, "a universal translation programme applicable to all languages" (Delavenay 1960, 47). Yehoshua Bar-Hillel acknowledged this requirement in his 1951 report on the state of MT research: "Whereas specific MT will, in all probability, continue to be mainly an application of trial-and-error investigations, general MT will require establishment of a *universal*, or at least *general grammar*" (Bar-Hillel 1964, 162; italics in original). Bar-Hillel recognized that this undertaking was directly connected to and dependent upon the seventeenth-century projects of universal language. Most proposals for a *characteristica universalis* or *grammatica universalis* proceed by first developing a list of primitive concepts that were assumed to be universal for all human cognition and transcendent of variation in linguistic expression. The *Real Character* of John Wilkins, for example, was grounded in a list of concepts that, he argued, had not been derived from one language but from the stock of concepts held in common by humanity. The foundation of Ramón Lull's *Ars Combinatoria* was a list of ideal entities that he collected in the *Tabula Generalis*, and the *characteristica universalis* proposed by Leibniz was grounded in an inventory of irreducible and universal primitives from which all expressions in any language could be generated. The development of general MT has proceeded in a similar fashion. Although researchers have generally rejected the universal language projects of the seventeenth century as naïve and unscientific, they have not rejected the fundamental concept of linguistic universals. Bar-Hillel (1964), for instance, does not reject the concept of universal grammar *tout court*; he rejects prior attempts to establish this universality through "metaphysical preconceptions and Aristotelian logic." As an alternative, he suggests formulating the universal character of general MT on scientific grounds—namely, "empirical open-mindedness, mathematical logic, and modern structural linguistics" (162). Following Bar-Hillel's suggestion, the discipline of MT has allied itself not with metaphysics but with linguistics and cognitive science. For this reason, the universal character proposed by MT lay not in a list of primary metaphysical entities but in the universal, deep structures of the linguistic faculty or the fundamental, general operation of human cognition.

In grounding universal translation in either a list of universal entities, as proposed by the universal language projects of the seventeenth century, or in linguistic universals, as proposed by contemporary science, general MT makes an assumption about the nature of language that is as ancient as Babel. It assumes that linguistic differentiation is not irreducible but derived from and subtended by a primordial universality and unity. This assumption has been a constitutive component of the discipline of MT from its inception. The application of computer technology to translation was initially suggested in a memorandum written by Warren Weaver, vice president of the Rockefeller Foundation. In this short but influential text, which according to Hutchins (1986) "launched machine translation as a scientific enterprise in the United States and subsequently elsewhere" (28), Weaver employed Babelian imagery to suggest that translation procedures be founded in the common, universal root of the natural languages:

> Think, by analogy, of individuals living in a series of tall closed towers, all erected over a common foundation. When they try to communicate with one another, they shout back and forth, each from his own closed tower. It is difficult to make the sound penetrate even the nearest towers, and communication proceeds very poorly indeed. But, when an individual goes down his tower, he finds himself in a great open basement, common to all the towers. Here he establishes easy and useful communication with the persons who have also descended from their towers. Thus may it be true that the way to translate . . . is not to attempt the direct route, shouting from tower to tower. Perhaps the way is to descend, from each language, down to the common base of human communication—the real but as yet undiscovered universal language. (Weaver 1955b, 23)

Weaver's post-Babelian narrative addresses not the *origin* of linguistic diversity but its possible resolution and remedy. He tells of a multiplicity of individual towers that indicate the isolation and incompatibility of each language. This diversity, however, is subtended by a common, universal substructure. For Weaver, this universal element is not a single tower situated on the plain at Shinar but a foundation upon which each differentiated tower has been constructed. Although there has been debate within the discipline of MT as to the true nature of this universal foundation, the field has generally accepted and operated within the basic structure of this architectonic.

The assumption of linguistic universality that has directed the efforts of general MT has two complications. First, despite the traditional reading of the Babelian narrative, linguistic variation is not necessarily derived from or subtended by a universal substrate—whether that be an original proto-language, universal grammar, or common cognitive capability. These formulations of linguistic variation have been informed by a metaphysics that comprehends diversity, in either form or number, as not only derived from an original unity but destined for reintegration into the same. From the story of the *symbolon* told by Aristophanes in Plato's *Symposium*, through the eschatology of Scholastic onto-theology, to Hegel's *Science of Logic*, Western metaphysics has generally conceived of diversity as derived from and directed toward an original unity and self-same identity. As James Bono (1995) explains it, "unity becomes the very ground for the possibility of diversity; and the diversity of natural forms becomes the occasion for the quest for an original unity" (185). This presumption of "unity within diversity," however, has recently been submitted to reevaluation. Jacques Derrida (1978), for example, following the work of Georges Bataille, has espoused a concept of heterology. This alternative formulation of diversity differs from that of the metaphysical tradition in that it comprises "an irreducible plurality that ceaselessly differs from itself" (Gasché 1986, 88). As such, it constitutes a fundamental variation that not only suspends the assumption of an original unity and self-same homogeneity but also resists any and all eschatological promises of returning to the same. The consequences of this heterology for the theory and practice of translation are explicated by Derrida in "Des Tours de Babel" (1985a), an essay about translation that was written for translation, but that nevertheless resists translation. In this reading of the Babelian narrative, Derrida suggests that linguistic variation is not the result of some catastrophic fragmentation of an original and essential totality but an irreducible and fundamental multiplicity of idioms that always already resists any and all attempts at totality. "The 'Tower of Babel' does not figure merely the irreducible multiplicity of tongues; it exhibits an incompletion, the impossibility of finishing, of totalizing, of saturating of completing something on the order of edification, architectural construction, system and architectonics" (Derrida 1985a, 165). According to the Derridean reading, linguistic variation is not a mere empirical problem to be overcome by some perfect translation or return to a universal idiom but a fundamental heterological variation within languages that renders translation an interminable task that is both necessary and impossible.

Similar conclusions have been generated from experimental research in the field of MT. Since its optimistic beginnings in the late 1940s, MT has experienced significant setbacks and failures. According to Hutchins and Somers (1992), the reality of MT has not lived up to its initial dreams: "There are no 'translating machines' which, at the touch of a few buttons, can take any text in any language and produce a perfect translation in any other language without human intervention or assistance. That is an ideal for the distant future, if it is even achievable in principle, which many doubt" (1). The failures that have been experience in MT research have not only led the discipline to pursue less ambitious goals—namely, specific MT of restricted text or machine-assisted translation tools[5]—but have also motivated researchers to question the basic assumptions that had initiated and informed the discipline in the first place. Alan Melby's *The Possibility of Language* (1995) undertakes a critical investigation of these "failures" in order to suggest new possibilities for reorganizing and reorienting the discipline. According to his assessment, MT has experienced significant complications and failures not because of technological limitations or imprecise modeling but because of a fundamental misunderstanding of the object and supposed objectivity of languages.

Second, even if one denies these complications and accepts the traditional reading of Babel without question, MT still faces a rather curious paradox. On the one hand, general MT, as it has been formulated by the discipline, is possible only if there is some kind of universal characteristic or general grammar that transcends and substantiates specific linguistic variation. However, if there *is* such a universal character, translation becomes ultimately obsolete and superfluous. Why, for example, would anyone bother with the difficulties of translating natural languages into and out of a universal medium of exchange, when it would be far more efficient to employ the universal character directly? On the other hand, if general MT is not possible because of the lack of any universal characteristic transcending linguistic variation, then translation is absolutely necessary, for there would be no other way to negotiate linguistic diversity. Ironically, universal MT is possible only if it is ultimately superfluous and necessary only if it is fundamentally impossible. In the end, MT, like the Babelian narrative that informs its efforts, recounts "the necessary and impossible task of translation, its necessity *as* impossibility" (Derrida 1985a, 171).

Postlinguistic Communication

Just as all men have not the same writing so all men have not the same speech sounds, but mental experiences, of which these are the primary symbols, are the same for all, as also are those things of which our experiences are the images.

Aristotle 1941, 16a: 5–8

The Aristotelian formulation proposes that while the materials of language are manifold and differentiated, the animating thought, as well as the experience of the things of which these thoughts are images, remains universal and unique. The logical sequel to translation endeavors, therefore, would involve a transcendence of the material of translation, namely language, by a kind of communicative interaction that is located in this universal, metalinguistic element. "The next logical step," according to McLuhan's (1995) estimations, "would seem to be, not to translate, but to by-pass languages." (80). This next step would circumvent the confusion of tongues and the complications of translation, situating communication in either of the homologous elements that have been determined to subtend and transcend linguistic difference. In this way, communication would be situated in either a neurological telecommunications system where minds are directly wired into other minds, which McLuhan (1995) has called "a general cosmic consciousness" (80), or in an immediate manipulation of the thing themselves, which virtual reality pioneer Jaron Lanier (1988) has dubbed "post-symbolic communication" (15).

McLuhan's formulation of a "general cosmic consciousness" is informed by the Scholastic tradition, which traces its roots to Aristotelian philosophy. The concept is directly associated with the "collective unconscious" of Henri Bergson's *Creative Evolution* (1998) and approximates the Noosphere that had been proposed by Pierre Teilhard de Chardin in *Phenomenon of Man* (1959). The noosphere, according to McLuhan's *Gutenberg Galaxy* (1962), consists in a "cosmic membrane that has been snapped around the globe by the electric dilation of our various senses" (32). This worldwide electric membrane constitutes a "technological brain for the world" (McLuhan 1962, 32), and the entire earth itself becomes a single mind/computer. In this global world-brain network, speech becomes obsolete and, with the passing of this principle of human division, the earth once again beholds the promise of universal harmony. "The condition of 'weightlessness,' that biologists say promises a physical immortality, may be paralleled by the condition of speechlessness that could confer a perpetuity of collective harmony and peace" (McLuhan 1995, 80). Such speechless communication approximates "angelic speech" as described by Saint Thomas Aquinas (1945) in the *Summa Theologica* (Q.CVII A.2): "For one angel to speak to another angel means nothing else but that by his own will he directs his mental concept in such a way that it becomes known to the other" (991). The global net would provide a conduit for this kind of direct intellectual interaction. In this network, interlocutors would converse by directly communicating their thoughts to one another, avoiding once and for all the complications that have been associated with language since the Babelian confusion.

The concept of speechless, direct neurological interaction, which is rooted in Scholastic philosophy, has been uploaded into the networks of cyberspace by the novel that introduced the neologism, William Gibson's *Neuromancer*. Gibson's protagonist, the console cowboy Case, interacts with the global matrix and the world of information by directly jacking his consciousness into the network through surgically implanted "Sendai dermatrodes" (Gibson 1984, 52). Case does not require any of the interface devices we commonly associate with computer-mediated communication (keyboards, mice, headphones, monitors, etc.). Instead, his disembodied consciousness is directly wired into the neuroelectric fabric of the global network (Gibson 1984, 5). In the cyberspatial matrix, Case is said to communicate at the level and speed of thought itself. This ideal cybernaut is no longer encumbered by the "meat" of the body,[6] just as his communicative interactions are no longer burdened with the materiality of language. Since the publication of *Neuromancer*, "the desire to have one's brain patched directly into cyberspace" (Branwyn 1993, 1) has not only been a staple of cyberpunk fiction but the promise of contemporary telematic technology. A 1997 television advertisement for MCI, for example, promotes the Internet as a utopian environment in which users are liberated from the problematic constraints of embodiment (gender, race, age, etc.), communicating with each other "mind to mind." This kind of technologically enabled "angelic speech" not only promises to repair the cacophony of language experienced in the wake of Babel but, like the tower itself, both approaches and threatens the heavens.

This form of computer-mediated mind-to-mind connection is facilitated by brain-computer interface (BCI) technologies. Currently there are two BCI methodologies: electroencephalogram (EEG) monitoring and implanted electrodes. EEG interface schemes employ systems that detect brain waves, trace changes in the waveform, and interpret these changes as commands for computer functions. Initial work in this area was undertaken by the U.S. Air Force as part of the "Pilot's Associate" project. One element of this five-part system was something the air force called *biocybernetics*, which was "research aimed at developing better communication, even integration between computers and humans" (Gray 1995b, 104–105). The air force's biocybernetics program sought to employ EEG monitoring both to track pilots' mind states and to control aircraft functions. Although the program was canceled in the late 1970s, research in EEG monitoring and control systems continues at the Naval Health Research Center, which studies "links between human cognition and psychophysiology, principally EEG and eye movements, to develop neural human-system interface (NHSI) technology" (Naval Health Research Center 1996). Additional EEG interface systems have been developed by the Department of Psychology and Cognitive Psychophysiology at the University of Illinois (Farwell and Donchin 1988) and have been demonstrated in cursor control systems (Wolpaw et al. 1991) and computer communication devices for handicapped users (Pfurtscheller, Flotzinger, and Kalcher 1993).

EEG-based systems, however, have two fundamental limitations that render them impractical for the proposed direct mind-to-mind communication. First, they are monodirectional; they "have no possibility of input to the brain" (Wright 1993, 3). Although changes in EEG can be interpreted to control various computer functions, the computer cannot in turn influence brain waves in order to communicate with the user. EEG interfacing, therefore, holds more promise for the control of prosthetics than it does for communicative interaction. Second, the range of control provided by the EEG form of BCI remains extremely limited. "Although leading researcher Jonathan Wolpaw has commented that 'in theory the brain's intentions should be discernible in the spontaneous EEG,' the sheer complexity of the brain's measurable activity produces EEG traces which present a formidable problem of interpretation" (Howard 1996, 1). According to Andrew Pollack (1993), "it is a major challenge to recognize from brain waves whether a person means 'yes' or 'no,' let alone to understand complex thoughts" (2). For this reason, all contemporary EEG interface systems have been restricted to highly specified tasks, such as the movement of a cursor on a monitor screen (Wolpaw et al. 1991; McFarland et al. 1993; Pfurtscheller, Flotzinger, and Kalcher 1993) or the selecting of an element from a number of preprogrammed options (Farwell and Donchin 1988). In the end, the EEG interface does not circumvent the problem of language, interpretation, or translation; it merely relocates it. As Pollack (1993) points out, "it's difficult enough to have a speech recognition device, but there you know the language. . . . With EEG signals, we really don't know the language the brain uses" (2).

The second brain-computer interface schema is more in line with the imagery of contemporary science fiction, taking the form of electrodes implanted directly into the user's neurological system. The main advantage of implanted electrodes over the EEG BCI is that it permits bidirectional communication. Although this option is still considered science fiction, advances in electrode configuration design show some promise. Researchers at Stanford University, for example, have developed a "microelectrode array capable of recording from and stimulating peripheral nerves" (Branwyn 1993, 3). A team at the Max Planck Institute for Biochemistry, under the direction of Peter Fromherz, has developed a silicon-neuron circuit that makes it possible to "write to and read from individual cells" (Hogan 1995, 2). Theoretically, implanted electrodes would facilitate direct, bidirectional communication not only between neurological systems and the computer but between different neurological systems wired into a common computer network. This bidirectional communication system, however, is still confronted with the complications of language. In order for the computer to write to and read from the brain, the system would first need to understand and manipulate what John von Neumann (1958) called "the language of the brain" (80). This "language"—which has also been called "language of thought" (Fodor 1975, 2), "neural code" (Whitefield 1984, 76), "brain program"

(Young 1987, 18), and "representation system" (Churchland 1986, 9)—constitutes a language before and beyond the natural languages. The implanted-electrode BCI, therefore, does not, properly speaking, transcend language or the complications of linguistic variation. It extends the *confusio linguarum* from the macrostructure of the organism to the microstructure of the neuron. In this way we are not, as John Young (1978) indicates by reference to Frederick Jameson (1972), really escaping the prison house of language, but are as it were enlarging it. The implanted-electrode BCI, therefore, does not necessarily overcome the confusion of tongues but transcribes the complications of linguistic variation within the neuron.

Jaron Lanier argues that virtual reality, like the direct neurological interaction initially described by McLuhan and exhibited within the discourse of contemporary science fiction, promotes a communicative system that will eventually render language an obsolete technology. The malleable, synthetic sensorium of virtual reality promotes what Lanier calls "post-symbolic communication." This concept was initially explained in a 1988 interview with Adam Heilbrun in the *Whole Earth Review*: "This means that when you're able to improvise reality as you can in Virtual Reality and then that's shared with other people, you don't really need to describe the world anymore because you can simply make any contingency. You don't really need to describe an action because you can create any action" (Lanier 1988, 15). According to Lanier, virtual reality promises a kind of interpersonal communication that is facilitated not by the manipulation of symbols or codes that refer to and describe things but by direct and immediate manipulation of the things themselves. Postsymbolic communication, then, cuts out the "middleman" of communicative interaction (Lanier 1993, 4). As Lanier explained it in an interview with Frank Biocca (Lanier and Biocca 1992): In VR

it is possible to do something that goes beyond sharing codes with people, because you can just make the stuff directly with them. The codes would otherwise be used to refer to these things. So, if you make a house in virtual reality, and there's another person there in the virtual space with you, you have not created a symbol for a house or a code for a house. You've actually made a house. It's that direct creation of reality; that's what I call post-symbolic communication. (161)

Commenting on the consequences of Lanier's proposal, Michael Benedikt (1993b) concludes that "language bound descriptions and semantic games will no longer be required to communicate personal viewpoints, historical events, or technical information. Rather, direct—if 'virtual'—demonstration and interactive experience of the 'original' material will prevail, or at least be a universal possibility" (12–13).

Lanier's formulation of postsymbolic communication, whereby "you actually make stuff instead of just referring to it" (Lanier 1993, 7), achieves the communicative possibilities initially presented by the school of language at the fictional Academy of Lagado, which is described in part 3 of Jonathan Swift's *Gulliver's Travels*. "Since words are only names for things, it would be more convenient for all men to carry about them such things as were necessary to express the particular business they are to discourse on. . . . Many of the most learned and wise adhere to the new scheme of expressing themselves by things; which hath only this inconvenience attending it, that if a man's business be very great, and of various kinds, he must be obliged, in proportion, to carry a greater bundle of things upon his back, unless he can afford one or two strong servants to attend him" (Swift 1965, 185). Virtual reality would not only realize the Lagadian system of expression by things but would also solve its only inconvenience. By employing virtual objects rather than material ones, VR would facilitate the storage, transportation, and manipulation of the elements employed for communicative purposes. Lanier's postsymbolic communication, therefore, would constitute the actualization and perfection of the system of discourse proposed by the Academy of Lagado.

In Lanier's projection of VR there would no longer be Babelian confusion or the need for translation between languages. Furthermore, there would not even be the problem of intralingual translation caused by the plurality of names referring to one thing within a given language. There would only be the thing. "In language,"

Lanier (1993) explained in an interview with David Jay Brown and Rebecca McClen-Novick, "we have a notion of quality, such as redness or pudginess or something. In postsymbolic communication, why bother with those things when you can bring a jar containing everything you consider pudgy. Then the concept of pudgy becomes unnecessary, because you can look at them all at once and experientially get what's alike about them" (5). According to Lanier, it is the shared, homogeneous experience of the thing itself that constitutes an ultimate, universal protocol to which everyone and anyone has equal access. Once again, the Academy of Lagado had projected the same opportunity for its system of converse. "Another great advantage, proposed by this invention was, that it would serve as a universal language, to be understood in all civilized nations. . . . And thus ambassadors would be qualified to treat with foreign princes, or ministers of state, to whose tongues they were utter strangers" (Swift 1965, 186).

Lanier's formulation of postsymbolic communication, however, is confronted with two complications. On the one hand, it presupposes a specific understanding of the nature of language—namely, words are signs that refer, ultimately, to things. This formulation, which was initially articulated in Aristotle's *De Interpretatione* and has been instrumental in the fields of philosophy, linguistics, and semiotics, has been submitted to critical reevaluation in the latter half of the twentieth century. Structural linguistics, for instance, has argued that language exceeds this indicative, referential formulation (Saussure 1959; Derrida 1974). For structural linguistics, "the key to language is not so much a connection between a word and a thing but an arbitrary designation that depended on a differential mark. Language for them is composed of binary oppositions of signifiers—I/you, black/white, and so forth—whose ability to have meaning hinges on the stable relation between the terms or what they term the 'structure.' Language is theorized as a vast machine for generating such differential relations" (Poster 1995, 63). According to this conceptualization, the signification of words is produced not by reference to a transcendental signified but through the differential relations situated within and between signs.

On the other hand, even if one accepts the Aristotelian conceptualization of language without question, Lanier's postsymbolic
communication does not necessarily escape symbolism or the ambiguity of the linguistic sign. Despite claims to the contrary, VR
cannot simply be divorced from the order of the symbolic. In the
first place, as argued by Simon Penny (1994), the virtually dissim-
ulated object is not identical to the object itself. The virtual cup is
not a cup per se. "It is not that simple: the cup in VR is a representation, a stereographic image—you can't drink out of it" (Penny
1994, 245). According to Penny's analysis, the virtual cup is still a
representation of a cup; therefore, a virtual object is no less symbolic than any other icon or word. Frank Biocca and Mark R. Levy
(1995b) point out "that a 3D model of a house can be as ambiguous
a sign as the word 'house'" (23). Although the 3D model may (or
may not) be a more effective means of coding the information, it is
still a sign that refers to and indicates something else. Finally,
Lanier's own explanations have led to some rather curious contradictions. VR, that which supposedly escapes description in and by
symbols, is produced by the computer. Computers, however, according to Lanier (1988), "live by description" (15). These descriptions are themselves designed and programmed through the manipulation of symbols. Far from escaping the limitations of
symbolic description, virtual reality is necessarily produced in and
by the manipulation of descriptive signs. VR's apparent flight
away from the symbolic is ironically produced and substantiated
by that from which it flees.

Deconstructing the Tower of Babel

When we say "Babel" today, do we know what we are naming?

Derrida 1985a, 165

The computer, which has been determined to be a machine of language, proposes technological solutions to the *confusio linguarum*,
returning the earth to the pre-Babelian condition of one language
for all. These restitutive endeavors, however, have been animated

and legitimated by an assumption that remains unquestioned. In particular, they presume that the initial conditions described in the narrative are original and perfect, while the subsequent effects of linguistic plurality are derivative and catastrophic. The reparation of Babel that is hardwired into the computer, therefore, presumes that the plurality of language constitutes a catastrophe that has befallen an original and perfect means of communication. Because this catastrophe is considered to be both damaging and derivative, its reparation is, consequently, both necessary and justified.

The various projects concerning the communicative potential of the computer and cyberspace have operated as if this interpretation of the Babelian myth was somehow self-evident and universal. There is, however, no necessity that the narrative be considered in this manner. It can be, and has been, read otherwise. Take for example the interpretation provided by George Steiner (1975) in his extended analysis of translation in *After Babel*: "The ripened humanity of language, its indispensable conservative and creative force live in the extraordinary diversity of actual tongues, in the bewildering profusion and eccentricity (though there is no center) of their modes. The psychic need for particularity, for 'in-clusion' and invention is so intense that it has, during the whole of man's history until very lately, outweighed the spectacular, obvious material advantages of mutual comprehension and linguistic unity. In that sense, the Babel myth is once again a case of symbolic inversion: mankind was not destroyed but on the contrary kept vital and creative by being scattered among tongues" (233). Steiner's reading suggests an inversion of the traditional interpretation of the Babelian myth. He intimates, evoking a Nietzschean trope, that the "catastrophe" of Babel, namely the multiplicity of languages, does not necessarily constitute a kind of damage to be repaired but a substantial advantage and gain. At Babel, humankind was not destroyed by confusion but was "kept vital and creative" through linguistic diversification. Consequently, the vitality and inventiveness fostered by the wide range of particular idioms is determined to outstrip any advantages that have been ascribed to universal comprehension. Steiner, however, does not stop at a simple inversion of the usual evaluation of linguistic difference, which would amount to little more than a kind of naïve reversal. On the contrary, he also releases a disruption of the metaphysical structure that has organized and legitimated this system. Accordingly, the differentiation of languages not only suggests a substantial advantage rather than a devastating loss, but this variation is not derived from or subtended by an original or primal identity. Instead, linguistic difference constitutes an original eccentricity that does not proceed from or possess a center. The multiplicity of languages, therefore, neither originates in nor aims at monolingualism. They constitute a primal, necessary, and irreducible multiplicity.

The interpretation provided by Steiner deconstructs the Tower of Babel. *Deconstruction*, however, does not indicate "to demolish" or "to dismantle." It constitutes a strategic intervention that necessarily takes the form of a double gesture of inversion and displacement.[7] Steiner's reading of Babel not only overturns the conceptual hierarchy that animates the traditional interpretation of the narrative, granting privilege and primacy to linguistic plurality over and against an original monolingualism, but simultaneously displaces the system that is overturned by emphasizing a fundamental and eccentric pluralism that does not derive from or fuse into a single and uniform center. Steiner's *After Babel*, therefore, not only occasions a general reassessment of the significance of the Babelian narrative but questions the project and goals of those endeavors that have been informed by its *mythos*. If, according to Steiner, the confusion of tongues is not an essential loss of a primordial homogeneity but a vital and creative heterogeneity, then the attempt to (re)establish a universal and ubiquitous idiom does not necessarily constitute a beneficent undertaking. Indeed, this endeavor may be allied with other interests and directed by alternative objectives. This possibility was assayed by Jacques Derrida (1985b) during the roundtable discussion on translation that was transcribed in *The Ear of the Other*:

What happens in the Babel episode, in the tribe of the Shems? Notice that the word "shem" already means *name*: Shem equals name. The Shems decide to raise a tower—not just in order to reach all the way to the heavens

but also, it says in the text, to make a name for themselves. . . . How will
they do it? By imposing their tongue on the entire universe on the basis of
this sublime edification. Tongue: actually the Hebrew word here is the word
that signifies lip. Not tongue but lip. Thus, they want to impose their lip on
the entire universe. Had their enterprise succeeded, the universal tongue
would have been a particular language imposed by violence, by force, by violent hegemony over the rest of the world. (100–101)

According to the Derridean reading, the Babelian fable does not
necessarily conform to the logic of a "paradise lost" scenario. The
monolingualism that was interrupted and resisted at Babel is neither original nor universal. It is, instead, allied with a kind of im-
perialistic violence. The "one lip," therefore, does not constitute a
perfectly transparent language to which everyone would have had
equal access. "Rather, the master with the most force would have
imposed his language on the world and, by virtue of this fact, it
would have become the universal tongue" (Derrida 1985b, 101).
The supposed universal idiom of the Babelian narrative, therefore,
is nothing more than a particular language that would have been
elevated to the position of universality by violent imposition. Yahweh, Derrida argues, opposes this hegemonic endeavor. His intervention is not a catastrophic interruption that destroys an original
perfection. His actions save the earth from the violence that would
have been imposed on a global scale had the Shems succeeded. In
this way, the so-called *confusio linguarum* that had been imposed
by Yahweh does not constitute a damaging loss of an original universality and communicative transparency but provides a kind of
protection from and resistance to the violence of totality and homogeneity. As Derrida (1985a) describes it, Yahweh's intervention
"interrupts the colonial violence or the linguistic imperialism" that
would have been imposed at Babel had the Semites succeeded in
their project (174).

If the monolingualism of the "Tower of Babel" can be interpreted as a kind of linguistic imperialism, then the various attempts to return the earth to this condition may also be correlative
with a kind of linguistic and cultural violence. The universal-

language movement, for example, has been criticized for its association with cultural imperialism and ethnocentrism. Early universal language projects, like the *Ars Magna* of Ramón Lull, were initially devised for the purposes of converting the heathen to Christianity. Not only was this missionary activity complicit with the colonial expansion of Europe but the choice of "universal" concepts and linguistic material demonstrate a distinct European predisposition. This "unconscious ethnocentrism," as Eco (1995, 69) calls it, continues to inform the language and linguistic projects associated with the computer and computer-mediated communication. First, the technologies of MT, brain-computer interface, and virtual reality were not (at least initially) developed for purposes of intercultural communication. All three technologies were initially funded and inaugurated under the U.S. Department of Defense for purposes of national security. MT not only began as an extension of wartime cryptanalysis by computer (Hutchins 1986, 24) but was motivated by the "fear of Soviet technological prowess (particularly after the launch of the first sputnik in 1957) [which] stimulated much governmental and military support for Russian-English translation" (Hutchins 1986, 15). The various techniques and technologies of brain-computer interfacing were initially devised and developed by the U.S. Air Force for controlling combat aircraft, and a significant portion of contemporary EEG BCI research is funded and coordinated by the U.S. Navy's Cognitive Psychophysiology Laboratory. VR technology was pioneered in simulator systems such as the Link Trainer, which was employed during World War II to train combat pilots, the U.S. Army's SIM-NET tank-battle simulation, and the U.S. Air Force's experiments with head-mounted display systems and haptic input/output devices. As Howard Rheingold (1991) confesses, "if necessity is the mother of invention, it must be added that the Defense Department is the father of technology; from the Army's first electronic digital computer in the 1940's to the Air Force's research on head-mounted displays in the 1980's, the U.S. military has always been the prime contractor for the most significant innovations in computer technology" (79–80). Consequently, the enabling technologies of computer-mediated communication are correlative with a particular vision of national defense and cultural hegemony. This is not to say that the technologies in question could not eventually be disentangled from the network of their own genealogy. Such disentanglement, however, is not automatic. It requires, in the first place, that one take this complicated paternity and its consequences seriously. As Penny (1994) advises, technologies are never neutral but are always products of a specific culture (248).

Second, the general project of MT and the efforts of postlinguistic communication (BCI and postsymbolic communication) have been formulated and organized according to a particular understanding of language and linguistic variation. Specifically, linguistic difference is considered to be an empirical problem that can be overcome and mediated through techniques that appeal to and employ fundamental and universal elements (i.e., an original protolanguage, universal grammar, common cognitive capability, or the "things themselves"). This approach, which proceeds under the assumption of "unity within diversity" or "identity in difference," belongs to and is justified by a specific philosophical and cultural tradition. It is not, therefore, properly speaking, universal. It is merely a particular concept of linguistic diversity that has been imposed on the world and, by virtue of this fact, has been considered to be universal. Consequently, the post-Babelian concord that has been encoded in computer technology from the beginning constitutes nothing more than the imposition of a particular and restricted understanding of language and linguistic diversity that is derived from and complicit with Western metaphysics. Finally, employing the "Tower of Babel" as a legitimating narrative for projects of universal communication is itself complicit with this ethnocentric trope. Although the "Tower of Babel" narrates an original, universal communion, it is a story that belongs to a particular culture and is narrated in one of the languages resulting from the Babelian confusion that it describes. Ironically, nominating Genesis 11:1–9 as the paradigm of universal communion determines universality from the position and in the language of one of the particulars. In this way, universal concourse is narrated through the imposition of one particular narrative form.

The "Tower of Babel" has been and continues to be one of the narratives anchoring and directing the research and rhetoric of computer-mediated communication. The significance of this myth, however, remains indeterminate. There is, as Derrida (1985a) points out, a kind of fundamental undecidability or confusion at work within the Babelian narrative itself. On the one hand, the narrative appears to justify and to ground the projects of universal language, MT, and postlinguistic communication—for it legitimates and directs the efforts of these projects by positing a fundamental unity that is not only the origin but also the programmed end of ontic, linguistic diversity. On the other hand, the narrative also connects the computer to an alternative reading, one that not only questions the Western metaphysical assumption of unity within diversity but criticizes its association with cultural imperialism and violence. In this way, the linguistic universality promised by the universal machine constitutes nothing more than one technique of a particular and restricted understanding of universality. In situating the significance of computer-mediated communication under the Tower of Babel, cyberspace cannot help but be informed by the babble of these competing interpretations or translations of the narrative. For this reason, the Babelian myth, rather than anchoring the computer to a single, universal purpose and mission, renders its significance particularly indeterminate, manifold, and contended. Far from determining a rigid and univocal meaning, the "Tower of Babel" opens computer technology to the babble of Babel and the interminable task of translation. From the perspective of mainstream efforts in computer-mediated communication, a perspective that is correlative with the Western metaphysical desire for universality and totality, this situation can only appear to be a devastating loss and confusion—for what is at stake are the very assumptions of universality and transparency that have been built into the computer from the beginning. From another perspective, however, this occurrence cannot help but appear to be otherwise—for the plurality that would have deformed the Babelian narrative can also be perceived as a significant advantage and gain, one which opens computer technology to a plurality of competing interpretations that make room for irreducible and contestatory positions.

Notes

1. See "Translation Technology Alternatives" (1996). For an introduction to and historical overview of the discipline of machine translation, see Hutchins (1986), Hutchins and Somers (1992), and Arnold et al. (1994).

2. Marshall McLuhan was canonized the "patron saint" of the telematic world in the initial issue of *Wired* magazine (July 1993). Since then, the name of Saint Marshall has been invoked in the masthead of every subsequent issue.

3. In her article on machine translation, Muriel Vasconcellos misspells Douglas Adam's "Babel Fish" as "babblefish." In doing so, she (either inadvertently or not) puts into play the linguistic confusion that has been determined to be the legacy of Babel and the object of translation.

4. A similar device, actually named the Universal Translator, has been incorporated into the standard equipment of Star Fleet in the science-fiction television series *Star Trek*. According to the *Star Trek Encyclopedia*, the Universal Translator is a "device used to provide real-time two-way translation of spoken languages" (Okuda, Okuda, and Mirek 1994, 361). In the original series, which made its debut in the mid–1960s, the Universal Translator was a hand-held device about the size of a flashlight (a graphic representation can be found in Franz Joseph's *Star Fleet Technical Manual*, 1975, T0:03:02:04). In the sequel, *Star Trek: The Next Generation* (as well as its spinoffs, *Deep Space Nine* and *Voyager*), the Universal Translator is incorporated as a piece of software residing in the ship's main computer. According to the *Star Trek Next Generation Technical Manual*, "the Universal Translator is an extremely sophisticated computer program that is designed to first analyze the patterns of an unknown form of communication, then to derive a translation matrix to permit real-time verbal or data exchanges" (Sternbach and Okuda 1991, 101). Contemporary MT programs rely on a permanent, resident knowledge source. "The most essential of the knowledge sources is the dictionary—a file of records containing the words and phrases of the source language against which the input text must be matched" (Vasconcellos 1993, 152). The Universal Translator of Star Fleet derives its knowledge source or "translation matrix" on the fly through an analysis of a representative language sample. It is therefore just as effective in translating a known language, like Klingon or Romulan, as it is translating a new and unknown idiom, like the languages of the Gorn or Kason.

The Universal Translator is a remarkable piece of technology for several reasons. First, it is virtually invisible. It is not present in the frame as a piece of equipment. This is extremely curious for a technoporn series like *Star Trek: The Next Generation*, which subsists as a kind of home-shopping network of futuristic gadgetry. Second, because of this invisibility, the Universal Translator is ubiquitous and omnipresent. It not only functions for ship-to-ship communications but also operates as an interpersonal translator when the away-team has left the starship and is engaged in negotiations with an alien life-form. This ubiquity is generally explained by the com-badge, which Star Fleet personnel wear on their uniform, and which supposedly ties all crew members into a communications network with the shipboard computer and the universal translation subroutine (Okuda, Okuda, and Mirek 1994, 361). However, translation services appear to be available even in those rare cases when the com-badge has been confiscated or disabled. Finally, the Universal Translator appears to be without operational limits. It does not seem to require any processing time or to rely on previously entered data for making its linguistic calculations.

Because of its utter transparency, efficiency, and ubiquity, viewers might question the very existence of the Universal Translator. There is, however, one episode in which the translator and its operations obtrude. Like the paradigmatic hammer in Martin Heidegger's (1962) analysis of equipmentality, this tool becomes manifest as such only through its breakdown and malfunction. The event is unique in *Star Trek: The Next Generation*, for it happens only once in the course of the *Enterprise's* five-year mission. It occurs in the episode "Darmok at Tenagra." In this installment, the *Enterprise* is sent to initiate diplomatic relations with the Tamarians, a race which had been labeled "unintelligible" by Star Fleet records. Captain Picard's initial statement is prescient as usual: "Indeed, but are they truly incomprehensible? In my experience communication is a matter of patience . . . imagination. I would like to think that these are qualities that we have in sufficient measure." These qualities so admired by the captain are immediately challenged by the Tamarians' first transmission: "Rey Angeri at Lunka. Rey of Luani. Luani under two moons. Jeari of Lumbi-a. Lumbi-a of cross roads, at Lunka. Lunka the sky grey." Although the Universal Translator has supplied English translations of Tamarian vocalizations, which we can (mis)understand as readily as the bridge crew, the meaning of their statements remains obscure. A similar problem occurs when Picard attempts to reply; the Tamarians are unable to understand Star Fleet. Diana Troi, the ship's counselor, expresses the frustration caused by the situation while explicitly marking the presence of the Universal Translator: "All our technology and experience, our Universal Translator, our years in space contacting more alien cultures than I can even remember. And we still can't even say 'hello' to these people."

Despite the presence of the Universal Translator, communication with the Tamarians remains nearly impossible. Although the discourse of this alien race can apparently be translated into understandable expressions, they speak in a curious idiom that resists translation. As Commander Data explains, "the Tamarians seem to be stating the proper names of individuals and locations." These proper names simultaneously necessitate and thoroughly resist translation. They, therefore, demonstrate what Jacques Derrida (1985a) calls "the necessary and impossible task of translation, its necessity as impossibility" (171). For this reason, the episode mainly consists of a rather dangerous language lesson for the captain, who eventually learns to speak Tamarian.

5. For a critical investigation of the practical limits of current MT technology, see Vasconcellos (1988), Newton (1992), and Hutchins and Somers (1992).

6. On technology, the body, and the dream of incorporeal interaction, see Chapter 5.

7. On the necessary and irreducible double gesture of deconstruction, see the Appendix.

5

CORPUS AMITTERE:
CYBERSPACE AND
THE BODY

For Case, who'd lived for the bodiless exultation of
cyberspace, it was the Fall. In bars he'd frequented as
a cowboy hotshot, the elite stance involved a certain
relaxed contempt for the flesh. The body was meat.

Gibson 1984, 6

A recent MCI television commercial has provided succinct articulation of what has been considered to be the general ethos of the Internet. "There is no race. There are no genders. There is no age. There are no infirmities." In this popular vision of cyberspace, the technology of computer-mediated communication is presented as the great cultural mediator, leveling the differences that have divided and segregated human beings. The rationale animating this utopian promise[1] lies in the technology's apparent disembodiment. Cyberspace, it has been argued, provides a system through which "people communicate mind to mind" without the problematic constraints imposed by the meat-interface of differentiated bodies. As Mark Dery explains in the introduction to *Flame Wars* (1994), "the upside of incorporeal interaction [is] a technologically enabled, postmulticultural vision of identity disengaged from gender, ethnicity, and other problematic constructions. On line, users can float free of biological and sociocultural determinants" (2–3).

From the beginning, cyberspace has been informed by prophetic tales that forecast a time when one will be able to connect one's consciousness directly to the network and surpass the cumbersome "meat" (Gibson 1984, 6) of his or her body. "Perhaps not since the Middle Ages," N. Katherine Hayles (1993) suggests, "has the fantasy of leaving the body behind been so widely dispersed through the population, and never has it been so strongly linked with existing technology" (173). This corporeal transcendence, which amounts to "nothing less than the desire to free the mind from the 'prison' of the body" (Biocca, Kim, and Levy 1995, 7), not only constitutes one of the controlling ideals of cyberspatial systems (cf. Gibson 1984; Biocca, Kim, and Levy 1995; Balsamo 1996; Hillis 1996; Interrogate the Internet 1996) but has been determined to comprise the essence of the age of information. "The central event of the 20th century," state Dyson et al., "is the overthrow of matter. In technology, economics, and the politics of nations, wealth—in the form of physical resources—has been losing value and significance. The powers of mind are everywhere ascendant over the brute force of things" (295). The fact that the Heaven's Gate cult worked on the Internet, engaged in ascetic practices that denigrated the flesh (celibacy and castration), and advocated procedures by which "to leave the containers of the body" is not a mere coincidence but a symptom of a general transcendentalism within the circuits of cyberculture.[2] Consequently, as argued by Anne Balsamo (1996), "promises of bodily transcendence, gender 'neutrality,' and race-blindness are the main planks of the ideology of the information age" (161).

The following chapter undertakes a critical examination of this "transcendentalist fantasy" (Dery 1996, 8). In particular, it investigates the history and consequences of this proclivity to be liberated from the meat of the body. The inquiry is oriented by two suspicions concerning the value of technology and the logic of emancipation. First, as Simon Penny (1994) has suggested, "all technologies are products of culture" (234). Technology, therefore, is never neutral but always inflected and influenced by specific ideologies and preconceptions. The transcendental pretensions of cyberculture are informed and substantiated by the conceptual divisibility of the mind from the body. This ideology, which is generally termed *dualism*, is associated with specific sociocultural circumstances and has its own complicated history and ethical consequences. Employing dualism as a legitimating discourse, therefore, not only deploys a specific metaphysical doctrine but incorporates all the social, political, and cultural implications that have been associated with it. Second, emancipation is never a simple operation. As G. W. F. Hegel (1987) points out in the addendum [*Zusatz*] to section 94 of the *Encyclopedia of the Philosophical Sciences*, "the one who merely flees is not yet free; in fleeing he is still conditioned by that from which he flees" (138). Liberation, therefore, is never a matter of mere flight or simple leavetaking.[3] For the very means of release are often bound up with and conditioned by the mechanisms and systematicity of domination. Emancipation from the body, therefore, may itself be materially conditioned, rendering corporeal transcendence far more complicated and embedded than it initially appears.

Despisers of the Body

We see the Internet as an expression of, and even the savior of high modernism. . . . It, above all else, promises the possibility of achieving the ends of the Enlightenment: a sense of mastery and escape from the limits of the frailties of incarnation.

Interrogate the Internet 1996, 125

In promising to facilitate bodily transcendence, cyberspace participates in a larger project that constitutes one of the defining elements of the modern ethos. The obvious point of intersection, and the one most often mobilized in the discourses of cyberspace, is René Descartes's *Meditations* (1988), which is said to have insti-

tuted not only modern philosophy but the "doctrine of dualism."
Dualism, the radical dissociation of the mind or soul (Descartes
1988, 74, n. 3, interestingly conflates the two terms), from the body,
does not, however, begin with Descartes. In Plato's *Cratylus* (1961),
for example, Socrates suggests that the word "body" (σῶμα) was
coined by the Orphic poets who considered the living soul (ψυχή)
to be incarcerated in the body as in a prison or grave (σῆμα)
(400c). This Orphic position is subsequently incorporated into the
Platonic corpus with the *Phaedo*, which is subtitled "On the Soul."
According to tradition, the *Phaedo* not only argues for the separa-
bility of the soul from the body but provides several "proofs" for
the soul's immortality (Loraux 1989). Similar "dualistic" formulations are essayed in Aristotle's *De Anima*, the Letters of St. Paul,
the works of the medieval neoplatonists (Plotinus, Augustine,
etc.), and the tradition of Scholasticism. Direct correspondence between cyberspace and the Judeo-Christian version of dualism is
demonstrated in the texts of William Gibson. In an August 1993 interview on National Public Radio, Gibson explained that *Neuromancer* was based, in a large part, on "some ideas I'd gotten from
reading D. H. Lawrence about the dichotomy of mind and body in
Judeo-Christian culture" (Dery 1996, 248). As Dery (1996) explains
by way of Jeffrey Meyers (1990), Lawrence had blamed St. Paul for
his "emphasis on the division of the body and spirit, and his belief
that the flesh is the source of corruption" (236).

The mind/body dichotomy, however, is not unique. This binary opposition participates in a general structure of dualism
that has been constitutive of the very fabric of the Western episteme. "The mind/body opposition," Elizabeth Grosz explains in
Volatile Bodies (1994),

> has always been correlated with a number of other oppositional pairs. Lat-
> eral associations link the mind/body opposition to a whole series of other
> oppositional (or binarized) terms, enabling them to function interchange-
> ably, at least in certain contexts. The mind/body relation is frequently corre-
> lated with the distinctions between reason and passion, sense and sensibil-
> ity, outside and inside, self and other, depth and surface, reality and

appearance, mechanism and vitalism, transcendence and immanence, temporality and spatiality, psychology and physiology, form and matter, and so on. (3)

Within the traditions of the West, these dualities are never situations of peaceful coexistence but constitute what Derrida (1981a) calls "violent hierarchies" (41). Such "dichotomous thinking," Grosz (1994) argues, "necessarily hierarchizes and ranks the two polarized terms so that one becomes the privileged term and the other its suppressed, subordinate, negative counterpart" (3). Within Western traditions, mind has been customarily situated above and has ruled over the body, which has consequently been understood as the negation of everything that is determined of and for mind. This determination, in turn, has been accomplished by mobilizing the elements of the other binary pairs that constitute the structural field of Western systems of knowing. Mind, for example, is associated with divinity, while the body is relegated to the realm of brute animality. Mind is determined to be an immortal form; the body is perishable material. Mind is whole or indivisible, while the body remains divisible. Mind is profound and essential, the body superfluous and merely accidental. "Through these associations," Grosz (1994) concludes, "the body is coded in terms that are themselves traditionally devalued" (4). Because of this precedence and privilege granted the mind over its negative and devalued counterpart, Nietzsche (1983a) characterized Western thought as composed of "despisers of the body" (146). Cyberspace and its promised emancipation from the body, therefore, is nothing other than a technological incorporation of this ancient and deprecatory practice.

Discourses that promise liberation from the body through technology mobilize and leverage this rich tradition. In this fashion, mind becomes posited as the essence of the person and is considered to be the source of one's true identity. The body and its complex of variations, on the contrary, is construed as a mere accident of biology, something that is inessential to who and what the individual actually is. Tracing the implications of this assumption, Laura Gurak (1997) writes: "It is almost as if we could simply plug a coaxial cable directly into another person's brain and get at their true self, avoiding the messiness of race, gender, and other of these darn confounding variables that get in the way of who we truly are" (1). According to this logic, differentiation in gender, race, physical ability, and age are considered to be mere externalities that do not effect or belong to one's essential being. This formulation is not only consistent with the metaphysical understanding of difference as "variations in and of the same" (cf. Bataille 1985) but has traditionally been deployed to substantiate antisexist and antiracist positions. In her *Inessential Woman* (1988), Elizabeth Spelman provides a succinct formulation of this procedure: "Since the body, or at least certain of its aspects may be thought to be the culprit, the solution may seem to be: Keep the person and leave the occasion for oppression behind. Keep the woman, somehow, but leave behind the woman's body; keep the Black person but leave the Blackness behind" (128). This formula for emancipation does not in any way challenge the dualisms that structure Western thought but employs its "despising of the body" as the necessary means by which to secure liberation from sexist and racist prejudice.

This procedure, however, is doubly problematic. First, as Gurak (1997) argues, "to imagine that a technology, any technology, could possibly allow us to separate our 'minds' from our social and emotional states encourages the worst kind of Cartesian thinking and detracts from our responsibility to learn how to live together in a diverse, complex democracy. It is dangerous to believe that you can escape into a space where issues of race and gender do not exist" (2). Second, and more fundamental, the doctrine of dualism does not challenge but has been the primary mechanism of prejudice and inequality. "In our cultural hermeneutics," writes Drew Leder (1990), "women have consistently been associated with the bodily sphere. They have been linked with nature, sexuality, and the passions, whereas men have been identified with the rational mind. This equation implicitly legitimizes structures of domination. Just as the mind is superior to and should rule the body, so men, it is suggested, should rule over women" (154). Similar associations have been made in the area of race and ethnicity. "Certain kinds, or 'races,' of people," Spelman (1988) argues, "have been held to be more body-like than others, and this has meant that they are perceived as more animal-like and less god-like. For example, in the *White Man's Burden*, Winthrop Jordan describes ways in which white Englishmen portrayed black Africans as beastly, dirty, highly sexual beings. Lillian Smith tells us in *Killers of the Dream* how closely run together were her lessons about evil of the body and the evil of Blacks" (127). Throughout Western traditions, therefore, mind has not been a value-neutral and universal component but has been associated with and has served to legitimate specific positions of cultural hegemony. Dualism, then, is not merely an abstract metaphysical formula. It is also a social and political principle that has substantiated and legitimated all kinds of prejudicial and exclusionary practices. Because of their associations with the body, certain persons and groups of people have been always and already excluded from the transcendental domain of the (white masculine) mind.

Employing dualism as a legitimating narrative of liberation and equality, therefore, is necessarily complicated by these associations. Such discourses promise liberation from sexist and racist prejudice by deploying a concept that reinscribes and reinforces the very ideology of sexism and racism from which one would be liberated. This procedure is not only potentially self-contradictory but insidious. It is contradictory insofar as it employs as a mechanism of social equality a dualistic formula that always and already excludes and marginalizes certain persons and groups of people. It is insidious, for it reinscribes traditional modes of domination and prejudice under the guise of liberation and equality. With the rhetoric circulated in the advertising of MCI, the fiction of cyberpunk, and the scholarly investigations initiated by Dery, Biocca, and others, computer technology has come to participate in these problematic operations. Through the naïve formulations posed in these texts, cyberspatial technologies come to substantiate and reinforce the very systems of oppression and prejudice they promise to supersede and surpass. What is needed in assessing the sociocultural significance of cyberspace, therefore, is not a blind faith in the emancipation and egalitarian rhetoric of technology but a critical engagement with the philosophical and cultural traditions that have come to empower and inform our employment and understanding of technological innovation. As Judith Butler (1990) suggests, "any uncritical reproduction of the mind/body distinction ought to be rethought for the implicit gender [and racial] hierarchy that the distinction has conventionally produced, maintained, and rationalized" (12).

The Matter of Cyberspace

No network connection at all makes you a digital hermit, an outcast from cyberspace. The Net creates new opportunities, but exclusion from it becomes a new form of marginalization.

Mitchell 1995, 18

The doctrine of dualism is not a mere abstract ideology. It is also a practical mechanism of actual social and political discrimination. By employing this doctrine as a legitimating discourse, cyberspace necessarily comes to participate in these exclusionary activities. As a result, individuals customarily associated with the body and materiality are always already restricted from participating in the incorporeal realm of cyberspace. This marginalization, however, does not remain at a mere ideological level. It is substantiated by the actual milieu of computer and telecommunications technology. Cyberspace, therefore, not only reiterates current systems of domination through its employment of the doctrine of dualism but reinforces this discrimination in practice. As Zillah Eisenstein (1998) notes, " Cybercommunications reflect and are structured by old systems of power. Many poor people, people of color, white women, homeless children, Africans, and others, are effectively excluded from the net. Without access there can be no participation" (32).

Currently, in order to enter and participate in the various cyberspaces created by the technology of the Internet, one needs, minimally, a computer, a modem, telephone service, and an Internet service provider (ISP). One's access to the transcendent, virtual realm, therefore, is materially conditioned. And it should be no surprise that those individuals who are materially restricted from accessing cyberspace are precisely those who have been traditionally marginalized because of their associations with the material of the body: women, people of color, and the impoverished. Transcending the body, therefore, is a luxury that belongs to a certain group of people for whom material limitations in general have not traditionally been an issue. In this way, "the Net is not only another way to divide the world into haves and have nots" (CAE 1997, 6), but this information apartheid actually adheres to and reinforces current systems of oppression and inequality.

Cyberspace has been and currently remains the domain of white males. In this matter, John Perry Barlow, cofounder of the Electronic Frontier Foundation, did not know to what extent he was right, with what exactitude he had described the evolving demographics of cyberspace. "Cyberspace is presently inhabited almost exclusively by mountain men, desperadoes and vigilantes, kind of a rough bunch" (Gans and Sirius 1991, 49). Recent studies concerning computer usage and Internet access corroborate this conclusion. According to a 1996 RAND report on computers and connectivity, the majority of netizens are male (68%), white (87%), college-educated (64%), and highly compensated (average annual household income of $59,000). This report not only found great discrepancies in access to cyberspace due to race, gender, and class but, by comparing the data obtained in 1996 with that from earlier studies conducted in 1993 and 1989, concluded that the gap between the information haves and have nots has been growing steadily (Anderson et al. 1995). Similar results have been obtained in the *Times Mirror* national survey of 1994, the 1995 Georgia Tech/Hermes survey of Web usage (Anderson et al. 1995; Hoffman, Novak, and Chatterjee 1996), the *Wired*/Merrill Lynch Forum "Digital Citizen" survey conducted in 1997 (Katz 1997), and Novak and Hoffman (1998). It should be noted, however, that available demographic information is currently limited to the United States and parts of Western Europe. Global statistics will obviously be more dramatic and potentially more disturbing, especially when one considers that 84 percent of computer users are found in North America and northern Europe (Ellwood 1996, 19), that an overwhelming majority (approximately 80%) of the world's population does not have access to basic telephone service (Telecommunications 1993, 5), and that only about 40% of people have daily access to electricity (Eisenstein 1998, 74). From a global perspective, therefore, cyberspace is and remains a luxury of the postindustrial "First World."

Proposed resolutions addressing these disturbing discrepancies generally take the form of extending access to equipment and services. Al Gore (1999), for example, in the first article of his "Digital Declaration of Independence," espouses a version of "universal access," by which every person on earth would be within walking distance of the "information superhighway" (14). And Barlow (1998), in a gesture that explicitly recalls the colonizing activities of Christian Europe four centuries earlier, promotes various activities that endeavor to bring the fiber-optic light of digital technology to the darkest jungles of Africa. These ethnocentric pretensions, however, are doubly problematic. First, they are disconnected from and uninformed by the well-documented history of the development of telecommunications technology. Shortly after its introduction, advocates of the telephone and the telephonic network promoted a concept of "universal service." Approximately one hundred years later, only one in five individuals throughout the world has access to a phone line. In fact, the ideal of universal service has not even been realized in so-called "developed" nations. In the United States, for example, "nearly one in five Black and Hispanic households do not have phone lines; among poor women heading households with small children, close to half do not" (Eisenstein 1998, 18; Benton Foundation 1994). If the goal of universal service has not been achieved with the low-tech equipment of the telephone, what makes one so sure that it will be effected with the more complex technology of the Internet?

Second, the technology of cyberspace is not a neutral tool but, as demonstrated through the experiences of the European exportation of other technologies (firearms, railroad, telegraph, etc.) to its colonies, is often employed and functions differently in different social situations and cultural contexts. Even if Internet access is effectively extended to the people who currently compose what is called the Third World, there is no guarantee that the technologies will operate within these diverse cultures in a way that is anything like that experienced in and expected by Western manufacturers, governments, and social institutions. "The Street," as Gibson (1993) has pointed out, "finds its own use for things" (29). Consequently, not only has the Internet often been considered "just another misunderstood 'white-man-thing'" (Dyrkton 1996, 55), but recent experiments with computer and computer-mediated communication technologies in the Third World have failed to provide the sociocultural liberation that has been espoused in the rhetoric of cyberspace theorists, equipment manufacturers, government administrators, and multinational telecos like MCI. Instead of providing, as Stephen Emmott (1995) suggests, "the best chance to date many such countries have for positive economic and social change" (5), computer-mediated communication systems have actually reinforced current socioeconomic inequities and systems of oppression. In June of 1991, for example, the Organization of American States embarked upon a plan to provide e-mail service to Caribbean and Latin American universities. Surveying the results of the SIRIAC (Integrated Informatic Resource System for Latin America and the Caribbean) program, Joerge Dyrkton (1996) made the following assessment: "E-mail represents a significant advance for the university as a place on the margin of the Third World but it is also a political tool in a very polarized, hierarchical society. E-mail can only exacerbate the gulf between classes; while it may help to rationalize the telephone system at various locations, it will not help realize appropriate sanitary facilities. The financially comfortable will learn to speak with computer literacy while the poor will continue in their world apart, just next door" (56). Consequently, the implementation and development of cyberspace technology outside the sphere of technological privilege, whether that be in what one used to call a Third World country or the West Side of Chicago, requires attention to the complexity of cultural specificity and not presumptuous, utopian assurances derived from the limited experience of privilege.

The question of technological access reduplicates and reinforces the complications encountered in the consideration of dualism. Cyberspace has been determined to provide liberation from the problematic constraints of the body, which most often entail the triumvirate of race, gender, and class. Access to this technologically enabled emancipation, however, is precisely dependent on one's race, gender, and class. Cyberspace is, in the words of Olu Oguibe (1996), a highly "dependent phenomenon" (p. 11). Consequently, bodily transcendence via the technology of computers, the Internet, and other forms of computer-mediated communication is a luxury that has been granted a group of individuals for whom race, gender, and class have rarely been problematic or restrictive. As Martin Spinelli (1996) reminds us, "the Internet is not some kind of *deus ex machina* of democracy. The net is only an emergent medium, existing in a specific context with a real set of material confines, and possibly with a real potential. But it is a potential that will remain unrealized if we allow the drive to virtualize to obscure its material base and economic realities of our culture" (14). For this reason, women, people of color, and the impoverished find themselves doubly excluded by the transcendentalist pretensions of cyberspace. They are not only always and already positioned outside the realm of mind through conceptual associations with materiality and the body, but they are practically limited in their access to technologies that would promise to facilitate this corporeal transcendence.

Virtual Discrimination

The language of the Internet, and not just its structure, is specific to the Western World.

Interrogate the Internet 1996, 126

The issue of access reduplicates in the material of cyberspace the privilege that has already been encoded and legitimated by the doctrine of dualism. One can participate in what Michael Benedikt

(1993b) calls the "common mental geography" of cyberspace (2), if and only if she already has appropriate access to the necessary equipment and basic technical skills. Rudimentary access to cyberspace, however, is only the beginning. Even those who have the opportunity to gain access to this alleged "civilization of the mind" (Barlow 1997, 23), discover that this domain of uncontaminated information where "people communicate mind-to-mind" reinscribes and uploads traditional forms of gender, race, and class bias that originate in and are substantiated by the problematic dualisms of Western metaphysics. As Barlow (1997) admits, without any sense of irony, "inside every working anarchy, there is an old boy network, and there is an old boy network in cyberspace" (24). Consequently, participation in the virtually utopia of cyberspace, where there is supposedly no race, gender, or class, requires that one also negotiate the "old boy network" that already dominates, informs, and configures this space.

Cyberspace, despite assurances to the contrary, is a space that is, in both its form and content, already ethnocentric and gendered. In the fictional account of *Neuromancer*, for example, the proper name bestowed on cyberspace is the *matrix* (Gibson 1984, 4). "In mathematics," as N. Katherine Hayles (1999) correctly points out, "'matrix' is a technical term denoting data that have been arranged into an n-dimensional array" (38). As it has been remarked in numerous places (Stone 1993; Penny 1995; Dery 1996; Hayles 1999), Gibson's vision of cyberspace accurately conforms to this mathematical formulation. As described in the novel (Gibson 1984) that first introduced the concept, cyberspace appears as a "bright lattices of logic" (5), "a graphic representation of data abstracted from the banks of every computer in the human system" (51), a "transparent 3D chess board extending to infinity" (52), and "an infinite blue space ranged with color-coded spheres strung on a tight grid of pale blue neon" (63). Furthermore, because Gibson's vision, as Stone (1993) has described it, "triggered a conceptual revolution among the scattered workers who had been doing virtual reality research for years" (99), this particular articulation has become the dominant form of extant cyberspaces. This is evident not only in the design approaches and practices of contemporary computer graphics but also in the cyberspaces created by low-bandwidth, text-based systems. "Online conferences," Stone writes (1993), "tend to visualize the conference system as a three-dimensional space that can be mapped in terms of Cartesian coordinates" (104).

Understood according to this specific technical formulation, the matrix of cyberspace appears to be neutral and universal—a pure mathematical concept that is beyond the mundane issues of gender, race, class, and cultural specificity. This, however, is not the case. On the one hand, mathematical concepts, like the organization of data in three-dimensional space, is neither natural nor universal. "Mathematical ideas," as Alan Bishop (1995) demonstrates, "are humanly constructed. They have a cultural history" (71). Consequently, the cyberspatial matrix, whether the one employed and described in Gibson's *Neuromancer* or the ones designed and navigated by the theorists and practitioners of contemporary computer graphics and virtual reality, employs a mathematical understanding and description of space that is distinctly Western. Not only are there other methods of conceiving of and organizing space (Bishop 1995, 72),[4] but this particular ethnocentrism is all too often obfuscated by the distinctly Western presumption that mathematics, in its Western form, constitutes the "language of nature" and the very "mind of the divine." On the other hand, *matrix* has another, older and more general denotation. The word is borrowed from the Latin *matrix*, which signifies womb. Gibson's "matrix" is, therefore, nominally gendered. She not only is female but incorporates all the biased descriptions Western thought has customarily assigned to the feminine. As a generation of feminist scholars have shown, Western traditions have defined woman as formless, passive, receptive, irrational, and fluid (cf. Grosz 1994; Balsamo 1996). These descriptions, they argue, have been used to justify all kinds of institutionalized sexism that approach the feminine and the female body as something to be dominated, regulated, and controlled by masculine rationality. The matrix of cyberspace is described and explained in terminology that is similar, if not exactly the same. Within the context of Gibson's *Neuromancer*

(1984) the cyberspatial matrix is presented as "flowing" (52), "fluid" (52), "unlimited" (63), and composed of "unthinkable complexity" (51). Conversely, the activities of the male protagonist, the cyberspace cowboy named simply Case, are predicated as a series of penetrations or "punches" (Gibson 1984, 63 and 115) into and through the insubstantial "nonspace of the matrix" (Gibson 1984, 63). In the final analysis, Gibson's "cyberspace," as he later describes it (Gibson 1993), is "slick and hollow—awaiting received meaning" (28).

The fictional cyberspace presented in Gibson's *Neuromancer* is already gendered female. Through this engendering, the novel presents and functions according to traditional gender stereotypes and biases. Cyberspace, arguable the main female character in the novel, remains for all intents and purposes passive, formless, and receptive, while Case, the cowboy hotshot, is presented as active and is primarily defined by his penetrations into this matrix. Consequently, the cyberspace of cyberpunk science fiction remains, as Fred Pfeil (1990) concludes, "stuck in a masculinist frame" (89). Not surprisingly, the various forms of extant cyberspace present similar gendered configurations. According to Simon Penny's (1995) analysis, "computer-graphics production—as seen in commercial cinema, video games, theme park rides, and military simulations—is dominated by a late adolescent Western male psyche and worldview" (231).[5] In the dominant form of video game cyberspace, for example, female characters are, as Eugene Provenzo (1999) points out, "often cast as individuals who are acted upon rather than as initiators of action" (100). And in the various text-based virtual realities of Internet relay chat (IRC), multiple-user domains (MUDs), and threaded discussion, female participants often find themselves at a considerable disadvantage. In her five-year study of communicative practices in cyberspace, Susan Herring (1999) found that women and men constitute distinctly different "discourse communities" (198). These different communities or cultures, she argues, are not "separate but equal. Rather, the norms and practices of masculine net culture, codified in netiquette rules, conflict with those of the female culture in ways that render cyberspace—or at least many 'neighborhoods' in cyber-space—inhospitable to women" (Herring 1999, 198). This inimical hostility finds its most problematic expression in the various forms of sexual harassment that have all too often been the unfortunate experience of wired women or users who employ recognizably fe-male pseudonyms. "If you have a female screen name and you en-ter the general chat area," one women reported to Gareth Bran-wyn (1994), "you're gonna get hassled" (232). The various cyberspaces of the Internet, therefore, clearly do have an "old boy network," and negotiating the hegemony of this network can be difficult if not humiliating for users who do not already belong to the club. Consequently, the incorporeal realm of cyberspace, whether fictional or extant, is not liberated from gender bias but ostensibly reinscribes and validates some of the more traditional and oppressive forms of gender inequality.

Finally, there is one remaining area in which the ethnocentrism of cyberspace is particularly powerful but all too often ignored. Gibson's cybernauts move through the matrix and encounter other users at the speed and in the form of thought. Because Gib-son's (1984) console cowboys have their sensorium directly wired into the matrix through "Sendai dermatrodes" (52), they not only are unencumbered by the "meat of the body" but are also appar-ently disengaged from the material of language.[6] Although this fictionalized form of direct "mind-to-mind" interaction informs the rhetoric and expectations of cyberspace, current technology operates otherwise. On the Internet, for example, the so-called dis-embodied interactions of cyberspace employ and require lan-guage. This is the case whether cyberspace is experienced in the strictly textual form of e-mail, IRC, and MUDs or the multimedia mode of the World Wide Web, enriched as it currently is with high-resolution graphics, virtual reality interfaces, and streaming audio and video. The language of the Internet, however, is neither universal nor uninformed by cultural privilege and specificity. From the beginning, American English has been the unofficial offi-cial language of cyberspace.[7] For this reason, Eisenstein (1998) ar-gues that "the phrase 'World Wide Web' images the world about as accurately as the baseball phrase 'The World Series'" (74).

The internationalizing of the English language in cybercommunication has not been decided by a global congress or international consortium. Its position is the direct result of ethnocentric privilege. As Britain extended her empire throughout the globe between the seventeenth and nineteenth centuries, English gradually achieved the status of an international idiom. It was not only the official language of the colonies, but, through the workings of various British cultural initiatives, most notably education, it was eventually imposed upon the indigenous colonized people. More recently, the economic and political dominance of the United States directly after World War II has had a similar linguistic effect. As American products and ideologies flooded the global market, the dominant language of the United States came to occupy a central position in international business and industry. The use and utility of English as a *lingua franca* cannot simply be disengaged from the history that has formed and substantiated it. The privileging of this idiom, although currently useful for running network infrastructure and facilitating intercultural dialogue, has come at a substantial expense—one that we should not be too quick to forget.

The utility of English as an international language has been secured through considerable cultural violence. This violence, however, is not limited to a particular time in history. It is not something that is either over and done or easily surpassed. Traces of its linguistic imperialism are currently manifest in the very texture of cyberspatial interaction. James Powell (1997), for instance, suggests that the "World Wide Web" be renamed the "English Wide Web." For "everything from browser menus, to the markup elements, right down to the normally invisible hypertext transfer protocol commands are in English" (188). Consequently, even web-sites that employ languages other than English find that the subtext of their discourse is necessarily organized, regulated, and controlled by HTML tags written in English. Because of this linguistic privilege, which for most American users and critics of cyberspace generally remains invisible, there are good reasons to be skeptical of any suggestion that cyberspace, in whatever form it takes, is liberated from and effaces ethnic privilege. As Joerg Wurzer (1999) accurately points out, "hinzu kommt, dass die lingua franca des Internets die englische Sprache ist, die den grössten Teil der Weltbevölkerung zu Ausländer im globalen Dorf macht" (1).[8]

Cyberspace, despite transcendental assurances circulating in the rhetoric of its advertising, technical specifications, and even theoretical treatises, is thoroughly gendered and ethnocentric. From the beginning, she not only constitutes a feminine matrix that incorporates all the (in)determinations of Western forms of misogyny but also is configured and functions in a manner that is culturally specific and literally exclusive. For this reason, Barlow, once again, did not know to what extent he was right. Cyberspace definitely has and is dominated by an "old boy network." And it is this exclusive Intranet that makes the experience of cyberspace, if one should be fortunate enough to have the privilege of access, particularly inhospitable for others. This situation, although currently dominant in both fictional and extant forms of cyberspace, does not necessarily preclude the development of alternative configurations and approaches. Such a possibility, however, is not automatic or guaranteed. Like all struggles against old boy networks and embedded forms of discrimination, it will require not simple assurances of equity and empty platitudes, which are often and ironically issued by the individuals already in the position of power, but a sustained and critical engagement with the complexities of its exclusionary system.

Conclusion

We have no reason to delude ourselves that any new technology, as such, promises any sort of sociocultural liberation.

Penny 1994, 247

From the beginning, cyberspace has been informed and directed by transcendentalist pretensions. It not only proposes liberation from the meat of the body but, in doing so, promises to surpass sociocultural restrictions that have been the source of prejudice, exclusion, inequality, and oppression. The projected eschatology of this transcendentalist thinking is nothing short of utopia—a global community emancipated from the problematic constraints of race, gender, age, infirmity, etc. This incorporeal exaltation, however, is not only informed by the ideology of dualism, which has its own complicated history and consequences, but remains a luxury that belongs to and continually reinforces particular forms of cultural hegemony. As Stone (1993) has recalled, "forgetting about the body is an old Cartesian trick, one that has unpleasant consequences for those bodies whose speech is silenced by the act of our forgetting; that is to say, those upon whose labor the act of forgetting the body is founded—usually women and minorities" (113). It is precisely through this form of *corpus amittere*, which aims at overcoming the meat or "data-trash" (Kroker and Weinstein 1994) of the body, that Western thought has instituted and accomplished a violent erasure of other bodies and the body of the other.[9] Therefore, the cyberspatial researchers and critics who forecast and celebrate a virtual utopian community that is, in the words of Dery (1994), "disengaged from gender, ethnicity, and other problematic constructions" (3) do so at the expense of those others who are always already excluded from participating in this magnificent, disembodied technocracy precisely because of their gender, ethnicity, class, and age. Far from resolving social inequities, this conceptualization of cyberspace perpetuates and reinforces current systems of privilege and domination, reinscribing traditional forms of mastery behind the façade of emancipation. In the end, what these various discourses *want to articulate* is resisted and undermined by what they are *compelled to articulate* because of the very metaphysical information they deploy and utilize.

This dissonance not only opens structural difficulties within the networks of cyberspace but, perhaps more important, implies disturbing ethical consequences. On the one hand, for those for whom material conditions have not been problematic, this transcendental rhetoric serves to obscure and to disguise current systems of privilege and oppression. In locating sociocultural emancipation in the transcendental promises of cyberspace, one not

only promotes a mode of liberation that does not in any way problematize or question current positions of cultural privilege but ob-
scures the fact that the very means of liberation is itself identical to
the mechanisms of oppression. For the privileged few, this form of
emancipation bolsters current modes of sovereignty while maintaining the façade of equity and democratization. On the other
hand, for those already excluded through their association with
materiality and the body, these empty promises of emancipation
reinscribe current systems of domination. This procedure is not
only contradictory but effectively legitimizes traditional forms of
oppression and prejudice under the sign of emancipation. Unfortunately, this operation has all too often been the experience of
those who have lived with and under oppression. Namely, what is
promoted as "liberation" amounts to little more than another form
of subjugation.

Confronting the effects of this technologically enabled *corpus
amittere*, however, like so many critical and oppositional undertakings, will be neither simple nor self-evident. The majority of approaches that endeavor to address and critique these issues
assume that the best way to oppose the transcendentalist pretensions of cyberspace is to reaffirm the body and the "reality of
lived bodily existence." This is precisely the strategy espoused and
employed by Allucquere Stone (1993), Michael Heim (1993), Ziauddin Sardar and Jerome Ravetz (1996), Zillah Eisenstein (1998),
and many others. Heim (1993), for example, concludes his examination of the ontology of cyberspace with this nostalgic plea: "As
we suit up for the exciting future in cyberspace, we must not lose
touch with Gibson's Zionites, the body people who remain rooted
in the energies of the earth. They will nudge us out of our heady
reverie in this new layer of reality. They will remind us of the living genesis of cyberspace, of the heartbeat behind the laboratory"
(107). And Stone (1993) finalizes her examination of the problem of
embodiment in cyberspace with the following conclusion: "No
matter how virtual the subject may become, there is always a body
attached. It may be off somewhere else . . . but consciousness remains firmly rooted in the physical" (111). In these and similar

cases the argument follows an intuitive and predictable logic. If the problem is the forgetting of the body, then the proper method for opposing this corporeal negligence, it seems, is to reaffirm and revalidate the experience of the body and embodiment. Corporeal reaffirmation, however, does not necessarily interrupt or escape the fundamental structure of the mind/body dichotomy. In fact, reaffirming the body only inverts the conceptual hierarchy that distinguishes the mind from the body. This sort of simple inversion, which replaces the traditional emphasis on the mind with that of the body, does little or nothing to change the structure of the established system. Although such an inversion can appear to be liberating and transgressive, it remains delimited and controlled by the hierarchy in which and on which it operates. Like so many revolutionary undertakings, this procedure simply reaffirms and maintains the opposition of mind and body, albeit in an inverted form.

What is necessary, therefore, is not a mere overturning and replacement of mind with body but a thorough *deconstruction* of this influential binary opposition. Such deconstruction will entail an irreducible double gesture of inversion and displacement (Derrida 1981a, 41) that does not simply negate, reconfirm, or neutralize the hierarchy in which and on which it operates. Although initially placing renewed emphasis on the body, this deconstruction will, in the words of Grosz (1994), provide for a new "notion of corporeality, which avoids not only dualism but also the very problematic of dualism that makes alternatives to it and criticisms of it possible" (22). Although the "corporeal feminism" of Grosz provides one attempt at the deconstruction of mind/body, it is Donna Haraway's (1991a, b) "cyborg" that has had the greatest influence in the fields of information science, communication technology, and cyberspace theory. In a gesture that is akin to but not the same as that promoted in Grosz's *Volatile Bodies*, Haraway's cyborg, a curious hybrid of cybernetic machine and organism, provides for a reconfiguration of subjectivity that not only complicates beyond repair the metaphysical dualisms that opposes mind and body but does so in a way that "avoids the problematic of dualism that make alternatives to it and criticisms of it possible." The next chapter engages and investigates this monstrous subject that is, from the perspective we now occupy—a perspective that is still rooted in the traditions of the Enlightenment—simultaneously terrifying and transgressive.

Notes

1. For a brief analysis of the utopian rhetoric employed by MCI, see Gurak (1997).

2. For a detailed examination of the Heaven's Gate Cult and its complex relationship to the technology of the Internet, see Robinson's (1997) analysis.

3. For an examination of the complexities of emancipation, see Gunkel 1998a.

4. "The conception of space which underlies Euclidean geometry is also only one conception—it relies particularly on the 'atomistic' and object-oriented ideas of points, lines, planes, and solids. Other conceptions exist, such as that of the Navajos where space is neither subdivided nor objectified, and where everything is in motion" (Bishop 1995, 72).

5. Although Penny (1994) is critical of contemporary practices in computer-graphics production and virtual reality design, he is by no means a pessimist. He cites recent work by Agnes Hegedus and Lynn Hershman Leesons as examples that experiment with and demonstrate alternative employments of computer-graphics technology (239–240).

6. This assumption is investigated and complicated in Chapter 4.

7. For a detailed analysis of the dominance of the English language on the Internet and its relationship to digitized forms of Americanization, see Gunkel 1997a.

8. Translation: "Because the lingua franca of the Internet is English, a majority of the world's people are made foreigners in the global village." I am grateful to Reinhold Wagnleitner of Salzburg University, who first brought this text to my attention.

9. For a critical examination of the fundamental exclusivity of Cartesian metaphysics, see Chang, *Deconstructing Communication* (1996).

b

ECCE CYBORG:
THE SUBJECT OF
COMMUNICATION

The 1990s may well be remembered as the beginning
of the cyborg era.

Kunzru 1997, 156

The figure of the cyborg, it appears, has thoroughly invaded and
infiltrated the contemporary scene. From the novels of Philip K.
Dick, Stanisław Lem, and Vonda McIntyre to the cinematic images
of *RoboCop*, the *Terminator*, and the Borg of *Star Trek: The Next
Generation*, contemporary culture seems to be saturated with images of complex cybernetic organisms that threaten to disrupt and
disturb the boundaries that have traditionally defined the human
subject. The cyborg, however, is not mere science fiction. For
many, it is not only a real possibility but a *fait accompli*. In her "Cyborg Manifesto,"[1] for example, Donna Haraway suggests that the
cyborg constitutes not merely a subject of fantasy but a contemporary social reality. "By the late twentieth century," she writes, "we
are all chimeras, theorized and fabricated hybrids of machine and
organism; in short we are cyborgs" (Haraway 1991b, 150). In the
wake of this influential essay, there has been an increased interest

in the cyborg[2] especially in the fields of information technology and computer-mediated communication. Indeed, in January 1997, *Wired* magazine uploaded Haraway's thesis into the mainstream of cyberculture, declaring the ominous "We are (already) Borg" (Kunzru 1997, 154).

How are we already cyborgs? In what way are we already as-similated into this theorized and fabricated hybrid of machine and organism? What does this hybridization mean for the subject of communication? What are the consequences of this figure that is both more and less than human for the discipline that takes *human communication* as its subject matter and the individual human sub-ject as its fundamental unit of analysis? What, in other words, does the cyborg mean for the concept of the communicative subject and the subject matter of communication? Does it announce the end of life and the study of communication as we have known it, or is it otherwise?

The cyborg, it will be argued in the following, does not consti-tute a new object to be investigated and comprehended according to the established methods and techniques of the discipline of communication. It constitutes a reconfiguration of the subject that not only undermines the concept of human subjectivity but threat-ens and promises to transform the very subject matter of the study of human communication. To dissimulate the apocalyptic tone of the Borg of *Star Trek: The Next Generation*, one could say that the cy-borg announces the end of the subject of communication as we have known it. Unlike the Borg, though, this termination does not take place as an external threat or catastrophe that could be avoided or resisted with any amount of strength. Instead, the cy-borg, true to its thoroughly monstrous configuration, has always and already infiltrated and determined the subject that it subse-quently appears to threaten. Consequently, the subject of commu-nication, it will be argued, is not only disrupted by but constitutes a privileged site for investigating and understanding the cyborg.

The demonstration of these apparently monstrous assertions will be divided into two parts. The first explores Haraway's po-tentially disturbing proclamation, "we are already cyborgs," questioning not only how and why *we* are already implicated in this theorized and fabricated hybrid but also inquiring about the scope and limitations of the pronoun. In other words, the first part asks the deceptively simple question, "who are we?" and attempts to deal with the not so simple responses. The second part takes up the conclusions of the first and, assuming that we are to some extent already implicated in the figure of the cyborg, explores the consequences of this reconfiguration of subjectivity for the theory and practice of communication. In taking this approach, the second part deploys and exhibits the double meaning of the phrase "the subject of communication," investigating the repercussions of the cyborg not only on the communicative subject but also within the subject matter of communication.

The End of Man

Man is an invention of recent date. And one perhaps nearing its end.

Foucault 1973, 387

The neologism *cyborg* originates in an article written by Manfred Clynes and Nathan Kline and published in the September 1960 edition of *Astronautics*. This short, speculative essay entitled "Cyborgs and Space" addressed the future of manned space flight, arguing that "altering man's bodily functions to meet the requirements of extraterrestrial environments would be more logical than providing an earthy environment for him in space" (Clynes and Kline 1995, 29). Within the course of this argument, Clynes and Kline proposed the word *cyborg* to name any "exogeneously extended organizational complex functioning as an integrated homeostatic system" (30–31). Since its introduction, the word has come to be employed to name any integrated synthesis of organism and machine into a hybrid system.[3] Consequently, as Gray, Mentor, and Figueroa-Sarriera (1995) argue in the Introduction to the *Cyborg Handbook*, "there are many actual cyborgs among us in society. Anyone with an artificial organ, limb or supplement (like a pacemaker), anyone programmed to resist disease (immunized) or drugged to think/behave/feel better (psychopharmacology) is technically a cyborg" (2). Understood in this fashion, N. Katherine Hayles (1995) estimates that somewhere around 10 percent of the current U.S. population are literally cyborgs. "A much higher percentage," she continues, "participate in occupations that make them into metaphoric cyborgs, including the computer keyboarder joined in a cybernetic circuit with the screen, the neurosurgeon guided by fiber optic microscopy during an operation, and the teen gameplayer in the local videogame arcade" (322).

There is, however, a more fundamental and conceptual level through which the cyborg makes its appearance. This conceptual cyborg, or what Brenda Brasher (1996) calls a "cultural cyborg" (813), constitutes simultaneously an extension of the concept developed by Clynes and Kline and the ideological ground upon which their work first becomes possible. This formulation of the cyborg is introduced in Donna Haraway's "Cyborg Manifesto." According to Haraway, "A cyborg exists when two kinds of boundaries are simultaneously problematic: 1) that between animals (or other organisms) and humans, and 2) that between self-controlled, self-governing machines and organisms, especially humans" (Gray, Mentor, and Figueroa-Sarriera 1995, 1). These boundary breakdowns, as Haraway illustrates, are particularly evident in contemporary, postmodern culture.[4] "By the late twentieth century in United States, scientific culture, the boundary between human and animal is thoroughly breached. The last beachheads of uniqueness have been polluted, if not turned into amusement parks—language, tool use, social behavior, mental events. Nothing really convincingly settles the separation of human and animal" (Haraway 1991b, 151–152). In addition, "late twentieth century machines have made thoroughly ambiguous the difference between natural and artificial, mind and body, self-developing and externally designed, and many other distinctions that used to apply to organisms and machines. Our machines are disturbingly lively, and we ourselves frighteningly inert" (Haraway 1991b, 152).

Nowhere is this dual erosion of the conceptual boundaries of the human more evident than in the Human Genome Project (HGP), a multinational effort to decode and map the totality of genetic information constituting the human species.[5] This project takes deoxyribonucleic acid (DNA) as its primary object of investigation. DNA, on the one hand, is considered to be the fundamental and universal element determining all organic entities, human or otherwise. Understood in this fashion, the difference between the human being and any other life-form is merely a matter of the number and sequence of DNA strings. Geneticists, for example, now estimate that there is a mere 1 percent variation in the ape and human genomes (cf. Kevles and Hood 1992). Consequently, the HGP's emphasis on DNA, the presumed universal substrate of all organic life, effectively dissolves the rigid boundaries that had once distinguished the human from the animal. On the other hand, the HGP, following a paradigm that has been central to modern biology, considers DNA to be nothing more than a string of information, a biologically encoded program that is to be decoded, manipulated, and run on a specific information-processing device.[6] This procedure allows for animal bodies to be theorized, understood, and manipulated as mechanisms of information. For this reason, Haraway (1991b) concludes that "biological organisms have become biotic systems, communications devices like others. There is no fundamental, ontological separation in our formal knowledge of machine and organism, of technical and organic" (177–178).

The cyborg, if we follow Haraway's formulation, is not just an enhanced or augmented human being. It is simultaneously more and less than what has been traditionally defined as human. It is the product of an erosion of the concept and definition of the human. This erosion promotes communication between the terms of a categorical distinction, resulting in a thorough contamination and pollution of the one by its other. For this reason, the cyborg is neither human nor its dialectically opposed other, that is, that in opposition to which the concept of the human has been traditionally defined and delimited (i.e., the animal and the machine). On the contrary, the cyborg constitutes a monstrous hybrid or what

Timo Siivonen (1996) calls an "oxymoronic undecidability" (227) that, like the feminist "mestiza" of Gloria Anzaldua (1987) or Trinh T. Minh-ha's (1991) postcolonial "inappropriate/d other," is situated in between conceptual opposites[7] or, as Derrida (1979) might articulate it, is "living on border lines." In this way, the cyborg, in affinity with other figures and strategies of postmodern criticism, short-circuits dualistic logic, which constitutes one of the cornerstones of Western thought. Western systems of meaning, it has been argued (Derrida 1981a; Haraway 1991b; Taylor 1993; Grosz 1994; Dery 1996), are structured by a network of conceptual oppositions, which include, among others, "mind/body, self/other, human/machine, nature/culture, natural/artificial, material/immaterial and reality/virtuality" (Taylor 1997, 269). The cyborg names a monstrous practice that deliberately fosters contamination across the boundaries that have divided and distinguished these oppositions. It constitutes an undecidable oxymoronic operation that is in between. In occupying this median position, however, the cyborg does not constitute a simple synthetic or dialectical resolution of the traditional opposition. It constitutes a kind of illegitimate and ironic practice that, as Haraway (1991b) explains it, holds incompatible things together without resolving into larger wholes (149) or seeking unitary identity (180). In doing so, the cyborg constitutes an irreducible and indeterminate *third term* that not only exceeds comprehension by the restricted, dualistic logic of Western thought but offers an alternative to either/or formulations that resists all forms of identification and dialectical mediation whether Hegelian, Marxian, or otherwise. The cyborg, therefore, intimates a way out of restricted dualistic thinking and dialectical reasoning. As Haraway (1991b) proposes, "cyborg imagery can suggest a way out of the maze of dualisms in which we have explained our bodies and our tools to ourselves" (181).

Generally speaking, the cyborg exceeds the concept of the human. It does not remain a mere enhancement or augmentation of "human nature," as Clynes and Kline had originally proposed or continue to argue (cf. Gray 1995a). It comprises an ideological implosion of the human. Consequently, as Claudia Springer (1996) points out, "the cyborg undermines the very concept of 'human'" (33). For those schooled in, supported by, and empowered through this concept, this conclusion can only appear to be a dangerous loss of everything that is near and dear. Indeed, at stake is one's very humanity. It is for this reason that the cyborg almost always appears under the guise of "dehumanization." As Haraway (1991b) points out, following the analysis of Zoe Sofia, "from one perspective, a cyborg world is about the final impositions of a grid of control on the planet, about the final abstraction embodied in a Star Wars apocalypse waged in the name of defense" (154). Popular conceptions of the cyborg as deployed in both science-fiction film and literature generally conform to this apocalyptic and dystopic configuration. From the mythical golem to *RoboCop* and the Borg of *Star Trek*, from Mary Shelley's *Frankenstein* to the *Terminator* and the replicants of *Blade Runner*, cyborgs have customarily been represented as a catastrophic counterforce to human dignity and survival.[8]

Although the cyborg necessarily provides the appearance of dehumanization, its significance may be otherwise. As Friedrich Nietzsche reminds us in light of that other, potentially terrifying "catastrophe" at the end of the nineteenth century, the death of God, such threats always have the potential to be otherwise. "These initial consequences, the consequences for ourselves, are quite the opposite of what one might perhaps expect: They are not at all sad and gloomy but rather like a new and scarcely describable kind of light, happiness, relief, exhilaration, encouragement, dawn" (Nietzsche 1974, 280). The cyborg does indeed announce something like the "end of the human." However, this termination is only a degeneration and loss if viewed from a perspective that still values and deifies the concept of the human and the traditions of humanism. From another perspective, this ending constitutes a kind of liberation that could supply interesting possibilities in excess of the limitations and restrictions of Western humanism. This perspective is not simply nihilistic or misanthropic; it constitutes a strategic position for alternative and oppositional approaches. "It is crucial to remember," Haraway

(1991b) writes, "that what is lost is often times virulent forms of oppression, nostalgically naturalized in the face of current viola- tion" (172). Indeed, for some time now, there has been a general suspicion surrounding the concept of the human and the values of humanism.[9] Martin Heidegger (1977) provides succinct articu- lation of this skepticism, which constitutes one of the main threads of postmodern criticism, in his "Letter on Humanism": "You ask: 'How can we restore the meaning of the word human- ism?' This question proceeds from your intention to retain the word 'humanism.' I wonder whether that is necessary. Or is the damage caused by all such terms still not obvious?" (195).

Humanism and the concept of the human have a definite ideo- logical history and have been informed and supported by specific political and sociocultural presuppositions. Recent work in critical theory (cf. Foucault 1973; Fraiberg 1993; Vitanza 1997), feminism (Haraway 1991b; Braidotti 1994; Grosz 1994) and postcolonial studies (Trinh 1989; Shome 1996), for example, have criticized the traditions of humanism and the concept of humanity for their ali- mentation with and justification of all kinds of sexist, ethnic, and racial violence. Justifying her employment of the cyborg in an es- say on AIDS, for example, Allison Fraiberg (1993) makes the fol- lowing argument: "By using the cyborg as a starting point, I'm saying that—and this is by no means an astounding observation— rhetorics of humanism and organicism have produced, are cur- rently producing, and, I dare say, will probably always produce, radical material inequities for the vast majority of people" (65). It is for this reason that Haraway (1991b) proposes the cyborg as a means to interfere in and eventually avoid contributing to the con- cept and legacy of humanism. "Perhaps," she suggests, "we can learn from our fusion with animals and machines how not to be Man, the embodiment of Western Logos" (173).

For Haraway (1991b), therefore, the cyborg appears under the sign and promise of liberation (149), offering compelling alterna- tives to the hegemony and logic of Western humanism. As a result, the cyborg has often been situated in alliance with postcolonial theory and practice. Like the cyborg, postcolonialism, as explained by Raka Shome (1996), "is about borderlands and hybridity. It is about cultural indeterminacy and spaces in between" (44). This association is deployed and operative throughout Haraway's manifesto. Not only is Haraway's cyborg compared to figures of postcolonial theory (i.e., Anzaldua's "mestiza" or Trinh's "inappropriate/d other"), but, as Andrew Ross points out, it is women of color, especially Asian technology workers, who seem to be "privileged as cyborgs" (Penley and Ross 1991, 12) in Haraway's text. This conclusion, however, is problematic, as Haraway candidly admits in response to Ross's comment. "My narrative partly ends up further imperializing, say, the Malaysian factory worker. If I were rewriting those sections of the Cyborg Manifesto I'd be much more careful about describing who counts as 'we,' in the statement, 'we are all cyborgs.' I would also be much more careful to point out that those are subject positions for people in certain regions of transnational systems of production that do not easily figure the situation of other people in the system" (Penley and Ross 1991, 12–13). In other words, the alternative, posthuman subjectivities introduced by the cyborg cannot, without precipitating a kind of neocolonial violence, be applied to cultures and peoples who have, in the customary estimations of Western humanism, never been fully human in the first place. Consequently, the "we" of Haraway's "we are all cyborgs" should be understood in a highly restricted sense, applying exclusively to those privileged peoples who always already reside within the systems of Western humanism. The cyborg should not be understood as a new, universal category simply replacing that of the human. It should be understood as a highly specific and strategic intervention simultaneously aimed at and situated within the history and ideology of Western thought. Elsewhere, Haraway (1991b) calls this kind of strategic and intentionally restricted operation "situated knowledge" (183). Although there is a certain affinity between Haraway's cyborg and the various figures and operations of postcolonial theory, they cannot be and never will be simply identical.

The cyborg signifies a crisis in and dissolution of the concept of the human situated within the horizon of Western humanism. It would, however, be inaccurate to say that the cyborg *causes* this conclusion. Rather, cyborgs initially come to be as the result of conceptual erosions that are always and already underway within the systems of Western thought. Within the intellectual traditions of the West, relations between the human and the animal and the animal and machine have been "border wars" (Haraway 1991b, 150). And these border wars have been going on for quite some time. As Bruce Mazlish (1993) demonstrates in the *Fourth Discontinuity*, the "concern about Man's animal and mechanical nature came forcefully together in the West in the seventeenth century and did so in terms of a debate over what was called the *animal-machine*" (14). In the *Discourse on Method*, for example, René Descartes (1988) had argued that animals were machines, making the famous comparison of animal bodies to the movement of clockwork mechanisms. By the early eighteenth century this mechanistic argument had been extended to human beings in Julien La Mettrie's *L'Homme-machine* [The Man Machine], which argued that "the human body is but a watch" (Mattelart 1996, 23). The controversies and debates surrounding these determinations characterized a great deal of scientific and philosophical discourse in the early modern period (cf. Mazlish 1993; Mattelart 1996). Haraway, therefore, does not produce or invent the boundary breakdowns that the cyborg presents. She simply traces the contours and consequences of border skirmishes or untenable "discontinuities" (Mazlish's term) that have been underway within and constitutive of Western intellectual history. The cyborg, therefore, does not cause the conceptual erosion of the human; it merely provides this dissolution with a name.[10]

This boundary breakdown of the concept of the human is particularly evident and operational within the discipline of communication studies. Consequently, the discipline constitutes one of the privileged site of cyborg hybridization and conceptual dissolution. As generally acknowledged, the modern science of communication originates with an important paper on communication theory published shortly after the end of World War II. As John Fiske explains in his *Introduction to Communication Studies* (1994),

"Shannon and Weaver's *Mathematical Theory of Communication* [1963] is widely accepted as one of the main seeds out of which Communication Studies has grown" (6).[11] Shannon and Weaver's "ground-breaking research" addressed telephonic systems, and their mathematical theory was devised as a means by which to calculate and improve the transmission rates of copper wire. Consequently, if we follow Fiske's characterization, one of the seeds out of which the study of human communication has grown (the organic metaphor is not accidental) is research in and theoretical perspectives derived from telecommunications technology. This conclusion has two related consequences. First, the study of human communication originates in and grows out of research in the technology and mechanisms of telecommunications. This curious genealogy situates "machinic" communication at the genetic center of a supposedly human activity. The influence of this mechanistic foundation can be perceived in the proliferation of telecommunication terminology in texts addressing the theory and practice of human communication—terms such as transmission/reception, coding/decoding, sender/receiver, signal/noise, etc. Second, the technology of telecommunications can no longer be understood as a technical addendum to supposedly natural forms of human communication. For the "natural" in this case is already defined and delimited by a technological system. This curious situation conforms to what Derrida (1973) calls the logic of the supplement: "The strange structure of the supplement appears here: by delayed reaction, a possibility produces that to which it is said to be added on" (89). In the development of communication studies, the technology of telecommunications comes to originate the "natural" form of human communication onto which one will want to say that it is subsequently added.

Communication studies is a discipline that not only participates in but initially promotes cyborg hybridization. It is an endeavor that effectively encourages dissolution of the distinctions that had separated the human organism from the machine. In other words, communication, through its very disciplinary genesis, is always and already part of a cyborg program. Within the discipline of communication, therefore, the cyborg does not constitute an external catastrophe that threatens a previously well-defined and pure concept of human communication. It does not, like the Borg of *Star Trek: The Next Generation*, appear on the view screens of this human enterprise as a big black box approaching from the frontier at ever-increasing speeds. Instead, the cyborg already constitutes what it subsequently appears to threaten. Consequently, the cyborg is not something that can be opposed or resisted with any amount of strength. As the Borg reiterate "Strength is irrelevant. Resistance is futile. You must comply." Resistance is futile not because the cyborg is that much stronger or better equipped than the human. It is futile because in the field of communication the cyborg already constitutes the position from which and for which one would establish resistance in the first place. Strength is irrelevant and resistance is futile because the very possibility of strength and the purpose of resistance has been established and substantiated by the cyborg itself. We have, therefore, always and already been assimilated. We are already Borg. This *a priori* dissolution of the concept of the human necessarily renders traditional, humanist presumptions ambiguous and questionable. As Mark Dery (1996) concludes, the "trespass across the once-forbidden zone between the natural and artificial, the organic and inorganic render much of what we know—or thought we knew—provisional" (244). This realization requires not only a rethinking of the technology of communication but a reorganization and reorientation of the subject of communication.

The Subject of Communication

Consciousness is really only a net of communication.

Nietzsche 1974, 298

The study of human communication, despite its diversity of methods and approaches, has traditionally privileged and organized its subject matter around a specific understanding of the communicative subject. As Briankle Chang (1996) argues in *Deconstructing Communication*, "despite its differing formulations, the central challenge facing all communication theories is the question how is individuality transcended?" (39). Consequently, as John Lannamann (1991) demonstrates in his study of the ideology of interpersonal communication, "the starting point for the observation of communication is often reduced to the individual" (187). This "individualist reduction" (Lannamann's term) is not only evident in Shannon and Weaver's model of communication, which privileges the intentional activity of the information source or sender (Shannon and Weaver 1963, 4), but is also present in Aristotle's theory of rhetoric with its emphasis on the orator as an "autonomous individual" (McGee 1982, 29) and, as Lannamann demonstrates, a majority of recent developments in communication theory. "Communication models," writes Lannamann, "based on Osgood's (1969) semantic differential, Fishbein's (1967) attitude hierarchy, Kelly's constructivism (Delia 1977; Kelly 1955), and Thibaut and Kelly's (1959) exchange theory share the common starting point of the individual" (188). This fundamental individualist orientation that is manifest in the various models and theories of communication is initially derived from a specific concept of human subjectivity that, as Chang (1996, 5) and Lannamann (1991, 188) argue, is indebted to Western metaphysics and the Enlightenment concept of the unitary, egocentric self. As Hari Kunzru (1997) describes it: "Ever since Descartes announced, 'I think, therefore I am,' the Western world has had an unhealthy obsession with selfhood. From the individual consumer to the misunderstood loner, modern citizens are taught to think of themselves as beings who exist inside their heads and only secondarily come into contact with everything else" (158). Under this rubric, communication has been understood as an activity that is intended and substantiated by a preestablished and unquestioned solitary subject. As Chang (1996) concludes: "The postulation of the solitary communicative subject thus becomes the precondition for theorizing about communication, for it legitimizes raising the question of communication to begin with and at the same time anticipates possible answers to it under the condition set by the problematic" (44). The cyborg, however, threatens and promises to undermine this restricted formulation of human subjectivity and its communicative activity.

The problematic of communication has always occupied a privileged position in the evolution of the concept of the cyborg. Early cyborg research, for example, sought methods and protocols for interconnecting technological apparatus and organic systems. The cyborg, as defined by Clynes and Kline (1995), depended upon technologies that incorporate "sensing and controlling mechanisms" capable of responding to and acting on the physiology of the organism (31). Facilitating and developing systems for this kind of machine-organism interface was definitive of cyborg research from the late 1950s through the early 1970s. The Pilot's Associate Program of the U.S. Air Force, for example, sought to design "communication links" that would foster an "intimate integration of the human with the machine" (Gray 1995b, 105). Similar efforts have been espoused by J.C.R. Licklider (1960), who advocated the development of "very close couplings" (1) between humans and electronic systems in his seminal "Man-Computer Symbiosis"; Patricia Cowing, who developed NASA's Autogenic Feedback System for physiological monitoring (Eglash 1995, 94); and Peter Fromherz, whose silicon-neuron circuit facilitates communication between organic cells and electronic systems (Hogan 1995, 2). These practical efforts in communications engineering, however, are made possible on the basis of a more fundamental and essential interconnection. The organism and machine communicate, in the first place, through a common, general concept of communication. "We have decided," wrote Norbert Wiener (1961), "to call the entire field of control and communication theory, whether in the machine or the animal, by the same name *cybernetics*" (11). Under the rubric of cybernetics, communication is posited as an isomorphism common to both organic entities and technological systems.[12] Because the cyborg, in whatever form it takes, names this interconnection of the organic and mechanical, it exists in terms of communication. As Haraway (1991b) concludes, "the cyborg is text, machine, body, and metaphor—all theorized and engaged in practice in terms of communication" (212). Communication, therefore, is not one operation among others in which the cyborg participates. It delimits the theoretical and practical *terms* under which cyborgs are generated. Or as Mark Amerika (1997) formulates it through parody of the *cogito ergo sum* of the self-certain and narcissistic Cartesian subject, "I link, therefore I am" (1).

Consequently, the cyborg does not constitute a preestablished individual subject that actively engages in the process of communication. It is itself subject to and initially activated by communicative interactions and linkages. In this way then, the cyborg introduces fundamental alterations in the concept of subjectivity, the activity of communication, and their perceived relationship. First, the cyborg does not constitute a subject in the Western metaphysical sense of the term. It is not a self-determined, autonomous, and active agent. Cyborg subjectivities, always in the plural and always in flux, are initially formed in and by the flow of information. Cyborg subjects, therefore, tend to be relational, variable, and essentially insubstantial. As Mark Poster (1995) argues: "if modernity or the mode of production signifies patterned practices that elicit identities as autonomous and rational, postmodernity or the mode of information indicates communication practices that constitute subjects as unstable, multiple, and diffuse" (32). The cyborg, consequently, shifts the emphasis from a presumed individual subject to the social and material conditions under which subjects are first created and made possible (Lannamann 1991, 192). Second, the communicative interactions productive of these polymorphic and relational subjectivities cannot be reduced to actions intended and deployed by some preconstituted subject. Hence, communication is not simply a matter of intentionality, which assumes an individual and self-sufficient subject that then decides to communicate. It consists of a complex of *unintentional signals* that are always and already circulating throughout a particular social network. In this way, communication necessarily takes on the appearance of *noise*.[13] However, unlike the negative concept initially developed in communication theory, noise no

longer constitutes the mere opposite of an intended and meaningful signal. It is not, as Shannon and Weaver (1963) suggest, "something added to the signal that was not intended by the information
source" (7). Rather, following subsequent developments in cybernetics and self-organizing systems, "'noise,' which had been seen
as a 'disturbance,' is now seen as a 'virtue'" (Mattelart and Mattelart 1992, 45). Cyborg subjectivities, therefore, do not, at least exclusively, originate or intend meaningful communicative interactions but are themselves the product of indeterminate exchanges.

This fundamental alteration in the status of and relationship between the subject and the activity of communication finds precedent in poststructuralist theories of language. In the essay entitled
Différance (1973), for example, Derrida, following the insights of
Ferdinand de Saussure, argues that "the subject (self-identical or
even conscious of self-identity, self-consciousness) is inscribed in
language, that he is a 'function' of the language. He becomes a
speaking subject only by conforming speech . . . to the system
of linguistic prescriptions taken as the system of differences"
(145–146). In other words, language is not simply a faculty or
tool that is possessed and employed by a sovereign and self-
determined speaking subject. "It is also a figurative, structuring
power that constitutes the subject who speaks as well as the one
that is spoken to" (Poster 1990, 14). Or as Carey (1990) argues,
"language is not merely a vehicle of communication in the nar-
rowed sense of a transmission system. . . . Language realizes a
mode of consciousness and being" (23). This understanding of the
construction of subjectivity and the function of communication is
not only substantiated by recent work in communication (Coward
and Ellis 1977; Lannamann 1991; Biesecker 1997) but has been the
practical experience of those who employ computer-mediated
communication (Stone 1995; Turkle 1995; Hayles 1997). In all cases,
it is argued/discovered that subjectivity is not a preconstituted
and individual essence that is subsequently communicated. Instead, subjects, plural and alterable, initially take form within
complex networks of communicative exchange. As Barbara
Biesecker (1997) explains, "in this view the sovereign or self-posit-

ing subject is displaced by a notion of identity as wholly or irreducibly relational: the self is only given by its structural position within a larger field of discursive forces or symbolic practices, the totality of which is indeterminable yet determining" (75). This formulation, however, does not imply that cyborgs simply overturn subjectivity for a kind of objectivism or indeterminate relativism, as a number of recent works, including Biesecker (1997) and Rushing and Frentz (1995), have argued. Cyborg subjects, true to their hybrid form, occupy a position that neither supports nor simply opposes traditional forms of subjectivity. "This is," argue Gray and Mentor (1995), "what makes the cyborg subject so interesting: on the one hand, it participates in a decentering of traditional subjectivity, of the metaphysics of presence, of the organic or essential identity and body; on the other, it offers a physical and bodily experience of what some feminists call strategic subjectivities" (229). Consequently, "the cyborg is a meeting place between those unwilling to give up notions of strategic subjectivities and those bent on the liberatory projects that assume the destruction of masterly, coherent selves, 'achieved (cultural) or innate (biological).' And the cyborg especially can be a place to learn a new conception of agency, what Judith Butler calls 'an instituted practice in a field of enabling constraints.'" (232). The cyborg, therefore, does not constitute the mere destruction or annihilation of the subject but delimits a postmodern subjectivity that *deconstructs* the presumptuous, sovereign individual of modernity without resolving into either naïve objectivism or simple relativisms.[14]

This inversion and displacement of the traditional relationship situated between subjectivity and the process of communication has been dramatized in *Star Trek: The Next Generation's* "The Best of Both Worlds."[15] In this, the final episode of the 1991 television season, Captain Picard is kidnapped by the Borg and transformed into the cybernetic organism Locutus of Borg. According to the structure of the narrative, the *Enterprise* and the entire ensemble called Star Fleet epitomize the traditional, humanist perspective and its validation of the individual, self-determined subject. Indeed, the *Enterprise* is composed of a confederation of individuals (Picard, Riker, Data, Troi, Crusher, Worf, etc.), each possessing his or her own characteristic strengths and weaknesses. As Picard, in characteristic modernist form, exclaims in response to the initial Borg threat: "My culture is based on freedom and self-determination!" The Borg, on the contrary, consist of a network of indeterminate and fluid proportions. Individual Borg entities are nothing more than functions of the network or nodal points within it. Borg subjectivities, therefore, are not conceptualized as preexisting, selfsame, or self-determining individuals. They are relational subjects constructed and reconstructed, based on the vicissitudes of the network. To paraphrase Mark Poster (1990), Borg subjects float, suspended between points of objectivity, being constituted and reconstituted in different configurations in relation to the arrangement of the occasion (11). Locutus of Borg, for example, is no longer the self-determinate, individual human subject called Captain Picard. As the Borg network explains it, "the entity you knew as Picard is no more." On the contrary, Locutus of Borg is delimited as nothing more than a temporary locus in the Borg network, a locus that serves the transitory requirement of locution. "It has been decided that a human voice will speak for us in all communication. You have been chosen to be that voice." From the perspective of the *Enterprise*, a perspective that is thoroughly grounded in the traditions of humanism and modern science, the Borg can appear as nothing less than monstrous, dangerous, and terrifying. For they interrupt and undermine the assumptions of individual subjectivity and agency, assumptions that are central to both modern science and the traditions of humanism. However, from another perspective, the Borg represent new affiliations and dangerous possibilities that have the potential to alter the way Westerners think about themselves and their technology.

This altered perspective necessarily introduces transformations in the way one considers the subject of communication, which should be understood in its double significance as both the communicative subject and the subject matter of a specific discipline. Once again, however, it would be a mistake to conclude that the cyborg intends or causes this alteration. For the cyborg does not threaten a pure and previously well-established concept of human communication as some external catastrophe that could be resisted or avoided with any amount of strength. It names a monstrous deformation of the subject of communication that has ironically always and already been underway within the discipline. The cyborg, therefore, does not necessarily introduce or advocate any new or revolutionary ideas. Instead it constitutes and names a nodal point that collects and coordinates a number of seemingly unrelated interventions that have questioned and criticized the subject of communication. First, by shifting the emphasis from the individual subject to the social and material conditions by which various subject positions become possible, the discipline of communication overcomes what Lannamann (1991) terms "the ideological pitfalls of individualism, subjectivity, and subjective intentionality" (195). According to Lannamann, "A subjectivist approach to interpersonal communication emphasizes subjective experience at the expense of recognizing the powerful influences of material conditions beyond the interpretive and rational control of the subject" (190). Under the individualist reduction, which is rooted in Western metaphysics, communication studies risk restricting themselves to the ideological assumptions and necessary limitations imposed by the modernist concept of the rational, self-determined subject. As Lannamann points out, "the danger of an uncritical acceptance of the subjectivist stance is that it limits research to a derivative of social process (the intrapsychic) while reifying the ideological belief that individuals are free subjects who are in control of their experience" (192). The cyborg provides an alternative formulation of the subject of communication that both defines communicative subjects "as cultural, not individual, manifestations, inseparably connected to social and historical processes" (187) and accounts for the "unintentional consequences of social interaction" (195).

Second, the technology of mediated communication has generally been understood as supplements to or extensions of natural forms of human concourse. Consequently, the subjectivist orientation and ideology have customarily been imported into the study of media and communication technology. As a result, the various technologies of communication are customarily understood as artificial aids extending the human subject's "natural" faculties. One is reminded, of course, of the slogans popularized in the work of Marshall McLuhan (1995): "The wheel is the extension of the foot," "the telephone is the extension of the ear," and "electronic media constitute an extension of the human nervous system." Consequently, technical devices have traditionally been regarded as prostheses for enhancing a particular human faculty, and their relative worth has been evaluated according to the pragmatic logic of efficiency. Jean-François Lyotard provides a succinct formulation of this approach in *The Postmodern Condition* (1984): "Technical devices originated as prosthetic aids for the human organs. . . . They follow a principle, and it is the principle of optimal performance: maximizing output and minimizing input. Technology is therefore a game pertaining not to the true, the just, or the beautiful, etc., but to efficiency: a technical 'move' is 'good' when it does better and/or expends less energy than another" (44). For the cyborg, however, technology does not remain a mere prosthetic aid for an already formed individual to deploy to his/her advantage or disadvantage. Technology participates in describing and constructing the very subject positions that come to be occupied by the cyborg. As Poster (1995) argues, "what is at stake in technical innovations is not simply an increased 'efficiency' of interchange, enabling new avenues of investment, increased productivity at work and new domains of leisure and consumption, but a broad and extensive change in the culture; in the way that identities are structured" (23–24). From a cyborg perspective, therefore, the fundamental question informing the consideration of communication technology and media is not "what can technology do for me?" but "how does technology enable and empower the very identity of this, or any other, subject position?" Consequently, "the machine is not an it to be animated, worshipped, and dominated. The machine is us, our processes, an aspect of our embodiment" (Haraway 1991b, 180).

Conclusion

I affirm at the same time: that existence is *communication*—that all representation of life, of being, and generally of "anything," is to be reconsidered
from this point of view.

Bataille 1988, 98

The cyborg designates nothing less than a radical alteration in the
subject of communication. Although originally proposed as a project for "man in space," the cyborg has become a potent conceptualization for alternative arrangements and understandings of subjectivity and the process of communication. In particular, the
cyborg constitutes a highly situated hybrid that does not adhere to
the categorical distinctions by which the human subject would be
distinguished and quarantined from its opposites. It is, therefore, a
devious monstrosity that not only challenges the boundaries that
had differentiated the human from the animal and the animal
from the machine but intentionally deforms the structure of all dualistic oppositions that construct and sustain Western epistemologies. The cyborg facilitates this by deconstructing the subject of
communication, inverting and displacing the causal, hierarchical
relationship customarily situated between the communicative
subject and the activity of communication. As a result of these
"noisy and illegitimate fusions" (Haraway 1991b, 176), the cyborg
calls for and encourages a thorough reevaluation of the humanist
presumptions and values that have informed and delimited traditional systems of knowledge, including the discipline of communication. The cyborg, therefore, does not constitute a new object to
be submitted to the discipline and study of human communication
but describes a fundamental transformation in the very subject of
communication.

This transformation, on the one hand, cannot help but appear to
be a kind of disciplinary crisis. The cyborg undermines the very
foundations of the study of communication, subverting not only
the human subject but deliberately short-circuiting the humanist
assumptions and values that have oriented and directed the sub-

ject matter of the discipline. Consequently, the cyborg appears as an apocalyptic figure that announces nothing less than the end of life as we have known it. Despite such appearances, however, this critical intervention does not necessarily signal the termination of the subject of communication. On the contrary, the cyborg, which exists in and by communication, occasions alternative approaches that exceed the restricted and closed systems of Western humanism. As Haraway (1991b) suggests, "the entire universe of objects that can be known scientifically must be formulated as problems in communications engineering or theories of the text. Both are cyborg semiologies" (163). Therefore, and on the other hand, the cyborg announces other approaches and schematics for understanding the subject of communication, proposing alternative conceptualizations that are purged of humanist pretensions and presuppositions. Under this formulation, the cyborg does not constitute a sad and gloomy twilight figure but designates "a new and scarcely describable kind of light, happiness, relief, exhilaration, encouragement, dawn" (Nietzsche 1974, 280). It is through the paradoxical figure of the cyborg that the subject of communication begins to disengage itself from the limited presuppositions and restricted possibilities imposed upon it by the traditions of humanism and modern science. Consequently, this fundamental alteration cannot help but affect and infect every aspect and corner of the discipline, eventually requiring a wholesale reassessment and reconceptualization that will encompass the entire subject of communication. In the end, however, it is not a matter of simply choosing the latter, apparently optimistic perspective over the former. The tension situated within the figure of the cyborg is neither a variable that is influenced by choice nor a dialectic that could be resolved through some kind of synthetic operation. Instead, following the precedent established by the cyborg, one must learn to see from both perspectives simultaneously. This kind of thoroughly monstrous double vision, which deforms and defies traditional forms of logic, is both fundamental and necessary for understanding the implications and consequences of the cyborg. As Haraway (1991b) insists, "single vision produces worse illusions than double vision or many-headed monsters" (154).

Although it is tempting to blame (or even credit) the cyborg for this apparently monstrous alteration and fundamental (re)configuration, such an assignment would be a mistake and grave misunderstanding. For the cyborg, as it has been demonstrated, does not befall the subject of communication as some newly introduced problem or external catastrophe. Unlike the Borg of *Star Trek: The Next Generation*, the cyborg neither threatens the human subject from the frontiers nor approaches as an external threat that could be thwarted or avoided. The cyborg, true to its thoroughly monstrous configuration, always and already inhabits and deforms the subject of communication. Functioning according to an ironic logic that Derrida names supplementarity, the cyborg already comprises and defines the subject of communication that it subsequently appears to threaten and denature. The cyborg, then, is not an external catastrophe that could be resisted with any amount of strength or resolve. It merely provides a name for an event that has been underway within and definitive of the subject of communication from the beginning. It is for this reason that cyborg assimilation is unavoidable and resistance is futile. We have, to paraphrase Hayles (1999), always been cyborg (291).

Notes

1. Haraway's "Cyborg Manifesto: Science, Technology, and Socialist Feminism in the Late Twentieth Century" was first published under the title "Manifesto for Cyborgs: Science, Technology, and Socialist Feminism in the 1980's" in *Socialist Review* 80 (1985): 65–108, and was subsequently included in her (1991b) collection of essays. A detailed explanation of the text's genesis and development is provided in a footnote appended to the latter. In the year of the essay's reprinting, Haraway discussed the development and impact of her work in an interview with Constance Penley and Andrew Ross. Summarizing the manifesto's initial context, Ross provides the following gloss: "One of the most striking effects of the Cyborg Manifesto was to announce the bankruptcy of an idea of nature as resistant to the patriarchal capitalism that had governed the Euro-American radical feminist counterculture from the early 70s to the mid-80s. In the technologically mediated everyday life of late capitalism, you were pointing out that nature was not immune to the contagions of technology, that technology was part of nature conceived as everyday social relations, and that women, especially, had better start using technologies before technology starts using them" (Penley and Ross 1991, 6). Although Haraway does not dispute this characterization, her reply indicates that she understands the context and effect of the "Cyborg Manifesto" oth-

erwise. "That is an interesting way to put it. I'm not sure what to say about that. What I was trying to do in the cyborg piece, in the regions that you're citing there, is locate myself and us in the belly of the monster, in a technostrategic discourse within a heavily militarized technology" (Penley and Ross 1991, 6). Whereas Ross understands the manifesto to be a specific reply to and argument against the antitechnology trend of a kind of goddess-worshipping feminism, Haraway understands the piece to have a much larger scope. For her, the manifesto constitutes a general intervention in a technoscientific episteme that has already interpolated who and what we are. As she explains in the short essay appended to the interview as a postscript, "the cyborg manifesto was written to find political direction in the 1980s in the face of the odd techno-organic, humanoid hybrids 'we' seemed to have become worldwide" (Haraway 1991a, 21).

2. Since the publication of Haraway's essay, the cyborg has materialized in a number of seemingly unrelated fields, e.g., feminism (Stabile 1994; Howell 1995; Sandoval 1995; Balsamo 1996), film studies (Pask 1995; Rushing and Frentz 1995; Springer 1996; Larson 1997; Bukatman 1997), environmental studies (Bennet 1993), literary criticism (Brown 1996; Lindberg 1996; Clayton 1996; Williams 1998), composition (Winkelmann 1995), philosophy and religion (Taylor 1993; Driscoll 1995; Brasher 1996; Davis 1998), interdisciplinary studies (Shanti 1993; Porush 1994; Biro 1994), science-fiction studies (Dunn and Erlich 1982; Harper 1995; Davidson 1996; Siivonen 1996; Casimir 1997), anthropology (Downey, Dumit, and Williams 1995; Downey 1995; Dumit 1995; Williams 1995; Hess 1995; Escobar 1996), sociology and cultural studies (Fraiberg 1993; Featherstone and Burrows 1995), and computer-mediated communication and information technology (Taylor and Saarinen 1994; Stone 1995; Turkle 1995; Kramarae 1995; Mitchell 1995; Dery 1996; Reid 1996; Hillis 1996; Ito 1997). The fact that the figure of the cyborg has become so thoroughly disseminated in this fashion and has often been employed in these various contexts in different if not contradictory ways is a symptom of and consequently anticipated by Haraway's characterization in the "Cyborg Manifesto." Because the cyborg constitutes an ironic and hybrid figure that blurs boundaries and occupies the space between logical, categorical, and ideological distinctions, it is only fitting that the cyborg constitute a site of difference, struggle, and controversy.

3. For a survey of the development of the concept of the cyborg in the wake of Clynes and Kline's influential article, see Halacy (1965) and Rorvik (1971).

4. Although these boundary breakdowns are particularly evident in postmodern culture, it has been argued that the delimitation of the human has always been a contested issue. For this reason, Halacy (1965) argues that "the cyborg's history begins around 1,000,000 B.C." (34).

5. For a critical investigation of the Human Genome Project, see Haraway (1997). For a critical examination of the recent concern with DNA in the biological sciences, see Doyle (1997).

6. Mattelart (1996) provides a brief account of the history of this approach:

> When, in 1948, Claude Shannon formulated the first mathematical theory of information and communication while in the service of Bell Telephone Laboratories, he borrowed heavily from biology's discoveries about the nervous system. Six years ear-

lier, in a famous book titled *What Is Life*, Erwin Schrödinger (1887–1961) had introduced into this branch of the life sciences the vocabulary of information and coding in order to explain the models of individual development contained in the chromosomes. The landmark discovery of DNA, the molecules present in the nucleus of each living cell, led to a further progression of the analogy. . . . To account for biological specificity, that is, what makes each individual unique, specialists in molecular biology used the communication model developed by Shannon. François Jacob, author of *The Logic of Life* (1970) and holder of a Nobel Prize in medicine and physiology obtained jointly with François Lwoff and Jacques Monod for their work on genetics, described heredity in terms of programs, information, messages, and codes. (302)

7. Although there is an affinity between the cyborg and the other interventionist figures of postcolonialism, feminism, and postmodernism, it would be erroneous simply to conclude that they are *identical*. Haraway is careful to distinguish the homogeneous tendency of identification, which reduces differences to an essential unity and, as a result, always engenders violent exclusions and appropriations, and critical affinities, which permit collaboration and coalition across irreducible, heterogeneous differences. For Haraway (1991b), the primary task for oppositional consciousness is "affinity not identity" (155).

8. For an analysis of the figure of the cyborg in science fiction literature and film, see Dunn and Erlich (1982), Shapiro (1993), Pask (1995), Harper (1995), Witwer (1995), Rushing and Frentz (1995), Boyd (1996), Davidson (1996), Harrison (1995), Springer (1996), Bukatman (1997), and Larson (1997). In examining the cyborg, the serious investigation of science fiction should not be underestimated. Haraway (1991b) not only recognizes that this genera constitutes one of the privileged sites in which cyborgs make their appearances (151), but she suggests that science-fiction writers are the "theorist[s] for cyborgs" (173). It is, therefore, in science-fiction literature and film that the boundary breakdowns between the human, the animal, and the machine are dramatized, theorized, and explored. It is for this reason that the second section of this essay turns to the analysis of an episode from the 1991 season of *Star Trek: The Next Generation*.

9. For a critical history of humanism, the concept of the human, and the development of antihumanism and posthumanism, see Davies (1997). For a philosophical critique of humanism, see Hartshorne (1969) and Ferry and Renaut (1990).

10. Mazlish (1993), unlike Haraway (1991b), does not advocate the employment of a neologism like *cyborg*. Mazlish engages in a kind of *paleonymy* that retains the name "human" while opening the concept to a general expansion and slippage in meaning. "I shall be arguing," Mazlish writes, "that human nature is not fixed, not a kind of Platonic ideal, but is rather an evolving identity" (7). Although retaining the word *human*, Mazlish traces a conceptual erosion that differs from the cyborg only in name. "My hope is that readers of this book will henceforth be persistently conscious of the machine question and will thoroughly and constantly perceive the meaning in their own lives of the interconnected nature of humans and machines. More pointedly, my aim is that readers will then feel deeply that they are that particular evolutionary creature whose origins are to be found in both the animal and the machine kingdoms, with the

animal and mechanical qualities together incorporated in the definition of human nature" (Mazlish 1993, 8). Hayles (1999) takes yet another approach, advocating the employment of another neologism to name this reconfiguration of the human being. She propose the term *posthuman,* which is derived from the work of Ihab Hassen. Hayles not only repeats a number of gestures and concepts associated with Haraway's cyborg but provides an extensive account of the role of cybernetics in constructing posthuman subjects. It would, however, be inaccurate to conclude that the posthuman constitutes a synonym for Haraway's cyborg. The cyborg, according to Haraway's determinations, is the result of a dual erosion of the boundaries that define and delimit the human. It is the product of a blurring of the boundaries that had attempted to distinguish the human from the animal and the animal from the machine. Although Hayles's posthuman also comprises a border identity, it is restricted to one of the two boundary breakdowns described by Haraway. Specifically, Hayles defines the posthuman as the product of an erosion of the border that had differentiated the human organism from the cybernetic mechanism: "The posthuman view configures human being so that it can be seamlessly articulated with intelligent machines. In the posthuman, there are no essential differences or absolute demarcations between bodily existence and computer simulation, cybernetic mechanism and biological organism, robot teleology and human goals" (3). Consequently, the posthuman articulates and is limited to one of the two boundary breakdowns that describe and constitute Haraway's figuration of the cyborg. For this reason, there is a potent affinity between Hayles's concept of the posthuman and Haraway's cyborg, but not an identity.

11. This remarkable sentence from Fiske (1994) may require some clarification. In stating that Shannon and Weaver's text is "accepted as one of the main seeds out of which Communication Studies has grown" (6), Fiske is neither claiming that this text constitutes the exclusive origin of the discipline of communication nor asserting that the statement itself is necessarily and unquestionably true. What his carefully constructed sentence does indicate is that Shannon and Weaver's text has, for better or worse, been acknowledged by communication scholars as *one* of the central elements that has shaped the theory and practice of communication studies. In citing Fiske, therefore, I intend neither to prove nor to disprove the statement, which would require nothing less than a critical history of the discipline of communication. The sentence is employed here as a general symptom, indicating how the field of communication studies has, in the latter half of the twentieth century, come to understand and conceptualize the development of its own disciplinary structure and practice.

12. Although *communication* is an isomorphism common to both organic and "machinic" systems, it would be a mistake to conclude that it constitutes *the* isomorphism. The science of cybernetics began, as Wiener explained, with two, communication and control. Subsequent developments in the science eventually added a third, computation. Although there have been attempts to reduce all cybernetics to communication (Wiener 1988), control (Beniger 1986), or computation (Morevac 1988), the fact is that none of these three can be said to be more fundamental than the others.

13. The relative position of the concept of *noise* in cybernetics has been the subject of significant internal debate and development. When Norbert Wiener initially introduced the science in his seminal text of 1948, he identified Claude Shannon, who formalized the *Mathematical Theory of Communication*, as one of the founding influences in the development of cybernetics (Wiener 1961, 10). The acknowledgment of Shannon's influence is reaffirmed and elaborated in Wiener's (1988) subsequent publication. In this sequel, which attempts to make the ideas of cybernetics "acceptable to a lay public" (15), Wiener credits both Claude Shannon and Warren Weaver with having assisted in making the nascent science of cybernetics a legitimate field of study: "Since then [1948] the subject has grown from a few ideas shared by Drs. Claude Shannon, Warren Weaver, and myself, into an established region of research" (Wiener 1988, 15–16). In Shannon's work on communication theory, which was eventually published in 1949 along with a lengthy introduction by Weaver, noise was formulated as a negative concept that is diametrically opposed to and a disruption of signal. Because of the lineage articulated by the "father of cybernetics," early forms of cybernetic research approached the issue of noise in ways that were consistent with Shannon's formulations. Subsequent developments in cybernetics, however, began to consider the concept otherwise. As early as the Seventh Conference on Cybernetics, an alternative approach was espoused by Donald MacKay. MacKay's work suggested that noise was not the mere opposite of signal but constituted the essence of information. These two different approaches to the concept of noise eventually resulted in two different directions for cybernetics—homeostasis and reflexivity. For an account of the historical developments and significant internal debates of cybernetics, see Hayles (1999).

14. All too often the distinction between these two operations is simply conflated, rendering deconstruction a sophisticated form of destructive analysis. As a result, theorists like Lannamann (1991) inappropriately assume that deconstruction must necessarily be followed by a kind of "reconstruction" (195), which, as demonstrated by Rushing and Frentz's (1995) proposal to reconstruct a "larger aspect of the human self" (25), always runs the risk of reestablishing the very object that would have been submitted to criticism in the first place. Deconstruction, however, does not indicate "to take apart." It does not, as Carey (1990) and others erroneously presume, signify "to break up," "to un-construct," or "to disassemble" (22). On the contrary, deconstruction comprises an irreducible *double gesture*, or what Biesecker (1997) calls "a two-step that, contrary to intellectual gossip, affirms rather than deplores radical possibility" (16). As characterized by Derrida (1982), this double gesture, or what is also called a *double science*, comprises both inversion and displacement. "Deconstruction cannot limit itself or proceed immediately to a neutralization: it must, by means of a double gesture, a double science, a double writing, practice an *overturning* of the classical opposition *and* a general *displacement* of the system. It is only on this condition that deconstruction will prove itself the means with which to *intervene* in the field of oppositions that it criticizes" (329). The cyborg exemplifies this double gesture in its deconstruction of the traditional relationship between the intending human subject and the activity of communication. First, the cyborg inverts the traditional

structure that privileges the intending speaking subject by placing its emphasis on the common material condition that first makes subjectivity possible. It does not, however, simply remain at this phase of inversion, which would constitute nothing less than a mere exchange of positions in the established system. Therefore, at the same time that the cyborg deploys this initial inversion, it also displaces this simple revolution by introducing a new concept of subjectivity, what one could call following Judith Butler "performative subjectivity," that "can no longer be, and never could be included in the previous regime" (Derrida 1981a, 42). For a detailed treatment of the strategy and implications of deconstruction, see the Appendix.

15. This illustration, which investigates only one moment in a single episode of *Star Trek: The Next Generation*, does not constitute a thorough case study of the Borg. Such an examination would require a perspicacious reading that would trace the development of this character from its initial introduction in *Star Trek: The Next Generation* though the television sequel *Voyager*, the *Star Trek* novels, the motion picture *Star Trek: First Contact*, and the CD-ROM-based interactive movie *Star Trek Borg*. For a detailed investigation of the Borg and their complex development as a character within the *Star Trek* universe, see Goulding (1995), Harrison et al. (1996), and Bernardi (1998). For a detailed analysis of the "Best of Both Worlds" episode, see Witwer (1995).

Appendix:
Deconstruction for Dummies

If there had been no computer, deconstruction could
never have happened.

Taylor and Saarinen 1994, Telewriting 9

Misunderstandings of deconstruction and what has sometimes been inappropriately termed the "method of deconstruction" or "deconstructivism" have become
something of an institutional (mal)practice. These misunderstandings are not,
however, the result of introducing complexity into the issue. They proceed from
simplifying all too quickly a complexity that has not been fully understood or ap-
preciated. Consequently, despite or because of these misappropriations and over-
simplifications, which some writers all too often apply to what they already mis-
understand, one must assert, in the first place, that deconstruction does not
indicate "to take apart" or "to un-construct." What it signifies is neither simply
synonymous with "destruction" nor the mere antithesis of "construction." As
Derrida (1993) points out, "the 'de-' of *de*construction signifies not the demolition
of what is constructing itself, but rather what remains to be thought beyond the
constructionist or destructionist schema" (147). For this reason, deconstruction is
something entirely other than what is understood and delimited by the conceptual opposition between construction and destruction. To put it schematically,
deconstruction is a kind of general strategy by which to intervene in this and all
other conceptual oppositions that have organized and regulated, and continue to
organize and regulate, Western systems of knowing. Such an operation, however,
does not, as it is often claimed, simply resolve into untruth or relativism but, true
to the strategy of deconstruction, intervenes in the system that first makes possible the meaning of and very difference between truth/falsity and determin-
ism/relativism.

Defining deconstruction or even describing a "method" of deconstruction is
exceedingly difficult if not impossible. This complication does not derive from
some "Derridean obscurantism" but is systemic and necessary. As Derrida (1993)
notes, "deconstruction does not exist somewhere, pure, proper, self-identical,
outside of its inscriptions in conflictual and differentiated contexts; it 'is' only
what it does and what is done with it, there where it takes place. It is difficult today to give a univocal definition or an adequate description of this 'taking place.'

This absence of univocal definition is not 'obscurantist,' it pays homage to a new, a very new *Aufklärung* [enlightenment or, literally, clearing-up]" (141). Despite the all but unavoidable employment of sentences with the grammatical and logical form of "S is P," deconstruction cannot, as Briankle Chang (1996) concludes, be adequately understood in this abstract and generalized form (119). Consequently, deconstruction is only what it does and what is done with it in a specific context. This has at least two consequences. First, deconstruction does not constitute, at least in the usual sense of the words, either a method or theory. "There is," as Derrida (1993) insists, "no one single deconstruction" (141) but only specific and irreducible instances in which deconstruction takes place. Because deconstruction cannot be abstracted and formalized apart from its specific performances, it cannot resolve into theory as opposed to practice or method as opposed to application. Although this renders deconstruction resistant to customary forms of methodological articulation and understanding, it is necessary and unavoidable if it is to be understood at all. This is, as Derrida (1993) is well aware, "precisely what gets on everyone's nerves" (141).

Second, because deconstruction is not a method in the usual sense of the word, one cannot learn or understand deconstruction by appealing to abstract formulas provided by Derrida or anyone else for that matter (and Derrida would be the first to question this appeal to an author's authority). Instead, the contours of deconstruction will have been traced only by "focusing on the actual operation of deconstruction, on what happens when deconstruction takes place" (Chang 1996, 119). Such a tracing was provided in an interview that Jean-Louis Houdebine and Guy Scarpetta staged with Derrida for the academic journal *Promesse* in 1971. In the course of this dialogue, Derrida, who was asked to reflect on the direction and development of his own work, provided a basic, albeit lengthy, characterization of deconstruction that was derived from and by considering the actual works and workings of deconstruction:

> What interested me then, which I am attempting to pursue along other lines now, was . . . a kind of *general strategy of deconstruction*. The latter is to avoid both simply *neutralizing* the binary oppositions of metaphysics and simply *residing* within the closed field of these oppositions, thereby confirming it. Therefore we must proceed using a double gesture, according to a unity that is both systematic and in and of itself divided, according to a double writing, that is, a writing that is in and of itself multiple, what I called, in "The Double Session" a *double science*. On the one hand, we must traverse a phase of *overturning*. To do justice to this necessity is to recognize that in a classical philosophical opposition we are not dealing with the peaceful coexistence of a *vis-à-vis*, but rather with a violent hierarchy. One of the two terms governs the other, or has the upper hand. To deconstruct the opposition, first of all, is to overturn the hierarchy at a given moment. To overlook this phase of overturning is to forget the conflictual and subordinating structure of opposition. Therefore one might proceed too quickly to a *neutralization* that in practice would leave the previous field untouched, leaving one no hold on the previous opposition, thereby preventing any means of *intervening* in the field effectively. . . . That being said—and on the other hand—to remain in this phase is still to operate on the terrain of and from the deconstructed system. By means of this double, and precisely stratified, dislodged and dis-

lodging, writing, we must also mark the interval between inversion, which brings low what was high, and the irruptive emergence of a new "concept," a concept that can no longer be, and never could be, included in the previous regime. (Derrida 1981a, 41–43)

Deconstruction is a general strategy for intervening in metaphysical oppositions. These oppositions do not just belong to a philosophy or even the discipline of philosophy. They are and have been constitutive of the entire fabric of what is called the Western episteme. As Mark Dery (1996) explains it: "Western systems of meaning are underwritten by binary oppositions: body/soul, other/self, matter/spirit, emotion/reason, natural/artificial, and so forth. Meaning is generated through exclusion: The first term of each hierarchical dualism is subordinated to the second, privileged one" (244). These binary oppositions, by which meaning is produced and regulated, inform and delimit forms of knowing within the horizon of what is called Western science, up to and including those by which one would describe and/or criticize this tradition as such. Deconstruction, therefore, constitutes a mode of *critical intervention* that takes aim at the binary oppositions by which Western systems of knowing, including itself, have been organized and articulated and does so in a way that does not simply neutralize or remain within the hegemony of the system. In this way, deconstruction is a general strategy for "thinking outside the box," where "the box" is defined as the total enclosure that delimits the possibilities of any kind of thought whatsoever.

Because of this somewhat complex undertaking, deconstruction, according to Derrida's characterization here and elsewhere (Derrida 1974, 1981b, 1982, and 1993), involves two related but irreducible operations or phases. The first consists of inversion. In a traditional metaphysical opposition the two terms are not equal. One is always given precedence over the other and, therefore, not only rules over it but determines this other as its negative and counterpart. As Derrida (1982) has explained elsewhere, "an opposition of metaphysical concepts is never the face-to-face of two terms but a hierarchy and an order of subordination" (329). The inversion of this hierarchy would, in the first place, "bring low what was high." This *revolutionary* gesture would overturn a specific binary opposition by inverting the relative positions occupied by its two, dialectically opposed terms. This inversion, however, like all revolutionary operations, does little or nothing to challenge the system that is overturned. In merely exchanging the relative positions occupied by the two metaphysical concepts, inversion still maintains, albeit in an inverted form, the binary opposition in which and on which it operates. Inversion, therefore, does not dispute the essential *structure* of the metaphysical opposition but only exchanges the relative positions occupied by its two components. Consequently, "mere inversion essentially changes nothing, for it still operates on the terrain of and from the deconstructed system."

Although deconstruction begins with a phase of inversion, inversion alone is not sufficient. For this reason, deconstruction comprises an irreducible *double gesture*, or what Barbara Biesecker (1997) calls "a two-step" (16), of which inversion is only the first phase. "We must," as Derrida (1981a) points out, "also mark the interval between inversion, which brings low what was high, and the irruptive emergence of a new 'concept,' a concept that can no longer be, and never could be, included in the previous regime" (42). Deconstruction, therefore, comprises both the overturning of a traditional metaphysical opposition and the ir-ruptive emergence of a new concept that is situated outside the scope and com-prehension of the system in question. This new "concept" is, strictly speaking, no concept whatsoever (which does not mean that it is simply the opposite of the conceptual order), for it always and already exceeds the system of dualities that define the conceptual order as well as the nonconceptual order with which the conceptual order is articulated (Derrida 1982, 329). This "concept," therefore, can only be called a concept by a kind of deliberate and transgressive *paleonymy*. This new concept is what Derrida (1981a) calls, by analogy, an *undecidable*. It is, first and foremost, what "can no longer be included within philosophical (binary) op-position, but which, however, inhabits philosophical opposition, resisting and disorganizing it, without ever constituting a third term, *without ever* leaving room for a solution in the form of speculative dialectics" (43). The undecidable new concept, then, occupies a position that is in between or in/at the margins of a tra-ditional metaphysical opposition. It is simultaneously neither/nor and either/or. It does not resolve into one or the other of the two terms that make up a meta-physical opposition nor constitute a third term that would mediate their differ-ence in a synthetic unity, à la Hegelian or Marxian dialectics. The undecidable, therefore, is positioned in such a way that it both inhabits and operates in excess of the binary oppositions by which and through which systems of knowledge have been organized and articulated. Consequently, it cannot be described or marked in language except (as is exemplified here) by engaging in what Derrida (1981a) calls a "bifurcated writing" (42), which compels the traditional philosophemes to articulate, however incompletely and insufficiently, what nec-essarily resists and displaces all possible articulation.

Finally, there neither is nor can be finality, for deconstruction comprises, as Derrida (1981a) insists within the space of the same interview, something of an "interminable analysis" (42). The analysis is *interminable* for two reasons. First, deconstruction, following the lesson of Hegel's speculative science, understands that it cannot simply situate itself outside what it deconstructs. Deconstruction always takes place as a parasitic operation that works within and by employing tools and strategies derived from a specific system. It cannot, therefore, simply re-move itself from this milieu and stand outside what defines and delimits its very possibility. For this reason, deconstruction is never simply finished with that in which and on which it operates but takes place as a kind of never-ending en-gagement with the systems in which it takes place and is necessarily situated. This is perhaps best exemplified by the following comment, provided by Derrida (1981a) toward the end of the interview with Houdebine and Scarpetta, which concerns the deconstructive reading of Hegel: "We will never be finished with the reading or rereading of Hegel, and, in a certain way, I do nothing other than at-tempt to explain myself on this point" (77). Second, because the metaphysical oppositions, on which and in which deconstruction works, comprise the very logic and possibility of discourse within the Western episteme, "the hierarchy of dual oppositions always seeks to reestablish itself" (Derrida 1981a, 42). Conse-quently, the result of deconstruction always risks becoming reappropriated into traditional metaphysical oppositions by which it comes to be articulated, ex-plained, and understood. This fact is probably best illustrated by considering the recent fate of deconstruction. Even though the practice of deconstruction, as ex-emplified and explained in the work of Derrida and others, exceeds the binary oppositions of destruction/construction, it is continually understood and ex-plained through association with forms of destructive criticism that come to be defined through opposition to the (positive) work of construction. For this rea-son, deconstruction must continually work against this form of reinscription that not only threatens its conclusions but is nevertheless a necessary and unavoid-able outcome. Consequently, deconstruction, unlike other forms of critical analy-sis that have a definite point of initiation and conclusion, is never simply finished with the object that it analyzes or able to bring its project to completion. This is, once again, one of those aspects of deconstruction that gets on everyone's nerves, precisely because it disturbs what Derrida (1993) has called "a good many habits and comforts" (127). However, the fact that this conclusion "hits a nerve" is not unimportant but, as Nietzsche (1974) had demonstrated, is an indication that the analysis grapples with a set of influential but as of yet unquestioned assump-tions, values, and prejudices.

References

Adams, Douglas. 1979. *The Hitchhiker's Guide to the Galaxy*. New York: Pocket Books.

Amerika, Mark. 1997. "Hypertextual Consciousness." (Internet.) Available at http://www.grammatron.com/htc1.0/intention.html.

Anderson, Benedict. 1983. *Imagined Communities*. New York: Verso.

Anderson, Robert H., Tora K. Bikson, Sally Ann Law, Bridger M. Mitchell, Christopher Kedzie, Brent Keltner, Constantijn Panis, Joel Pliskin, and Padmanabhan Srinagesh. 1995. "Universal Access to E-Mail: Feasibility and Societal Implications" (MR–650-MF). (Internet.) Available at http://www.rand.org/publications/MR/MR650/.

Anzaldua, Gloria. 1987. *Borderlands/La Frontera: The New Mestiza*. San Francisco: Spinster/Aunt Lute.

Appadurai, Arjun. 1996. *Modernity at Large: Cultural Dimensions of Globalization*. Minneapolis: University of Minnesota Press.

Argyle, Katie, and Rob Shields. 1996. "Is There a Body in the Net?" In *Cultures of Internet: Virtual Spaces, Real Histories, Living Bodies*, edited by Rob Shields. London: Sage Publications.

Aristotle. 1907. *De Anima*, translated by R. Hicks. Cambridge, Mass.: Harvard University Press.

_____. 1941. *De Interpretatione*. In *The Basic Works of Aristotle*, edited and translated by Richard McKeon. New York: Random House.

_____. 1982. *Poetics*, translated by W. Hamilton Fyfe. Cambridge, Mass.: Harvard University Press.

_____. 1991. *Rhetoric*, translated by J. H. Freese. Cambridge, Mass.: Harvard University Press.

Arnold, Doug, Lorna Balkan, R. Lee Humphreys, Siety Meijer, and Louisa Sadler. 1994. *Machine Translation: Introductory Guide*. Cambridge, Eng.: Blackwell. Also available at http://clwww.essex.ac.uk/~doug/book/book.html.

Ashcroft, Bill, Gareth Griffiths, and Helen Tiffin, eds. 1995. *The Post-Colonial Studies Reader*. New York: Routledge.

Aukstakalnis, Steve, and David Blatner. 1992. *Silicon Mirage: The Art and Science of Virtual Reality*. Berkeley: Peachpit Press.

Austin, John L. 1957. *How to Do Things with Words*. Cambridge, Mass.: Harvard University Press.

Bailey, Cameron. 1996. "Virtual Skin: Articulating Race in Cyberspace." In *Immersed in Technology: Art and Virtual Environments*, translated by Mary Anne Moser and Douglas MacLeod. Cambridge, Mass.: MIT Press.

Bakis, Henry, and Edward Mozley Roche. 1997. *Developments in Telecommunications: Between Global and Local*. Aldershot, Eng.: Ashgate.

Balsamo, Anne. 1996. *Technologies of the Gendered Body: Reading Cyborg Women*. Durham, N.C.: Duke University Press.

Bar-Hillel, Yehoshua. 1964. *Language and Information: Selected Essays on Their Theory and Application*. Reading, Mass.: Addison-Wesley.

Barlow, John Perry. 1990. "Being in Nothingness." *Mondo 2000* (Summer): 34–43.

_____. 1994. "Jack In, Young Pioneer!" (Internet.) Available at http://www.eff.org/pub/publications/john_perry_barlow/jack_in_young_pioneer.article.

_____. 1997. "A Declaration of the Independence of Cyberspace." In *Binäre Mythen/Binary Myths*, edited by Edeltraud Stiftinger and Edward Strasser. Proceeds of the 14 Sept.1996 conference Binary Myths—The Renaissance of Lost Emotions held in Vienna, Austria. Vienna: Zukunfts werkstätte.

_____. 1998. "Africa Rising: Everything You Know About Africa Is Wrong." *Wired* 6, no. 1: 142–158.

_____. 1999. "The Economy of Ideas: A Framework for Rethinking Patents and Copyright in the Digital Age." In *CyberReader*, edited by Victor Vitanza. Boston: Allyn and Bacon.

Bataille, Georges. 1985. *Vision of Excess: Selected Writings 1927–1939*, edited and translated by Allan Stoekl. Minneapolis: University of Minnesota Press.

_____. 1988. *Inner Experience*, translated by Leslie Anne Boldt. Albany: State University of New York Press.

Baudrillard, Jean. 1983. *Simulations*, translated by Paul Foss, Paul Patton, and Philip Beitchman. New York: Semiotext(e).

Benedikt, Michael. 1993a. "Cyberspace: Some Proposals." In *Cyberspace: First Steps*, edited by Michael Benedikt. Cambridge, Mass.: MIT Press.

_____. 1993b. Introduction to *Cyberspace: First Steps*, edited by Michael Benedikt. Cambridge, Mass.: MIT Press.

Beniger, James R. 1986. *The Control Revolution: Technological and Economic Origins of the Information Society*. Cambridge, Mass.: Harvard University Press.

Bennett, Jane. 1993. "Primate Vision and Alter-Tales." In *In the Nature of Things: Language, Politics, and the Environment*, edited by Jane Bennett and William Chaloupka. Minneapolis: University of Minnesota Press.

Bennington, Geoffrey. 1993. *Jacques Derrida*. Chicago: University of Chicago Press.

Benton Foundation. 1994. *Universal Service and the Information Superhighway*. Benton Foundation Communications Policy Briefing 1. Washington: Benton Foundation.

Berger, Peter L., and Thomas Luckmann. 1966. *The Social Construction of Reality: A Treatise in the Sociology of Knowledge*. New York: Doubleday.

Bergson, Henri. 1998. *Creative Evolution*, translated by Arthur Mitchell. New York: Dover.

Bernardi, Daniel L. 1998. *Star Trek and History: Race-ing Toward a White Future*. New Brunswick, N.J.: Rutgers University Press.

Bertol, Daniela, and David Foell. 1997. *Designing Digital Space: An Architect's Guide to Virtual Reality*. New York: John Wiley and Sons.

Bhabha, Homi K. 1994. "Of Mimicry and Man: The Ambivalence of Colonial Discourse." *October* 28 (spring): 125–133..

Biesecker, Barbara. 1997. *Addressing Postmodernity: Kenneth Burke, Rhetoric and a Theory of Social Change*. Tuscaloosa: University of Alabama Press.

Biocca, Frank, Taeyong Kim, and Mark R. Levy. 1995. "The Vision of Virtual Reality." In *Communication in the Age of Virtual Reality*, edited by Frank Biocca and Mark R. Levy. Hillsdale, N.J.: Lawrence Erlbaum Associates.

Biocca, Frank, and Mark R. Levy. 1995a. Preface to *Communication in the Age of Virtual Reality*, edited by Frank Biocca and Mark R. Levy. Hillsdale, N.J.: Lawrence Erlbaum Associates.

_____. 1995b. "Virtual Reality As a Communication System." In *Communication in the Age of Virtual Reality*, edited by Frank Biocca and Mark R. Levy. Hillsdale, N.J.: Lawrence Erlbaum Associates.

Biro, Matthew. 1994. "The New Man As Cyborg: Figures of Technology in Weimar Visual Culture." *New German Critique* 62: 71–110.

Bishop, Alan J. 1995. "Western Mathematics: The Secret Weapon of Cultural Imperialism." In *The Postcolonial Studies Reader*, edited by Bill Ashcroft, Gareth Griffiths, and Helen Tiffin. New York: Routledge.

Bolter, Jay David. 1991. *Writing Space: The Computer, Hypertext, and the History of Writing*. Hillsdale, N.J.: Lawrence Erlbaum Associates.

Bono, James J. 1995. *The Word of God and the Languages of Man: Interpreting Nature in Early Modern Science and Medicine*, vol. 1, *Ficino to Descartes*. Madison: University of Wisconsin Press.

Booth, A. Donald, L. Brandwood, and J. Cleave. 1958. *Mechanical Resolution of Linguistic Problems*. London: Butterworths.

Boyd, Katrina G. 1996. "Cyborgs in Utopia: The Problem of Radical Difference in *Star Trek: The Next Generation*." In *Enterprising Zones: Critical Positions on* Star Trek, edited by Taylor Harrison, Sarah Projansky, Kent A. Ono, and Elyce Rae Helford. Boulder: Westview Press.

Boyer, M. Christine. 1996. *CyberCities: Visual Perception in the Age of Electronic Communication*. New York: Princeton Architectural Press.

Braidotti, Rosi. 1994. *Nomadic Subjects: Embodiment and Sexual Difference in Contemporary Feminist Theory*. New York: Columbia University Press.

Branwyn, Gareth. 1993. "The Desire to Be Wired." *Wired* 1, no. 4: 92–94. Also available at http://www.wired.com/wired/archive/1.04/desire.to.be.wired.html.

_____. 1994. "Compu-Sex: Erotica for Cybernauts." In *Flame Wars: The Discourse of Cyberculture*, edited by Mark Dery. Durham, N.C.: Duke University Press.

Brasher, Brenda E. 1996. "Thoughts on the Status of the Cyborg: On Technological Socialization and Its Link to the Religious Function of Popular Culture." *Journal of the American Academy of Religion* 64: 809–830.

Bromberg, Heather. 1996. "Are Muds Communities? Identity, Belonging and Consciousness in Virtual Worlds." In *Cultures of Internet: Virtual Spaces, Real Histories, Living Bodies*, edited by Rob Shields. Thousand Oaks, Calif.: Sage Publications.

Brook, James, and Iain A. Boal, eds. 1995. *Resisting the Virtual Life*. San Francisco: City Lights.

Brooks, Frederick. 1988. "Grasping Reality Through Illusion: Interactive Graphics Serving Science." *CHI'88 Proceedings*: 1–11. Reading, Mass.: Addison-Wesley.

Brown, Richard. 1996. "Marilyn Monroe Reading *Ulysses*: Goddess or Post-cultural Cyborgs?" In *Joyce and Popular Culture*, edited by R. B. Kershner. Gainesville: University of Florida Press.

Brunn, Stanley D., and Thomas R. Leinbach. 1991. *Collapsing Space and Time: Geographic Aspects of Communication and Information*. London: HarperCollins Academic.

Bryson, Norman. 1983. *Vision and Painting: The Logic of the Gaze*. New Haven: Yale University Press.

Bukatman, Scott. 1997. *Blade Runner*. London: BFI.

Burke, Kenneth. 1966. *Language As Symbolic Action: Essays on Life, Literature, and Method*. Berkeley: University of California Press.

Butler, Judith. 1990. *Gender Trouble: Feminism and the Subversion of Identity*. New York: Routledge.

Cairncross, Frances. 1997. *The Death of Distance: How the Communications Revolution Will Change Our Lives*. Boston: Harvard Business School Press.

Calvert, Clay. 1997. "Hate Speech and Its Harms: A Communication Theory Perspective." *Journal of Communication* 47, no. 1: 4–19.

Calvino, Italo. 1994. "Collezione di Sabbia," translated by Rob Wittig. In *Invisible Rendezvous*. Middletown, Conn.: Wesleyan University Press.

Carey, James W. 1989. *Communication As Culture: Essays on Media and Society*. New York: Routledge.

———. 1990. "The Language of Technology: Talk, Text, and Template As Metaphors for Communication." In *Communication and the Culture of Technology*, edited by Martin J. Medhurst, Alberto Gonzalez, and Tarla Rai Peterson. Pullman: Washington State University Press.

Carnegie Mellon University, Language Technologies Institute. 1996. Center for Machine Translation—Projects. (Internet.) Available at http://www.lti.cs.cmu.edu/Research/cmt-projects.html.

Casimir, Viviane. 1997. "Data and Dick's Deckard: Cyborg As Problematic Signifier." *Extrapolations* 38, no. 4: 278–291.

Chang, Briankle. 1996. *Deconstructing Communication: Representation, Subject, and Economies of Exchange*. Minneapolis: University of Minnesota Press.

Chesher, Chris. 1993. "Colonizing Virtual Reality: Construction of the Discourse of Virtual Reality, 1984–1992." *Cultronix* 1, no. 1: 1–29. (Internet.) Available at http://www.eng.cmu.edu/cultronix/chesher/.

Churchland, Patricia S. 1986. *Neurophilosophy: Toward a Unified Science of the Mind-Brain*. Cambridge, Mass.: MIT Press.

CITAC. 1999. "Chinese/English Machine Translation System." (Internet.) Available at http://citac-mt.com/products.htm.

Clayton, Jay. 1996. "Concealed Circuits: Frankenstein's Monster, the Medusa, and the Cyborg." *Raritan* 15: 53–69.

Clifford, James. 1992. "Traveling Cultures." In *Cultural Studies*, edited by Lawrence Grossberg, Cary Nelson, and Paula Treichler. New York: Routledge.

Clynes, Manfred E., and Nathan S. Kline. 1995. "Cyborgs and Space." In *The Cyborg Handbook*, edited by Chris Hables Gray. New York: Routledge, 1995.

Columbus, Christopher. 1989. *The Diario of Christopher Columbus's First Voyage to America (1492–1493)*, translated by Oliver Dunn and James E. Kelly, Jr. Norman: University of Oklahoma Press.

_____. 1993. "Letters to Queen Isabella." In *Discovering and Transforming*, edited by David Krause. New York: Harcourt Brace.

Conrad, Joseph. 1988. *Heart of Darkness*. New York: Norton.

Cooley, Charles Horton. 1962 [1901]. *Social Organization*. New York: Schocken Books.

Coward, R., and J. Ellis. 1977. *Language and Materialism: Developments in Semiology and the Theory of the Subject*. London: Routledge.

Critical Art Ensemble (CAE). 1994. *The Electronic Disturbance*. New York: Autonomedia.

_____. 1997. "Utopian Promises—Net Realities." (Internet.) Available at http://www.well.com/user/hlr/texts/utopiancrit.html.

Dathorne, O. R. 1994. *Imagining the World: Mythical Belief versus Reality in Global Encounters*. Westport, Conn.: Bergin & Garvey.

Davidson, Cynthia. 1996. "Riviera's Golem, Haraway's Cyborg: Reading *Neuromancer* As Baudrillard's Simulation of Crisis." *Science-Fiction Studies* 23: 188–198.

Davies, Tony. 1997. *Humanism*. New York: Routledge.

Davis, Erik. 1998. *Techgnosis: Myth, Magic, and Mysticism in the Age of Information*. New York: Harmony.

Delavenay, Emile. 1960. *An Introduction to Machine Translation*. New York: Frederick A. Praeger.

Delia, Jesse G. 1977. "Constructivism and the Study of Human Communication." *Quarterly Journal of Speech* 63: 66–83.

Denning, Dorothy E. 1996. "Concerning Hackers Who Break into Computer Systems." In *High Noon on the Electronic Frontier: Conceptual Issues in Cyberspace*, edited by Peter Ludlow. Cambridge, Mass.: MIT Press.

Derrida, Jacques. 1973. "Différance." In *Speech and Phenomenon*, edited and translated by David B. Allison. Evanston, Ill.: Northwestern University Press.

_____. 1974. *Of Grammatology*, translated by Gayatri Chakravorty Spivak. Baltimore: Johns Hopkins University Press.

_____. 1976. "The Retrait of Metaphor." *Enclitic* 2, no. 2: 5–33.

_____. 1978. *Writing and Difference*, translated by Alan Bass. Chicago: University of Chicago Press.

_____. 1979. "Living On: Border Lines," translated by James Hulbert. In *Deconstruction and Criticism*, edited by Harold Bloom. New York: Seabury.

_____. 1981a. *Positions*, translated by Alan Bass. Chicago: University of Chicago Press.

_____. 1981b. *Disseminations*, translated by Barbara Johnson. Chicago: University of Chicago Press.

_____. 1982. *Margins of Philosophy*, translated by Alan Bass. Chicago: University of Chicago Press.

_____. 1985a. *Des Tours de Babel*. In *Difference in Translation*, edited and translated by Joseph F. Graham. Ithaca: Cornell University Press.

_____. 1985b. "Roundtable on Translation," translated by Peggy Kamuf. In *The Ear of the Other*, edited by Christie V. McDonald. New York: Schocken Books.

_____. 1993. *Limited Inc.*, translated by Samuel Weber and Jeffrey Mehlman. Evanston, Ill.: Northwestern University Press.

Dery, Mark. 1994. "Flame Wars." In *Flame Wars: The Discourse of Cyberculture*, edited by Mark Dery. Durham, N.C.: Duke University Press.

_____. 1996. *Escape Velocity: Cyberculture at the End of the Century*. New York: Grove Press.

Descartes, René. 1988. *Discourse on Method* and *Meditations on First Philosophy*. In *Descartes: Selected Philosophical Writings*, edited and translated by John Cottingham, Robert Stoothoff, and Dugald Murdoch. Cambridge, Eng.: Cambridge University Press.

Dewey, John. 1916. *Democracy and Education*. New York: Macmillan.

Dibbell, Julian. 1994. "A Rape in Cyberspace; or, How an Evil Clown, a Haitian Trickster Spirit, Two Wizards, and a Cast of Dozens Turned a Database into a Society." In *Flame Wars: The Discourse of Cyberculture*, edited by Mark Dery. Durham, N.C.: Duke University Press.

Dillon, Andrew. 1996. "Book Review of S. J. Emmott's *Information Superhighways: Multimedia Users and Futures*." *The Information Society* 12, no. 3: 335–336.

Dixon, Joan Broadhurst, and Eric J. Cassidy. 1998. *Virtual Futures: Cyberotics, Technology, and Post-Human Pragmatism*. New York: Routledge.

Dizard, Wilson. 1997. *Meganet: How the Global Communications Network Will Connect Everyone on Earth*. Boulder: Westview Press.

Doheny-Farina, Stephen. 1996. *The Wired Neighborhood*. New Haven: Yale University Press.

Downey, Gary Lee. 1995. "Human Agency in CAD/CAM Technology." In *The Cyborg Handbook*, edited by Chris Hables Gray. New York: Routledge.

Downey, Gary Lee, Joseph Dumit, and Sarah Williams. 1995. "Cyborg Anthropology." In *The Cyborg Handbook*, edited by Chris Hables Gray. New York: Routledge.

Doyle, Richard. 1997. *On Beyond Living: Rhetorical Transformations of the Life Sciences*. Stanford: Stanford University Press.

Driscoll, Mark. 1995. "Eyephone, Therefore I Am: Miki Kiyoshi on Cyborg-Envy in *Being and Time*." In *Prosthetic Territories: Politics and Hypertechnologies*, edited by Gabriel Brahm and Mark Driscoll. Boulder: Westview Press.

Druckrey, Timothy, and Ars Electronica, eds. 1999. *Ars Electronica: Facing the Future*. Cambridge, Mass.: MIT Press.

Dumit, Joseph. 1995. "Brain-Mind Machines and American Technological Dream Marketing: Toward an Ethnography of Cyborg Envy." In *The Cyborg Handbook*, edited by Chris Hables Gray. New York: Routledge.

Dunn, Thomas P., and Richard D. Erlich, eds. 1982. *The Mechanical God: Machines in Science Fiction*. Westport, Conn.: Greenwood Press.

Dutton, William. 1995. "Driving into the Future of Communications? Check the Rear View Mirror." In *Information Superhighways: Multimedia Users and Futures*, edited by Stephen J. Emmott. San Diego: Academic Press.

Dyrkton, Joerge. 1996. "Cool Runnings: The Coming of Cyberreality in Jamaica." In *Cultures of Internet: Virtual Spaces, Real Histories, Living Bodies*, edited by Rob Shields. London: Sage Publications.

Dyson, Esther, George Gilder, George Keyworth, and Alvin Toffler. 1996. "Cyberspace and the American Dream: A Magna Carta for the Knowledge Age." *Information Society* 12, no. 3: 295–308. Also available at http://www.pff.org:80/position.html.

Eco, Umberto. 1995. *The Search for the Perfect Language*, translated by James Fentress. Cambridge, Eng.: Blackwell.

Edwards, Gavin. 1996. "Dejpu'bogh hov rur qablli!*" *Wired* 4, no. 8: 84–93. Also available at http://www.wired.com/wired/archive/4.08/es.languages. html.

Eglash, Ron. 1995. "An Interview with Patricia Cowings." In *The Cyborg Handbook*, edited by Chris Hables Gray. New York: Routledge.

Eisenstein, Zillah. 1998. *Global Obscenities: Patriarchy, Capitalism, and the Lure of Cyberfantasy*. New York: New York University Press.

Ellwood, Wayne. 1996. "Seduced by Technology: The Information Highway." *New Internationalist* 286: 2–18.

Elmer-Dewitt, Philip. 1994. "Battle for the Soul of the Internet." *Time: The Strange New World of the Internet—Battles on the Frontiers of Cyberspace* 144, no. 4: 50–57.

Emmott, Stephen J. 1995. Introduction to *Information Superhighways: Multimedia Users and Futures*, edited by Stephen J. Emmott. New York: Academic Press.

Enloe, Cynthia. 1990. *Bananas, Beaches, and Bases*. Berkeley: University of California Press.

Escobar, Arturo. 1996. "Welcome to Cyberia: Notes on the Anthropology of Cyberculture." In *Cyberfutures: Culture and Politics on the Information Superhighway*, edited by Ziauddin Sardar and Jerome R. Ravetz. New York: New York University Press.

Farwell, L. A., and E. Donchin. 1988. "Talking Off the Top of Your Head: Toward a Mental Prosthesis Utilizing Event-Related Brain Potentials." *Electroencephalography and Clinical Neurophysiology* 70: 510–523.

Featherstone, Mike, and Roger Burrows, eds. 1995. *Cyberspace, Cyberbodies, Cyberpunk: Cultures of Technological Embodiment*. London: Sage Publications.

Ferguson, Russell, Martha Gever, Trinh T. Minh-ha, and Cornel West, eds. 1990. *Out There: Marginalization and Contemporary Cultures*. Cambridge, Mass.: MIT Press.

Ferry, Luc, and Alain Renaut. 1990. *French Philosophy of the Sixties: An Essay on Antihumanism*, translated by Mary H. S. Cattani. Amherst: University of Massachusetts Press.

Fishbein, Martin. 1967. "A Behavior Theory Approach to the Relations Between Beliefs About an Object and the Attitude Toward the Object." In *Readings in Attitude Theory and Measurement*, edited by Martin Fishbein. New York: John Wiley and Sons.

Fisher, Scott. 1981. "Viewpoint Dependent Imaging: An Interactive Stereoscopic Display." *Proceedings SPIE*: 360–367.

Fiske, John. 1994. *Introduction to Communication Studies*, 2d ed. New York: Routledge.

Fodor, Jerry A. 1975. *The Language of Thought*. Cambridge, Mass.: Harvard University Press.

Foster, Derek. 1997. "Community and Identity in the Electronic Village." In *Internet Culture*, edited by David Porter. New York: Routledge.

Foucault, Michel. 1973. *The Order of Things: An Archaeology of the Human Sciences*, translated by Alan Sheridan. New York: Vintage Books.

Fraiberg, Allison. 1993. "Of Aids, Cyborgs, and Other Indiscretions: Resurfacing the Body in the Postmodern." In *Essays in Postmodern Culture*, edited by Eyal Amiran and John Unsworth. Oxford, Eng.: Oxford University Press.

Freedman, David H., and Charles C. Mann. 1997. *@Large: The Strange Case of the World's Biggest Internet Invasion*. New York: Simon and Schuster.

Fuentes, Carlos. 1988. *Myself with Others: Selected Essays*. New York: Farrar, Straus & Giroux.

_____. 1993. "Discovery." In *Discovering and Transforming*, edited by David Krause. New York: Harcourt Brace.

Fuller, Mary, and Henry Jenkins. 1995. "Nintendo® and New World Travel Writing: A Dialogue." In *CyberSociety: Computer Mediated Communications and Community*, edited by Steve Jones. London: Sage Publications.

Furness, Thomas A. 1993. "Greetings from the General Chairman." In *IEEE Virtual Reality Annual International Symposium*. Piscataway, N.J.: IEEE.

Fusco, Coco. 1995. *English Is Broken Here*. New York: New Press.

Gans, David, and R. U. Sirius. 1991. "Civilizing the Electronic Frontier." *Mondo 2000* 3 (Winter): 45–49.

Gasché, Rodolphe. 1986. *The Tain of the Mirror: Derrida and the Philosophy of Reflection*. Cambridge, Mass.: Harvard University Press.

Gerbner, George. 1997. *The Crisis of the Cultural Environment: Media and Democracy in the 21st Century*. [Videotape.] Northampton, Mass.: Media Education Foundation.

Gibson, William. 1984. *Neuromancer*. New York: Ace Books.

_____. 1987. *Burning Chrome*. New York: Ace Books.

_____. 1993. "Academy Leader." In *Cyberspace: First Steps*, edited by Michael Benedikt. Cambridge, Mass.: MIT Press.

Giroux, Henry A. 1992. *Border Crossings*. New York: Routledge.

Godlewska, Anne, and Neilson Voyne Smith, eds. 1994. *Geography and Empire*. Cambridge, Eng.: Blackwell.

Gómez-Peña, Guillermo. 1997. "The Virtual Barrio @ The Other Frontier." (Internet.) Available at http://www.telefonica.es/fat/egomez.html.

Gore, Albert. 1993. "Remarks by the Vice President at the National Press Club Newsmaker Luncheon," 21 Dec. (Internet.) Available at http://www.pub.whitehouse.gov/uri-res/I2R?urn:pdi://oma.eop.gov.us/1993/12/21/5.text.1.

_____. 1994a. "Remarks As Delivered by Vice President Al Gore to the Superhighway Summit," 11 Jan. (Internet.) Available at http://www.whitehouse.gov/WH/EOP/OVP/other/superhig.txt.

_____. 1994b. "Remarks Prepared for Delivery by Vice President Al Gore—International Telecommunications Union," 21 Mar. (Internet.) Available at http://www.iitf.nist.gov/documents/speeches/032194_gore_giispeech.html.

_____. 1999. "Putting People First in the Information Age." In *Masters of the Wired World: Cyberspace Speaks Out*, edited by Anne Leer. London: Financial Times Management.

Goulding, J. 1995. *Aliens and Conquest: A Critique of American Ideology in* Star Trek *and Other Science Fiction Adventures*. Toronto: Sisyphus.

Gray, Chris Hables. 1995a. "An Interview with Manfred E. Clynes." In *The Cyborg Handbook*, edited by Chris Hables Gray. New York: Routledge.

_____. 1995b. "Science Fiction Becomes Military Fact." In *The Cyborg Handbook*, edited by Chris Hables Gray. New York: Routledge.

Gray, Chris Hables, and Steven Mentor. 1995. "The Cyborg Body Politic and the New World Order." In *Prosthetic Territories: Politics and Hypertechnologies*, edited by Gabriel Brahm and Mark Driscoll. Boulder: Westview Press.

Gray, Chris Hables, Steven Mentor, and Heidi J. Figueroa-Sarriera. 1995. "Cyborgology: Constructing the Knowledge of Cybernetic Organisms." In *The Cyborg Handbook*, edited by Chris Hables Gray. New York: Routledge.

Grosz, Elizabeth. 1994. *Volatile Bodies: Toward a Corporeal Feminism*. Bloomington: Indiana University Press.

Guisnel, Jean. 1997. *Cyberwars: Espionage on the Internet*, translated by Gui Masai. New York: Plenum Trade.

Gunkel, Ann Hetzel, and David J. Gunkel. 1997. "Virtual Geographies: The New Worlds of Cyberspace." *Critical Studies in Mass Communications* 14, no. 2: 123–137.

Gunkel, David J. 1997a. "The Empire Strikes Back Again: The Cultural Politics of the Internet." *Computers and Society* 27, no. 4: 18–21.

_____. 1997b. "Scary Monsters: Hegel and the Nature of the Monstrous." *International Studies in Philosophy* 29, no. 2: 23–46.

_____. 1997c. "What's the Matter with Architecture." In Ben Nicholson's *Thinking the Unthinkable House* (CD-ROM). Chicago: The Renaissance Society at the University of Chicago.

_____. 1998a. "Escape Velocity: Exodus and Postmodernism." *Soundings* 81, nos. 3–4: 437–459.

_____. 1998b. "Virtually Transcendent: Cyberspace and the Body." *Journal of Mass Media Ethics* 13, no. 2: 111–123.

_____. 1999. "Lingua Ex Machina: Computer-Mediated Communication and the Tower of Babel." *Configurations* 7, no. 1: 61–89.

_____. 2000a. "Rethinking Virtual Reality: Simulation and the Deconstruction of the Image." *Critical Studies in Media Communication* 17, no. 1: 45–62.

_____. 2000b. "We Are Borg: Cyborgs and the Subject of Communication." *Communication Theory* 10, no. 3: 30–45.

Gurak, Laura J. 1997. "Utopian Visions of Cyberspace." *Computer Mediated Communications* (May): 1–2. (Internet.) Available at http://www.december.com/cmc/mag/1997/may/last.html).

Hafner, Katie, and John Markoff. 1991. *Cyberpunk: Outlaws and Hackers on the Computer Frontier*. New York: Touchstone.

Halacy, D. S. 1965. *Cyborg: Evolution of the Superman*. New York: Harper and Row.

Haraway, Donna. 1991a. "The Actors Are Cyborg, Nature Is Coyote, and the Geography Is Elsewhere: Postscript to 'Cyborgs at Large.'" In *Technoculture*,

edited by Constance Penley and Andrew Ross. Minneapolis: University of
Minnesota Press.
_____. 1991b. *Simians, Cyborgs, and Women: The Reinvention of Nature*. New York:
Routledge.
_____. 1997. *Modest_witness@second_millennium. femaleman_meets_ oncomouse*[TM]:
Feminism and Technoscience. New York: Routledge.
Harmon, Willis W., and Howard Rheingold. 1984. *Higher Creativity: Liberating the
Unconscious for Breakthrough Insights*. New York: J.P. Tarcher.
Harper, Mary Catherine. 1995. "Incurably Alien Other: A Case for Feminist Cy-
borg Writers." *Science-Fiction Studies* 22: 399–421.
Harper's Forum. 1999. "Is Computer Hacking a Crime?" In *CyberReader*, edited by
Victor Vitanza. Boston: Allyn and Bacon.
Harrison, Taylor. 1995. "Weaving the Cyborg Shroud: Mourning and Deferral in
Star Trek: The Next Generation." In *Enterprising Zones: Critical Positions on Star
Trek*, edited by Taylor Harrison, Sarah Projansky, Kent A. Ono, and Elyce
Rae Helford. Boulder: Westview Press.
Harrison, Taylor, Sarah Projansky, Kent A. Ono, and Elyce Rae Helford, eds. 1996.
Enterprise Zones: Critical Positions on Star Trek. Boulder: Westview Press.
Hartmann, Frank. 1999. *Cyber.Philosophy—Medientheoretische Auslotungen*. Vienna:
Passagen Verlag.
Hartshorne, Charles. 1969. *Beyond Humanism: Essays in the Philosophy of Nature*.
Lincoln: University of Nebraska Press.
Harvey, David. 1969. *Explanation in Geography*. New York: St. Martin's Press.
Hayles, N. Katherine. 1993. "The Seductions of Cyberspace." In *Rethinking Tech-
nologies*, edited by Verena Andermatt Conley. Minneapolis: University of
Minnesota Press.
_____. 1995. "The Life Cycle of Cyborgs: Writing the Posthuman." In *The Cyborg
Handbook*, edited by Chris Hables Gray. New York: Routledge.
_____. 1996a. "Embodied Virtualities; or, How to Put Bodies Back into the Pic-
ture." In *Immersed in Technology: Art and Virtual Environments*, edited by
Mary Anne Moser and Douglas MacLeod. Cambridge, Mass.: MIT Press.
_____. 1996b. "Boundary Disputes: Homeostasis, Reflexivity, and the Founda-
tions of Cybernetics." In *Virtual Realities and Their Discontents*, edited by
Robert Markley. Baltimore: Johns Hopkins University Press.
_____. 1997. "Virtual Bodies and Flickering Signifiers." (Internet.) Available at
http://englishwww.humnet.ucla.edu/Individuals/Hayles/Flick.html.
_____. 1999. *How We Became Posthuman: Virtual Bodies in Cybernetics, Literature
and Informatics*. Chicago: University of Chicago Press.
Heaven's Gate. 1997. *Heaven's Gate Homepage*. (Internet.) Available at http://
www.heavensgate.com.
Hegel, Georg Wilhelm Friedrich. 1977. *Phenomenology of Spirit*, translated by A. V.
Miller. New York: Oxford University Press.
_____. 1987. *Encyclopedia of the Philosophical Sciences*, translated by William Wal-
lace. New York: Oxford University Press.
_____. 1989. *Science of Logic*, translated by A. V. Miller. Atlantic Highlands, N.J.:
Humanities Press International.

Heidegger, Martin. 1962. *Being and Time*, translated by John Macquarrie and Edward Robinson. New York: Harper and Row.

_____. 1971. *Poetry, Language, Thought*, translated by Albert Hofstadter. New York: Harper and Row.

_____. 1977. "Letter on Humanism," translated by Frank A. Capuzzi. In *Martin Heidegger: Basic Writings*, edited by David Farrell Krell. New York: Harper and Row.

Heilmann, Luigi. 1963. "J. J. Becker: Un Precursore della Traduzione Meccanica." *De homine* 7–8: 131–134.

Heim, Michael. 1993. *The Metaphysics of Virtual Reality*. New York: Oxford University Press.

_____. 1995. "The Design of Virtual Reality." In *Cyberspace, Cyberbodies, Cyberpunk: Cultures of Technological Embodiment*, edited by Mike Featherstone and Roger Burrows. London: Sage Publications.

_____. 1998. *Virtual Realism*. Oxford, Eng.: Oxford University Press.

Helm, Mary W. 1988. *Ulysses' Sail: An Ethnographic Odyssey of Power, Knowledge, and Geographical Distance*. Princeton: Princeton University Press.

Hermes Project. 1996. (Internet.) Available at http://www-personal.umich.edu/~sgupta/hermes/.

Herring, Susan. 1999. "Bringing Familiar Baggage to the New Frontier: Gender Differences in Computer-Mediated Communication." In *CyberReader*, edited by Victor Vitanza. Boston: Allyn and Bacon.

Hess, David J. 1995. "On Low-Tech Cyborgs." In *The Cyborg Handbook*, edited by Chris Hables Gray. New York: Routledge.

Hillis, Ken. 1996. "A Geography of the Eye: The Technologies of Virtual Reality." In *Cultures of Internet: Virtual Spaces, Real Histories, Living Bodies*, edited by Rob Shields. Thousand Oaks, Calif.: Sage Publications.

_____. 1999. *Digital Sensations: Space, Identity, and Embodiment in Virtual Reality*. Minneapolis: University of Minnesota Press.

Hoffman, Donna. L., Thomas P. Novak, and Patrali Chatterjee. 1996. "Commercial Scenarios for the Web: Opportunities and Challenges." *Journal of Computer Mediated Communication* 1, no. 3. (Internet.) Available at http://www.ascusc.org/jcmc/vol1/issue3/hoffman.html.

Hogan, Hank. 1995. "Wetware." *High Technology Careers Magazine*. (Internet.) Available at http://www.hightechcareers.com/docs695/wetware.html.

Howard, Toby. 1996. "Beyond the Big Barrier." (Internet.) Available at http://www.cs.man.ac.uk/aig/staff/toby/writing/PCW/bci.html. Originally published in *Personal Computer World*, Feb. 1996.

Howell, Linda. 1995. "The Cyborg Manifesto Revisited: Issues and Methods for Technocultural Feminism." In *Postmodern Apocalypse: Theory and Cultural Practice at the End*, edited by Richard Dellamora. Philadelphia: University of Pennsylvania Press.

Hulme, Peter. 1986. *Colonial Encounters: Europe and the Native Caribbean*. New York: Methuen.

Hunter, Lynette. 1999. *Critiques of Knowing: Situated Textualities in Science, Computing and the Arts*. New York: Routledge.

Hutchins, W. John. 1986. *Machine Translation: Past, Present, Future*. New York: John Wiley and Sons.

Hutchins, W. John, and Harold L. Somers. 1992. *An Introduction to Machine Translation*. New York: Academic Press.

International Business Machines (IBM). 1996a. "When Will the Networked World Arrive?" (Internet.) Available at http://www.ibm.com/IBM/ar95/sv_static/index.html.

_____. 1996b. "The Future of Computing." (Internet.) Available at http://www.ibm.com/IBM/ar95/sv_static/index.html.

_____. 1997. "Solutions for a Small Planet." (Internet.) Available at http://www.ibm.com/sfasp/index.html.

Interrogate the Internet. 1996. "Contradictions in Cyberspace: Collective Response." In *Cultures of Internet: Virtual Spaces, Real Histories, Living Bodies*, edited by Rob Shields. London: Sage Publications.

Ito, Mizuko. 1997. "Virtually Embodied: The Reality of Fantasy in a Multi-User Dungeon." In *Internet Culture*, edited by David Porter. New York: Routledge.

Jameson, Frederick. 1972. *The Prison House of Language: A Critical Account of Structuralism and Russian Formalism*. Princeton: Princeton University Press.

Johnson, Mark, and George Lakoff. 1980. *Metaphors We Live By*. Chicago: University of Chicago Press.

Jones, Steven G., ed. 1995. *CyberSociety: Computer-Mediated Communication and Community*. Thousand Oaks, Calif.: Sage Publications.

Jones, Steven G. 1997a. "The Consequences of Interaction in Electronic Communities." In *Binäre Mythen/Binary Myths*. Proceedings of the 14 Sept. 1996 conference Binary Myths—The Renaissance of Lost Emotions held in Vienna, Austria, edited by Edeltraud Stiftinger and Edward Strasser. Vienna: Zukunftswerkstätte.

Jones, Steven G., ed. 1997b. *Virtual Culture: Identity and Communication in Cybersociety*. Thousand Oaks, Calif.: Sage Publications.

Jones, Steven G. 1998. "Understanding Micropolis and Compunity." *Electronic Journal of Communication—La Revue Electronique de Communication* 8, nos. 3–4: 1–10. (Internet.) Available at http://www.cios.org/getfile\jones_V8N398.

Jordan, Winthrop P. 1974. *The White Man's Burden*. New York: Oxford University Press.

Joseph, Franz. 1975. *Star Fleet Technical Manual*. New York: Ballantine.

Katz, Jon. 1997. "The Digital Citizen: The Surprising Results of the First in-Depth Survey." *Wired* 5, no. 12: 68–82.

Kaufmann, Walter. 1969. Editor's Introduction to Friedrich Nietzsche's *Genealogy of Morals and Ecce Homo*. New York: Vintage Books.

Kelly, George A. 1955. *The Psychology of Personal Constructs*. New York: Norton.

Kendrick, Michelle. 1996. "Cyberspace and the Technological Real." In *Virtual Realities and Their Discontents*, edited by Robert Markley. Baltimore: Johns Hopkins University Press.

Kern, Stephen. 1986. *The Culture of Time and Space: 1880–1918*. Cambridge, Mass.: Harvard University Press.

Kevles, Daniel J., and Leroy Hood. 1992. *The Code of Codes: Scientific and Social Issues in the Human Genome Project*. Cambridge, Mass.: Harvard University Press.

Kramarae, Cheris. 1995. "A Backstage Critique of Virtual Reality." In *Cybersociety: Computer-Mediated Communication and Community*, edited by Steve Jones. Thousand Oaks, Calif.: Sage Publications.

Kroker, Arthur, and Michael A. Weinstein. 1994. *Data Trash: The Theory of the Virtual Class*. New York: St. Martin's Press.

Krueger, Myron. 1977. "Responsive Environments." *Proceedings of the National Computer Conference*, pp. 423–433.

_____. 1991. *Artificial Reality II*. Reading, Mass.: Addison-Wesley.

Kunzru, Hari. 1997. "You Are Borg." *Wired* 5, no. 2: 154–159. Also available at http://www.wired.com/wired/5.02/features/ffharaway.html.

Landow, George P. 1992. *Hypertext: The Convergence of Contemporary Critical Theory and Technology*. Baltimore: Johns Hopkins University Press.

Lanier, Jaron. 1988. "A Portrait of the Young Visionary." (Internet.) Available at http://www.well.com/user/jaron/vrint.html.

_____. 1993. "Jaron Lanier—Virtual Genius." *Magical Blend Magazine* 48. (Internet.) Available at http://magical.eden.com/Backissue/Backissue5.html.

Lanier, Jaron, and Frank Biocca. 1992. "An Insider's View of the Future of Virtual Reality." *Journal of Communication* 42, no. 4: 150–172.

Lannamann, John W. 1991. "Interpersonal Communication Research As Ideological Practice." *Communication Theory* 1, no. 3: 179–203.

Larson, Doran. 1997. "Machine As Messiah: Cyborgs, Morphs, and the American Body Politic." *Cinema Journal*, 36, no. 4: 57–75.

Laurel, Brenda. 1991. *Computers As Theatre*. Reading, Mass.: Addison-Wesley.

Leary, Timothy. 1994. *Chaos and Cyber Culture*. Berkeley: Ronin.

_____. 1999. "The Cyberpunk: The Individual As Reality Pilot." In *CyberReader*, edited by Victor Vitanza. Boston: Allyn and Bacon.

Leder, Drew. 1990. *The Absent Body*. Chicago: University of Chicago Press.

Leed, Eric J. 1991. *The Mind of the Traveler: From Gilgamesh to Global Tourism*. Boulder: Basic Books.

Leeson, Lynn Hershman. 1996. *Clicking In: Hot Links to a Digital Culture*. Seattle: Bay Press.

Lenert, Edward M. 1998. "A Communication Theory Perspective on Telecommunications Policy." *Journal of Communication* 48, no. 4: 3–23.

Lernout and Hauspie Speech Products. 1988. "PowerTranslator Pro." (Internet.) Available at http://www.lhsl.com/.

Levy, Steven. 1984. *Hackers: Heroes of the Computer Revolution*. New York: Anchor Press.

Licklider, J. C. R. 1960. "Man–Computer Symbiosis." (Internet.) Available at http://memex.org/licklider.html. Originally published in *IRE Transactions on Human Factors in Electronics* HRE–1 (Mar. 1960).

Licklider, J. C. R., and Robert W. Taylor. 1968. "The Computer As a Communication Device." Available at http://memex.org/licklider.html. Originally published in *Science and Technology* (Apr. 1968).

Lindberg, Kathryne V. 1996. "Prosthetic Mnemonics and Prophylactic Politics: William Gibson Among the Subjectivity Mechanisms." *Boundary II* 23, no. 2: 47–83.

Littman, Jonathan. 1996. *The Fugitive Game: On-Line with Kevin Mitnick.* New York: Little, Brown.

———. 1997. *The Watchman: The Twisted Life and Crimes of Serial Hacker Kevin Poulsen.* New York: Little, Brown.

Lopez, Barry. 1992. *The Rediscovery of North America.* New York: Vintage.

Loraux, Nicole. 1989. "Therefore, Socrates Is Immortal," translated by Janet Lloyd. In *Zone 4: Fragments for a History of the Human Body*, edited by Michel Feher. New York: Zone.

Lubar, Steven. 1993. *InfoCulture.* Boston: Houghton Mifflin.

Ludlow, Peter, ed. 1996. *High Noon on the Electronic Frontier: Conceptual Issues in Cyberspace.* Cambridge, Mass.: MIT Press.

Lyotard, Jean-François. 1984. *The Postmodern Condition: A Report on Knowledge,* translated by Geoffrey Bennington and B. Massumi. Minneapolis: University of Minnesota Press.

Maddox, Brenda. 1972. *Beyond Babel: New Directions in Communications.* London: André Deutsch.

Markley, Robert. 1996. "Introduction: History, Theory and Virtual Reality." In *Virtual Realities and Their Discontents*, edited by Robert Markley. Baltimore: Johns Hopkins University Press.

Martin, James. 1978. *The Wired Society.* Englewood Cliffs, N.J.: Prentice-Hall.

Marvin, Carolyn. 1988. *When Old Technologies Were New: Thinking About Electric Communication in the Late Nineteenth Century.* New York: Oxford University Press.

Mattelart, Armand. 1994. *Mapping World Communication: War, Progress, Culture,* translated by Susan Emanuel and James A. Cohen. Minneapolis: University of Minnesota Press.

———. 1996. *The Invention of Communication,* translated by Susan Emanuel. Minneapolis: University of Minnesota Press.

———. 2000. *Networking the World: 1794–2000,* translated by Liz Carey-Libbrecht and James A. Cohen. Minneapolis: University of Minnesota Press.

Mattelart, Armand, and Michele Mattelart. 1992. *Rethinking Media Theory: Signposts and New Directions,* translated by James A. Cohen and Marian Urquidi. Minneapolis: University of Minnesota Press.

Mazlish, Bruce. 1993. *The Fourth Discontinuity: The Co-Evolution of Humans and Machines.* New Haven: Yale University Press.

McFarland, D. J., G. W. Neat, R. F. Read, and J. R. Wolpaw. 1993. "An EEG-Based Method for Graded Cursor Control." *Psychobiology* 21, no. 1: 77–81.

McGee, Michael Calvin. 1982. "A Materialist's Conception of Rhetoric." In *Explorations in Rhetoric: Studies in Honor of Douglas Ehninger*, edited by Ray E. McKerrow. Glenview, Ill.: Scott, Foresman.

McLuhan, Marshall. 1962. *The Gutenberg Galaxy: The Making of Typographic Man.* Toronto: University of Toronto Press.

———. 1995. *Understanding Media: The Extensions of Man.* Cambridge, Mass.: MIT Press.

McLuhan, Marshall, and Eric McLuhan. 1988. *The Laws of Media: The New Science.* Toronto: University of Toronto Press.

Melby, Alan K. 1995. *The Possibility of Language.* Philadelphia: John Benjamins.

Mentor, The. 1986. "Hacker's Manifesto; or, The Conscience of a Hacker." *Phrack* 1, no. 7: 3. (Internet.) Available at http://www.fc.net/phrack/files/PO7/PO7-3.html.

Meyers, Jeffrey. 1990. *D. H. Lawrence.* New York: Alfred A. Knopf.

Miller, L. Chris. 1993. "Babelware for the Desktop: Personal Computer and Workstation Translation Software Offers You the Most Affordable Access to MT." *BYTE* 18, no. 1: 177–183.

Mitchell, William J. 1995. *City of Bits: Space, Place, and the Infobahn.* Cambridge, Mass.: MIT Press.

_____. 1999. *E-topia: Urban Life, Jim—But Not As We Know It.* Cambridge, Mass.: MIT Press.

Momaday, N. Scott. 1992. "Becoming of the Native: Man in America Before Columbus." In *America in 1492,* edited by Alvin M. Josephy. New York: Alfred A. Knopf.

Morevac, Hans. 1988. *Mind Children: The Future of Robot and Human Intelligence.* Cambridge, Mass.: Harvard University Press.

Morgan, Conway Lloyd, and Giuliano Zampi. 1995. *Virtual Architecture.* New York: McGraw-Hill.

Morningstar, Chip, and F. Randall Farmer. 1993. "The Lessons of Lucasfilm's Habitat." In *Cyberspace: First Steps,* edited by Michael Benedikt. Cambridge, Mass.: MIT Press.

Morris, Meaghan. 1988. *The Pirate's Fiancé.* New York: Verso.

Morse, Margaret. 1996. "Nature Morte: Landscape and Narrative in Virtual Environments." In *Immersed in Technology: Art and Virtual Environments,* edited by Mary Anne Moser and Douglas MacLeod. Cambridge, Mass.: MIT Press.

_____. 1998. *Virtualities: Television, Media Art, and Cyberculture.* Bloomington: Indiana University Press.

Moser, Mary Anne, and Douglas MacLeod, eds. 1996. *Immersed in Technology: Art and Virtual Environments.* Cambridge, Mass.: MIT Press.

Mungo, Paul, and Bryan Clough. 1992. *Approaching Zero: The Extraordinary Underworld of Hackers, Phreakers, Virus Writers and Keyboard Criminals.* New York: Random House.

Naval Health Research Center. 1996. "Neural Human-Systems Interface Development." (Internet.) Available at http://www.nhrc.navy.mil/Rsch/Code 223/wuis6429.html.

Nealon, Jeffrey T. 1998. *Alterity Politics: Ethics and Performative Subjectivity.* Durham, N.C.: Duke University Press.

Negroponte, Nicholas. 1970. *The Architecture Machine.* Cambridge, Mass.: MIT Press.

_____. 1975. *Soft Architecture Machines.* Cambridge, Mass.: MIT Press.

_____. 1995. *Being Digital.* New York: Vintage.

Newton, John. 1992. *Computers in Translation: A Practical Appraisal.* New York: Routledge.

Nietzsche, Friedrich. 1966. *Beyond Good and Evil*, translated by Walter Kaufmann. New York: Vintage Books.

_____. 1969. *Genealogy of Morals and Ecce Homo*, translated by Walter Kaufmann. New York: Vintage Books.

_____. 1974. *The Gay Science*, translated by Walter Kaufmann. New York: Vintage Books.

_____. 1983a. *Thus Spoke Zarathustra*, translated by Walter Kaufmann. In *The Portable Nietzsche*, edited by Walter Kaufmann. New York: Penguin Books.

_____. 1983b. *Twilight of the Idols*, translated by Walter Kaufmann. In *The Portable Nietzsche*, edited by Walter Kaufmann. New York: Penguin Books.

Nille, Jack M., F. Roy Carlson, Paul Gray, and Gerhard J. Hanneman. 1976. *The Telecommunications Transportation Tradeoff: Options for Tomorrow*. New York: John Wiley and Sons.

Norris, Christopher. 1982. *Deconstruction: Theory and Practice*. New York: Methuen.

Novak, Thomas P., and Donna L. Hoffman. 1998. "Bridging the Digital Divide: The Impact of Race on Computer Access and Internet Use." (Internet.) Available at http://ecommerce.vanderbilt.edu/papers/race/science.html.

Oguibe, Olu. 1996. "Forsaken Geographies: Cyberspace and the New World 'Other.'" (Internet.) Available at http://www.telefonica.es/fat/eoguibe.html.

Okuda, Michael, Denise Okuda, and Debbie Mirek. 1994. *The Star Trek Encyclopedia*. New York: Pocket Books.

Osgood, Charles E. 1969. "The Nature and Measurement of Meaning." In *The Semantic Differential Technique*, edited by James G. Snider and Charles E. Osgood. Chicago: Aldine.

Oslin, George P. 1992. *The Story of Telecommunications*. Macon, Ga.: Mercer University Press.

Pask, Kevin. 1995. "Cyborg Economies: Desire and Labor in the *Terminator* Films." In *Postmodern Apocalypse: Theory and Cultural Practice at the End*, edited by Richard Dellamora. Philadelphia: University of Pennsylvania Press.

Patton, Phil. 1986. *Open Road: A Celebration of the American Highway*. New York: Simon and Schuster.

Penley, Constance, and Andrew Ross. 1991. "Cyborgs at Large: Interview with Donna Haraway." In *Technoculture*, edited by Constance Penley and Andrew Ross. Minneapolis: University of Minnesota Press.

Penny, Simon. 1992. "Virtual Reality As the End of the Enlightenment Project." (Internet.) Available at http://www-art.cfa.cmu.edu/www-penny/text/VR_Dia_.html.

_____. 1994. "Virtual Reality As the Completion of the Enlightenment Project." In *Cultures on the Brink: Ideologies of Technology*, edited by Gretchen Bender and Timothy Druckrey. Seattle: Bay Press.

Penny, Simon, ed. 1995. *Critical Issues in Electronic Media*. Albany: State University of New York.

PENSEE. 1998. (Internet.) Available at http://www.oki.co.jp/OKI/RDG/English/java/pensee/index.html.

Pfeil, Frederick. 1990. *Another Tale to Tell: Politics and Narrative in Postmodern Culture*. London: Verso.

Pfurtscheller, Gert, Doris Flotzinger, and Joachim Kalcher. 1993. "Brain-Computer Interface: A New Communication Device for Handicapped Persons." *Journal of Microcomputer Applications* 16: 293–299.

Pimentel, Ken, and Kevin Teixeira. 1993. *Virtual Reality: Through the New Looking Glass*. New York: Intel/Windcrest/McGraw-Hill.

Plato. 1961. *Cratylus*, translated by Benjamin Jowett. In *The Collected Dialogues of Plato*, edited by Edith Hamilton and Huntington Cairns. New York: Random House.

———. 1982. *Timaeus*, translated by R. B. Bury. Cambridge, Mass.: Harvard University Press.

———. 1987. *Republic*, translated by Paul Shorey. Cambridge, Mass.: Harvard University Press.

———. 1990. *Phaedo*, translated by Harold North Fowler. Cambridge, Mass.: Harvard University Press.

Pollack, Andrew. 1993. "Computers Are Starting to Take Humans' Wishes As Their Commands." *New York Times*, 9 Feb. Also available at http://www.cs.man.ac.uk/aig/staff/toby/research/bci/nyt.txt.

Pool, Ithiel de Sola. 1990. *Technologies Without Boundaries: On Telecommunications in a Global Age*. Cambridge, Mass.: Harvard University Press.

Porter, David, ed. 1997. *Internet Culture*. New York: Routledge.

Porush, David. 1994. "The Rise of Cyborg Culture; or, The Bomb Was a Cyborg." *Surfaces* 4, no. 205: 1–32.

Poster, Mark. 1990. *The Mode of Information: Poststructuralism and Social Context*. Chicago: University of Chicago Press.

———. 1995. *The Second Media Age*. Cambridge, Mass.: Polity Press.

Powell, James. 1997. *HTML Plus!* Belmont, Calif.: Wadsworth.

Provenzo, Eugene F. 1999. *Video Kids: Making Sense of Nintendo*. Cambridge, Mass.: Harvard University Press.

Reid, Elizabeth M. 1996. "Text-Based Virtual Realities: Identity and the Cyborg Body." In *High Noon on the Electronic Frontier: Conceptual Issues in Cyberspace*, edited by Peter Ludlow. Cambridge, Mass.: MIT Press.

Reifler, Erwin. 1951. *MT*. Seattle: University of Washington Press.

Rethinking Columbus. 1991. Milwaukee: Rethinking Schools.

Rheingold, Howard. 1991. *Virtual Reality*. New York: Summit Books.

———. 1993. *The Virtual Community: Homesteading on the Electronic Frontier*. New York: Addison-Wesley.

Robins, Kevin. 1995. "Cyberspace and the World We Live In." In *Cyberspace, Cyberbodies, Cyberpunk: Cultures of Technological Embodiment*, edited by Mike Featherstone and Roger Burrows. London: Sage Publications.

Robins, Kevin, and Frank Webster. 1999. *Times of the Technoculture: From the Information Society to the Virtual Life*. New York: Routledge.

Robinson, Wendy. 1997. "Heaven's Gate: The End?" *Journal of Computer Mediated Communication* 3, no. 3 (Dec.). (Internet.) Available at http://www.ascusc.org/jcmc/vol3/issue3/robinson.html.

Rorvik, David M. 1971. *As Man Becomes Machine: The Evolution of the Cyborg.* New York: Doubleday.

Rose, Mark H. 1979. *Interstate: Express Highway Politics 1941–1956.* Lawrence: Regents Press of Kansas.

Rosenbaum, Ron. 1971. "Secrets of the Little Blue Box." *Esquire,* Oct., pp. 116–124.

Ross, Andrew. 1991a. *Strange Weather: Culture, Science, and Technology in the Age of Limits.* London: Verso.

————. 1991b. "Hacking Away at the Counterculture." In *Technoculture,* edited by Constance Penley and Andrew Ross. Minneapolis: University of Minnesota Press.

Rötzer, Florian. 1998. *Digitale Weltenwürfe: Streifzüge durch die Netzkultur.* Munich: Carl Hanser Verlag.

Rushing, Janice Hocker, and Thomas S. Frentz. 1995. *Projecting the Shadow: The Cyborg Hero in American Film.* Chicago: University of Chicago Press.

Ryan, Marie-Laure. 1994. "Immersion vs. Interactivity: Virtual Reality and Literary Theory." *Postmodern Culture* 5, no. 1: 1–20. (Internet.) Available at http://muse.jhu.edu/journals/postmodern_culture/v005/5.1ryan.html.

Said, Edward W. 1978. *Orientalism.* New York: Random House.

Sandoval, Chela. 1995. "New Sciences: Cyborg Feminism and the Methodology of the Oppressed." In *The Cyborg Handbook,* edited by Chris Hables Gray. New York: Routledge.

Sardar, Ziauddin. 1996. "Alt.civilization.faq: Cyberspace As the Darker Side of the West." In *Cyberfutures: Culture and Politics on the Information Superhighway,* edited by Ziauddin Sardar and Jerome R. Ravetz. New York: New York University Press.

Sardar, Ziauddin, and Jerome R. Ravetz. 1996. "Introduction: Reaping the Technological Whirlwind." In *Cyberfutures: Culture and Politics on the Information Superhighway,* edited by Ziauddin Sardar and Jerome R. Ravetz. New York: New York University Press.

Saussure, Ferdinand de. 1959. *A Course in General Linguistics,* translated by W. Baskin. New York: Harper and Row.

Schroeder, Ralph. 1996. *Possible Worlds: The Social Dynamic of Virtual Reality Technology.* Boulder: Westview Press.

Schubert, Klaus. 1992. "Esperanto As an Intermediate Language for Machine Translation." In *Computers in Translation: A Practical Appraisal,* edited by John Newton. New York: Routledge.

Schuman, Bruce. 1988. "Utopian Computer Networking: America's New Central Project." (Internet.) Available at http://www.rain.org/~origin/ucs.html.

Shannon, Claude E., and Warren Weaver. 1963. *The Mathematical Theory of Communication.* Urbana: University of Illinois Press.

Shannon, Robert E. 1975. *System Simulation: The Art and Science.* Englewood Cliffs, N.J.: Prentice-Hall.

Shanti, Alys. 1993. "Cyborgs in the n-Dimension: The Heretical Descent of Non-Euclidean Geometry." *Constructions* 8: 57–82.

Shapiro, Michael A., and Daniel G. McDonald. 1995. "I'm Not a Real Doctor but I Play One in Virtual Reality: Implications of Virtual Reality for Judgments

About Reality." In *Communication in the Age of Virtual Reality*, edited by Frank Biocca and Mark R. Levy. Hillsdale, N.J.: Lawrence Erlbaum Associates.

Shapiro, Michael J. 1993. "'Manning' the Frontiers: The Politics of (Human) Nature in *Blade Runner.*" In *In the Nature of Things: Language, Politics, and the Environment*, edited by Jane Bennett and William Chaloupka. Minneapolis: University of Minnesota Press.

Shields, Rob. 1996. "Virtual Spaces, Real Histories, and Living Bodies." In *Cultures of Internet: Virtual Spaces, Real Histories, Living Bodies*, edited by Rob Shields. London: Sage Publications.

Shome, Raka. 1996. "Postcolonial Interventions in the Rhetorical Canon: An 'Other' View." *Communication Theory* 6, no. 1 (Feb.): 40–59.

Siivonen, Timo. 1996. "Cyborgs and Generic Oxymorons: The Body and Technology in William Gibson's Cyberspace Trilogy." *Science-Fiction Studies* 23: 227–244.

Slatalla, Michelle, and Joshua Quittner. 1996. *Masters of Deception: The Gang That Ruled Cyberspace*. New York: HarperPerennial.

Slouka, Mark. 1995. *War of the Worlds: Cyberspace and the High-Tech Assault on Reality*. New York: Basic Books.

Smith, Lillian. 1961. *Killers of the Dream*. New York: Norton.

Smith, Ralph Lee. 1972. *The Wired Nation—Cable TV: The Electronic Communications Highway*. New York: Harper and Row.

Spelman, Elizabeth V. 1988. *Inessential Woman: Problems of Exclusion in Feminist Thought*. Boston: Beacon Press.

Spiller, Neil. 1998. *Digital Dreams: Architecture and the New Alchemic Technologies*. New York: Whitney Library of Design.

Spinelli, Martin. 1996. "Radio Lessons for the Internet." *Postmodern Culture* 6, no. 2. (Internet.) Available at http://muse jhu.edu/journals/postmodern_culture/v006/6.2spinelli.html.

Spivak, Gayatri Chakravorty. 1988. *In Other Worlds: Essays in Cultural Politics*. New York: Routledge.

Springer, Claudia. 1996. *Electronic Eros: Bodies and Desire in the Postindustrial Age*. Austin: University of Texas Press.

Stabile, Carol A. 1994. *Feminism and the Technological Fix*. Manchester, Eng.: Manchester University Press.

Stefik, Mark. 1996. *Internet Dreams: Archetypes, Myths, and Metaphors*. Cambridge, Mass.: MIT Press.

Steiner, George. 1975. *After Babel*. New York: Oxford University Press.

Stenger, Nicole. 1993. "Mind Is a Leaking Rainbow." In *Cyberspace: First Steps*, edited by Michael Benedikt. Cambridge, Mass.: MIT Press.

Stephenson, Neal. 1993. *Snow Crash*. New York: Bantam Spectra.

Sterling, Bruce. 1986. *Mirrorshades: The Cyberpunk Anthology*. New York: Arbor House.

_____. 1990. "Cyberspace (TM)." *Interzone* 41 (Nov.): 54.

_____. 1992. *The Hacker Crackdown: Law and Disorder on the Electronic Frontier*. New York: Bantam Books.

Sternbach, Rich, and Michael Okuda. 1991. *Star Trek Next Generation Technical Manual*. New York: Pocket Books.

Stone, Allucquere Rosanne. 1993. "Will the Real Body Please Stand Up?: Boundary Stories About Virtual Cultures." In *Cyberspace: First Steps*, edited by Michael Benedikt. Cambridge, Mass.: MIT Press.

———. 1995. *The War of Desire and Technology at the Close of the Mechanical Age*. Cambridge, Mass.: MIT Press.

Stratton, Jerry. 1994. "The Joy of Access: What Is the Net?" (Internet.) Available at http://www.acusd.edu/ac/help/?Joy.

Sutherland, Ivan. 1965. "The Ultimate Display." *Proceedings of the International Federation of Information Processing Congress* 2: 506–508.

Swift, Jonathan. 1965. *Gulliver's Travels*. Oxford: Basil Blackwell.

Taylor, Mark. 1993. *Nots*. Chicago: University of Chicago Press.

———. 1997. *Hiding*. Chicago: University of Chicago Press.

Taylor, Mark, and Esa Saarinen. 1994. *Imagologies: Media Philosophy*. New York: Routledge.

Taylor, Paul A. 1999. *Hackers: Crime in the Digital Sublime*. New York: Routledge.

Technology for America's Economic Growth. 1993. Available at http://simr02.si.ehu.es/DOCS/nearnet.gnn.com/mag/10_93/articles/clinton/clinton.tech.html?information+superhighway.

Teilhard de Chardin, Pierre. 1959. *Phenomenon of Man*, translated by Bernard Wall. New York: Harper.

Telecommunications Survey. 1993. *Economist*, Oct., 1–27.

Tepper, Michele. 1997. "Usenet Communities and the Cultural Politics of Information." In *Internet Culture*, edited by David Porter. New York: Routledge.

Thibaut, John W., and Harold H. Kelly. 1959. *The Social Psychology of Groups*. New York: John Wiley and Sons.

Thomas Aquinas. 1945. *Summa Theologica*. In *Basic Writings of Saint Thomas Aquinas*, vol. 1, edited and translated by Anton C. Pegis. New York: Random House.

Todd, Loretta. 1996. "Aboriginal Narratives in Cyberspace." In *Immersed in Technology: Art and Virtual Environments*, edited by Mary Anne Moser and Douglas MacLeod. Cambridge, Mass.: MIT Press.

Todorov, Tzvetan. 1984. *The Conquest of America*, translated by Richard Howard. New York: HarperCollins.

Tomas, David. 1993. "Old Rituals for New Space: Rites de Passage and William Gibson's Cultural Model of Cyberspace." In *Cyberspace: First Steps*, edited by Michael Benedikt. Cambridge, Mass.: MIT Press.

Translation Technology Alternatives. 1993. *BYTE* 18, no. 1: 169–171.

Trinh T. Minh-ha. 1989. *Woman, Native, Other: Writing, Postcoloniality and Feminism*. Bloomington: Indiana University Press.

———. 1991. *When the Full Moon Waxes Red: Representation, Gender, and Cultural Politics*. New York: Routledge.

Turkle, Sherry. 1995. *Life on the Screen: Identity in the Age of the Internet*. New York: Simon and Schuster.

United States Advisory Council on the National Information Infrastructure (USAC—NII). 1996. *A Nation of Opportunity: Realizing the Promise of the*

Information Superhighway. Washington, D.C.: U.S. Government Printing Office.

Unwin, Tim. 1992. *The Place of Geography*. New York: Longman Scientific and Technical.

Vasconcellos, Muriel. 1988. *Technology As Translation Strategy*. Binghamton: State University of New York Press.

_____. 1993. "Machine Translation: Translating the Languages of the World on a Desktop Computer Comes of Age." *BYTE* 18, no. 1: 152–159.

Virilio, Paul. 1993. "The Third Interval: A Critical Transition," translated by Tom Conley. In *Rethinking Technologies*, edited by Verena Andermatt Conley. Minneapolis: University of Minnesota Press.

_____. 1995. *The Art of the Motor*, translated by Julie Rose. Minneapolis: University of Minnesota Press.

Vitanza, Victor. 1997. *Negation, Subjectivity and the History of Rhetoric*. Albany: State University of New York Press.

Vitanza, Victor, ed. 1999. *CyberReader*. Boston: Allyn and Bacon.

Von Neumann, John. 1958. *The Computer and the Brain*. New Haven: Yale University Press.

Weaver, Warren. 1955a. "The New Tower." In *Machine Translation of Languages*, edited by William N. Locke and A. Donald Booth. Cambridge, Mass.: MIT Press.

_____. 1955b. "Translation." In *Machine Translation of Languages*, edited by William N. Locke and A. Donald Booth. Cambridge, Mass.: MIT Press.

Web, Jack E. 1967. *Space: The New Frontier*. Washington, D.C.: U.S. Government Printing Office.

Wertheim, Margaret. 1999. *The Pearly Gates of Cyberspace: A History of Space from Dante to the Internet*. New York: W.W. Norton.

Whitefield, Ian Cunliffe. 1984. *Neurocommunications: An Introduction*. New York: John Wiley and Sons.

Wiener, Norbert. 1961. *Cybernetics; or, Control and Communication in the Animal and the Machine*. Cambridge, Mass.: MIT Press.

_____. 1988. *The Human Use of Human Beings: Cybernetics and Society*. New York: Da Capo Press.

Wilbur, Shawn P. 1997. "An Archaeology of Cyberspaces: Virtuality, Community, Identity." In *Internet Culture*, edited by David Porter. New York: Routledge.

Williams, David. 1998. "The Politics of Cyborg Communication: Harold Innis, Marshall McLuhan, and *The English Patient*." *Canadian Literature* 156: 30–55.

Williams, Raymond. 1967. *Communications*. New York: Barnes and Noble.

_____. 1976. *Keywords: A Vocabulary of Culture and Society*. New York: Oxford University Press.

Williams, Sarah. 1995. "'Perhaps Images at One with the World Are Already Lost Forever': Visions of Cyborg Anthropology in Post-Cultural Worlds." In *The Cyborg Handbook*, edited by Chris Hables Gray. New York: Routledge.

Winkelmann, Carol L. 1995. "Electronic Literacy, Critical Pedagogy, and Collaboration: A Case for Cyborg Writing." *Computers in the Humanities* 29: 431–448.

Winograd, Terry. 1984. "Computer Software for Working with Languages." *Scientific American* 251: 131–142.

Wittig, Rob. 1994. *Invisible Rendezvous: Connection and Collaboration in the New Landscape of Electronic Writing*. Middletown, Conn.: Wesleyan University Press.

Witwer, Julia. 1995. "The Best of Both Worlds: On *Star Trek's* Borg." In *Prosthetic Territories: Politics and Hypertechnologies*, edited by Gabriel Brahm and Mark Driscoll. Boulder: Westview Press.

Wolpaw, Jonathan R., D. J. McFarland, G. W. Neat, and C. A. Forneris. 1991. "An EEG-Based Brain-Computer Interface for Cursor Control." *Electroencephalography and Clinical Neurophysiology* 78: 252–259.

Woolley, Benjamin. 1992. *Virtual Worlds*. New York: Penguin.

Wresch, William. 1996. *Disconnected: Haves and Have-nots in the Information Age*. New Brunswick, N.J.: Rutgers University Press.

Wright, Andrew. 1993. "On Designing a Brain–Computer Interface: After All, Computers Were Once Science Fiction, Too." (Internet.) Available at http://www.cs.man.ac.uk/aig/staff/toby/research/bci/andrew-wright. txt.

Wurzer, Joerg. 1999. "Der Vermeintliche Sprung über Kulturelle Gräben." *Telepolis*. (Internet.) Available at http://www.heise.de/tp/deutsch/inhalt/co/ 2640/1.html.

Young, John Z. 1978. *Programs of the Brain*. New York: Oxford University Press.

_____. 1987. *Philosophy and the Brain*. New York: Oxford University Press.

Zaleski, Jeffrey P. 1997. *The Soul of Cyberspace: How New Technology Is Changing Our Spiritual Lives*. San Francisco: HarperEdge.

Index